PIONEER AVIATORS

AND THE PLANES THEY FLEW

FRANK E. HITCHENS

Acorn Books
www.acornbooks.uk

Published in 2023 by
Acorn Books
www.acornbooks.co.uk

Acorn Books is an imprint of
Andrews UK Limited
www.andrewsuk.com

Contents

Introduction

This book starts with the very early pioneers of balloon flight from the mid-1700s up to the end of the 1800s, when flight with heavier-than-air airplanes was being attempted by several pioneers of the day. The success of the Wright brothers' first flight in 1903, marked the start of the *Pioneer Age of Aviation*, which lasted through 4 August 1914, the start of WWI, with technical advancements in aviation picking up momentum from 1909 with Bleriot's crossing of the English Channel.

The Wright brothers can be considered as experimental glider pilots, amateur aircraft constructors, aviation enthusiasts and demonstration pilots, etc. It was mostly individuals who built the first aircraft, which were very frail, unstable and underpowered. The first flight attempts were made as straight-line short hops, keeping the wings level with the aim to just remain airborne for as long as possible; turning flight came later. The early planes slowly improved in performance, but it was to be ten years after the Wright brothers first flight before the 100-mph mark was exceeded. Airships for military and commercial use were coming of age and light aircraft were being used by sport and private pilots in their attempts to become airborne and compete for the various competitions and prize money offered by several wealthy businessmen to encourage aviation progress.

Although the Wright brothers in America had achieved the first powered and controlled flight, it was in Europe where aviation was quickly adopted by pioneer pilots and plane manufacturers, initially from France and then followed by Germany and England. The first manufacturers to become established in America was the Boeing Company in 1916 followed by the Curtiss-Wright Company finding success in the 1920s.

France was the leader in producing aircraft engines, which were soon chosen by the British aircraft builders. From 1909, engines were being developed with more power, which helped to improve the performance of the early planes, which was further increased with the advent of WWI, with both sides trying to outperform the other; air superiority had arrived.

The years from the end of WWI to the start of WWII, were known as the *Golden Age Years of Aviation*. It was the time when civil aviation made rapid advances in aircraft design to improve performance, thanks to NACA (pre-NASA) in America and similar research establishments in Germany and England. The monoplane designs dominated the scene with improved streamlining to reduce drag and more powerful engines to increase speed and performance. The retractable undercarriage became standard equipment on high-performance planes, also to reduce drag and increase the speed. Variable-pitch and later, constant-speed propellers replaced the fixed-pitch propellers on higher performance aircraft. Other noticeable improvements included the tractor-engine/propeller combination becoming the favoured layout, as opposed to pusher props. The days of the wood and fabric covered biplanes were numbered.

Altitude, speed and distance records were being made and broken by the new breed of adventurous pioneer pilots. For example, the flights of Alcock and Brown, and Charles Lindbergh across the Atlantic was a great leap forward in trans-oceanic flights. World War One fighter pilots returning from the war, took to barnstorming around America, flying their planes into any spare available landing space in fields, etc. From there, they entertained the locals with daring manoeuvres and gave many people their first experience of flight. Eventually, the pilots would band together to put on displays, known as flying circuses, which became the advent of air shows, still enjoyed by many thousands of spectators and plane enthusiasts around the world today. The barnstorming pilots also turned to air racing and flew the air mail routes and in turn, became pilots of the fledgling airlines. Many airlines lasted for a relatively short period, other airlines have survived for many years, some to the present day, such as the Dutch airline, KLM. Long-distance, trans-oceanic flights were being made more frequently, new air routes were being added to the international airlines and aircraft became more versatile and were used as useful tools in polar exploration, by the military and for other general duties.

Forty-four years after the Wright brother's famous flight, USAF pilot Charles (Chuck) Yeager (1923-2020) exceeded Mach One on 14 October 1947 leading up to the space age; the Russian, Yuri Gagarin (1934-1968) becoming the first man in space followed by the first American in space, Alan Shepard (1923-1998). They were the pioneers of the *Space Age* paving the way for today's astronauts.

An American organisation known as *The Early Birds of Aviation*, recognises 598 pioneer aviators who have flown balloons, gliders and powered aircraft from the day of the Wright brother's first flight up to 17 December 1916 (the Wright's anniversary). Aviation pioneers are defined as those people (pilots, scientists, designers and builders, etc) who have pushed the envelope to improve aircraft performance and safety by their efforts in flight-testing, studies of aerodynamics, aircraft design and construction techniques, etc. This book includes pilots who have made significant flights right up to the end of the 20th century. All are considered within this work as pioneers of their day, having contributed to the progress of aviation. Other records have been made and broken since the start of the 21st century, but for this work they are not considered as pioneers, but modern-day record makers and breakers and achievers. They are great achievers in their own right.

This work records the various stages of the early years of flight and individual pilots and flights of importance and interest. It is impossible to include all aviation pioneers within this work therefore, a brief introduction to a select few of the more famous pioneer pilots is included along with details of the planes they flew. A selection of photographs of their historic aircraft (or a photo of the same type) illustrates this work. All photographs are from the author's collection, with the exception of the photo of the US Navy's *Truculent Turtle*, which was donated by the *National Museum of Naval Aviation in Pensacola,* Florida, to whom I truly grateful.

Most of these aircraft are now housed in museums around the world due to their importance in the part they have played in the world's aviation history and as a tribute to those early *pioneer pilots and the planes they flew*. Without their efforts, and sacrifices, we would not have the aviation industry of today.

A quote from Otto Lilienthal:

> *"To invent an airplane is one thing, to build one is something else, but to fly is everything".*

Frank Hitchens
Wellington, New Zealand

1 – The Early Pioneers

The Quest Begins

Mans' quest to fly as free as the birds can be traced back to South American, Chinese and Greek mythology, where stories from South America and Asia talk about air battles in the sky. In India, ancient writings talk about *Vimanas*, flying chariots, able to fly through the air and into outer space powered by mercury-driven engines. They were equipped for battle or long-distance flying, or so the story goes.

It is claimed the kite was invented in China circa 5th century BC, by philosophers Mozi and Lu Ban, which were used for military and civilian use and also for punishment of criminals. Chinese history reveals prisoners of Emperor Gao Yang Wenxuan (526-559) from Northern Qi in China, were forced to make experimental jumps from a tower attached to giant-size man-carrying kites; Yuan Huangtou was reported to be the only prisoner to have survived his jump, only to be executed shortly after.

Other stories have been told of people jumping from high places in an attempt to fly with self-made wings, usually ending with their loss of life or serious injury. Back in the year 1010 in England, Brother Eilmer, a Benedictine monk jumped from the 150-feet high Abbey tower at Malmesbury and managed to cover a distance of 650 feet. He was injured on landing, breaking his legs and was left partially disabled. In 1507, an Italian who used his British name of John Damien, jumped from the highest point of Stirling Castle in Scotland with self-made wings covered with chicken feathers, intending to fly to France. He didn't fly very far, crashing to the ground and breaking his thighbone. He later claimed that eagle feathers in place of chicken feathers would have enabled him to fly much further. Other tower-jumping attempts were tried in later years up until the early 19th century, but success was not forthcoming.

In Southern Peru, South America, straight-line geometric shapes and figures of animals and birds cover the barren desert landscape, now well-known as the Nazca lines. But, how were they laid out covering such a large area? They are believed to have been made about 1,500 years ago. Erich von Daniken, claims they were made by space aliens as landing strips for their visiting spacecraft; others claim the local Nazca people used hot air balloons to guide the layout of the lines. Moreover, the textiles made by the Nazca people are decorated with flying machines! The question remains, were they further advanced with hot air balloons than the Montgolfier brothers of the 1700s, or were the Nazca people visited by aliens? Or, maybe there is some other logical answer yet to be found?

Daedalus & Icarus

Greek mythology presents the more familiar story of Daedalus and his son Icarus, circa 180-120 BC. Daedalus built a pair of wings from feathers and wax for himself and his son Icarus to escape from the prison of King Minus on the island of Crete. Icarus was warned by his father not to fly too high because the sun would melt the wax and the feathers would be lost. He was also warned not to fly too close to the sea because the sea water moisture would also destroy his wings. Disregarding his father's warning, Icarus flew too high and the sun melted the wax and he dropped into the sea and was drowned. Daedalus continued flying and landed in Sicily 350 miles (560 km) further on! This story of Daedalus and his son Icarus introduced the saying, *"Don't fly too close to the sun"*.

In recent times, archaeologists have found drawings of modern-day airplanes and helicopters amongst ancient hieroglyphics in an archaeological site. Are these drawings genuine or fakes? Have these aircraft flown before, aeons ago? It remains a mystery. From 559 AD to 1633 AD several attempts at flight are purported to have taken place; however, there is no confirmed evidence to any of these claims.

Leonardo da Vinci

So much for mythology and dubious stories with unconfirmed claims. We now move forward to Leonardo da Vinci (1452-1519) born in the Tuscan district in Italy, he is now famed as a far-sighted inventor and artist. Up until circa 1505, he studied bird flight and human anatomy with visions of the future where man would to take to the air as the birds do. Amongst many other things, he made diagrams of a possible hang glider, a rigid-frame parachute and a crude form of airscrew for his helicopter design, but they were never built. Leonardo da Vinci also designed an ornithopter-type plane (man-powered flapping wings); although he also claimed that a man did not have the strength to operate the wings of an ornithopter to emulate bird flight. It was not until 1797 when da Vinci's various sketches were published, which showed he was the first to view the problems of flight from a technical viewpoint. However, that did not stop men from trying to fly like the birds and in 1811, Albrecht Berblinger built an ornithopter in which he tried to fly and landed in the River Danube at Ulm in Bavaria.

A century before Leonardo da Vinci, Father Francesco Lana de Terzi (1631-1687) was a man of many talents, being a Professor of physics, a mathematician and a naturalist. His claim to fame came in 1670, with his design of a ship-shaped airship using a sail for forward propulsion and four large vacuum spheres for lift. His theory claimed the spheres being devoid of air would make them lighter than the ambient air and produce sufficient lift to raise his airship with six people on board. It appears he didn't consider how to extract the air from the copper spheres or the fact the spheres if devoid of air, would collapse under ambient air pressure. What was needed was a medium lighter than air to provide the required lift; this was soon to come. Although his design was a failure, he did gain the accolade of the 'first pioneer of aeronautics'.

The 18th Century Ballooning Era

The hot air balloon (or aerostat) is said to have originated from the sky lanterns, which were made in China around the 3rd century BC. The sky lanterns are small, paper balloons with a candle inside to provide the heat for buoyancy.

In Lisbon, Portugal, a little-known Brazilian priest, Bartolomeu Lourenco de Gusmao (1685-1724) is claimed to have flown a small, unmanned hot air paper balloon on 8 August 1709. Gusmao's balloon, named as the *Passarola*, rose to a height of 13 feet (4 metres) and was viewed by King John V of Portugal and his Portuguese court. This balloon flight is said to have occurred some seventy-four years before the Montgolfier brother's famous first flight. It was the forerunner of the hot air balloon revolution of the eighteenth century.

The Montgolfier brothers

The year 1783, was a prominent year when aviation history was first made; the true dawn of aviation. It was the start of the man-carrying balloon era, preceding the manned gliders and powered-aircraft as we know it today.

Two Frenchmen, brothers Jacques-Étienne Montgolfier (1745-1799) and Joseph-Michel Montgolfier (1740-1810) from the town of Annonay in France, were not academics as were some of the other pioneers of that era. However, they were able to design their first balloon, the *Aerostat Reveillon* and build it in their father's papermaking factory. They first experimented with the use of steam and later 'smoky air', which they called electric smoke to give their model balloons buoyancy. The Montgolfier brothers, found success when they made the first flight of their unmanned, hot air balloon at Annonay on the 25 April 1783. Their balloon had a diameter of approximately 39 feet (12 m) containing a volume of 28,000 cubic feet (790 m3), which rose to a height of an estimated 1,000 feet (305 m). This was followed by their second demonstration flight on 4 June 1783. These flights were followed by their first *tethered* balloon flight, which carried aloft a duck, rooster and a sheep; the world's first creatures to become airborne. This flight was demonstrated on 19 September 1783 at the Palace of Versailles in Paris, witnessed by King Louis XVI and Queen Marie Antoinette of France. The balloon drifted for about two miles (3 km) landing safely about eight minutes later.

Their father had banned the brothers from making a flight in their balloon; however, Jacques-Étienne Montgolfier was officially recognised as the world's first man to become airborne in a tethered hot air balloon rising to a height of around 82 feet (25 metres) on 15 October 1783, from the Chateau de la Muette, at the Bois de Boulogne in Paris.

Hot air balloons are now known today as the Montgolfier type.

Rozier & d'Arlandes

Later, that same day in October 1783, Jean-Francois Pilatre de Rozier (1754-1785) a physics and chemistry teacher, also made a tethered flight in the Montgolfier's balloon. On 21 November 1783, Rozier made another ascent at the Bois de Boulogne in Paris, in company with the Marquis Francois Laurent le Vieux d'Arlandes (1742-1809) an army officer, to become the first humans to become airborne in *free-flight*. They were flying in a Montgolfier hot air balloon, the *Reveillon* measuring 49 feet (15 m) wide and 72 feet (22 m) high, with a capacity of 70,000 cubic feet and weighing in at 1,600 lbs. Flying just above the town's rooftops, the world's first aeronauts covered a distance of 5.5 miles (9 km) from Chateau de la Muette before landing at Butte-aux-Cailles, what is now known as the Place d'Italie in Paris, after drifting with the breeze for about twenty-five minutes. They were considered to be heroes for completing the world's first free-flight in a hot air balloon.

Jean-Francois de Rozier's life was cut short while flying with Pierre Romain; they both died on 15 June 1785 when their hot air balloon, designed by Rozier, deflated in flight and crashed near Wimereux in the Pas-de-Calais during an attempt to be the first to cross the English Channel by air. They were the world's first known air accident fatalities.

The Roziere type of balloon has two separate gas bags, one bag has heated air while the second bag is unheated, allowing more control over the altitude flown and the desired course; this type of balloon is favoured by long-distance balloon pilots. Although the invention of the hot air balloon performed well enough to allow the early aeronauts to become airborne, it was soon replaced by the hydrogen type balloon introduced by Professor Jacques Alexander Charles (1746-1823).

Henry Cavendish

In 1766, Henry Cavendish (1731-1810) a scientist, philosopher, theoretical chemist and physicist, is noted amongst other things for his discovery of hydrogen gas, which is lighter than air. It became the buoyancy gas of choice and despite it being a highly flammable gas, it was readily available to aeronauts, as balloon pilots are known,. It replaced burning straw and the like to provide buoyancy for hot air balloons used by the first pioneers.

After the Hindenburg disaster of 1937 in New Jersey, USA, hydrogen was deemed to be too dangerous for use in balloons and airships and was mostly replaced by helium, which was introduced at a later date as a much safer gas, being less flammable and providing the same amount of lift as hydrogen. Initially, helium was more readily available in the USA until around the 1960s when helium also became available in Europe. Propane gas is now commonly used for modern hot air balloon flights, carried in containers in liquid form and burned as a vapour at the rate of about fifteen gallons per hour.

Jacques Charles & The Robert Brothers

Two more famous pioneer aeronauts were Nicolas-Louis Robert (1760-1820) and his brother, Anne-Jean Robert (1758-1820). They were both employed as engineers to build the airtight gas balloons for Frenchman, Jacques Charles, mentioned above, a scientist, inventor and designer of the first hydrogen balloon, and a Paris resident. Jacques Charles pioneered the use of hydrogen as a source of lift for their balloons as opposed to the hot air method used by the Montgolfier brothers. Hydrogen balloons were named as *Charliere* balloons for their inventor, Jacques Charles.

They launched the world's first unmanned hydrogen gas-filled balloon from the Champ de Mars where the Eiffel Tower now stands, on the 27 August 1783, which after drifting a few miles came down by the village of Gonesse on the outskirts of Paris; the local people destroyed it, not knowing what it was.

A few weeks later, Charles and Robert made the first manned flight in a hydrogen-filled balloon on 1 December 1783, departing from near Paris and flew 27 miles (43 km) to land two hours later at Nesles-la-Vallee. Their departure was witnessed by an estimated crowd of around 400,000 local people. During their flight, they carried a thermometer and barometer to take the first readings of atmospheric temperature and air pressure above the earth's surface. Radiosondes (weather balloons) are now used frequently to make readings of atmospheric variables and transmit them back to their meteorological stations by telemetry.

All hot air balloons drift with the wind having no form of propulsion or any method of steering a course. However, some historians claim the first dirigible airship (Latin for steerable) was the *La Caroline*, which made its first flight on 15 July 1784 with Nicolas-Louis Robert and his brother, Anne-Jean Robert accompanied by M. Collin-Hullin and Louis Philippe II (1747-1793) the Duke of Chartres. The flight from Saint Cloud to Meudon lasted 45-minutes in the airship designed by Jacques Charles and reached an estimated height of 14,800 feet (4,500 m). On the 19 September 1784, it claimed the record for the first flight of 115 miles (186 km) when it flew from Paris to Beuvry near Bethune in the north of France, flown by the Robert brothers and M. Collin-Hullin.

The *La Caroline* had an elongated shape, as do all dirigibles, as opposed to the rounded shape of hot air balloons. Boat oars were trialled as a form of propulsion and steering, but of course, these proved to have no effect at all. Therefore, having no propulsive power it could not be steered and so it was not a true dirigible airship. The first powered dirigible was flown by Henri Gifford on 24 September 1852, as we shall see shortly.

Jean Baptiste Meuniere (1754-1793) is credited with inventing the dirigible balloon, although his project was never completed.

Jean-Pierre & Sophia Blanchard

Jean-Pierre Blanchard (1753-1809) an inventor and pioneer aeronaut had made his first successful balloon flight on 2 March 1784 in a hydrogen gas balloon launched from the Champ de Mars in Paris, where Jacques Charles and Nicolas-Louis Robert had departed from the previous year. Blanchard is also recognised as the first aeronaut to use a propeller driven by man-power to propel his airship, in 1784.

Jean-Pierre Blanchard made the first balloon flights in several other countries including Holland, Germany, the USA and England, where he later moved to live. He made several balloon flights in England before his attempt to cross the English Channel to France with American, John Jeffries (1745-1819). Together, they successfully made the first ever flight across the English Channel from Dover to Guines in France, in a hydrogen gas balloon on 7 January 1785. Their balloon had ornithopter-type flapping wings presumably to propel their balloon.

Blanchard went to America and made the first ever balloon flight there on 9 January 1793. His departure from Philadelphia in Pennsylvania was witnessed by a large crowd including President George Washington. Blanchard landed in New Jersey, a distance of about 25 miles (40 km).

Blanchard further developed the parachute, which was first mooted by Leonardo da Vinci; his design was copied by Sebastian Lenormand (1757-1837) in 1783 to be claimed as the first practical parachute. Blanchard tested his own parachute by dropping it from a balloon with a dog in its basket. The parachute was made of silk and was foldable, unlike earlier parachutes which were held open by a framework. Blanchard used his parachute to save himself in 1793 when his balloon failed. Unfortunately, in 1808 he died after falling from his balloon at The Hague in Holland, presumably without a parachute.

The first female aeronaut was Sophia Blanchard (1778-1819) the widow of Jean-Pierre Blanchard. She made a solo balloon flight at Toulouse in France on 18 August 1805. She was also the first woman to make a balloon flight in Germany when she became airborne at Frankfurt. She was also the first female air fatality when her hydrogen balloon caught fire and crashed on 6 July 1819. The fire was caused by her igniting fireworks from her balloon overhead an exhibition at the Tivoli Gardens in Paris.

Moving on… As the use of hot air balloons progressed, they were put to good use for scientific experiments. For example, in 1804, Joseph Gay-Lussac (1778-1850) a chemist and physicist and Jean-Baptiste Biot (1774-1862) an astronomer, mathematician and a physicist, ascended to 23,018 feet (7,016 metres) in a hot air balloon to collect measurements of the composition of the atmosphere and to study the earth's magnetic field.

On 26 June 1794, a 10-hour battle between France and Austria during the Battle of Fleurus was observed from a balloon for the first time, enabling

France to outwit its enemy. During the American Civil War of 1861-1865, hot air balloons were used for the first time in warfare by the American, Union Army Balloon Corps as observation platforms. Balloons have also been used by other foreign armies for observation.

Henry Coxwell & James Glaisher

In 1862, Englishman, Henry Tracey Coxwell (1819-1900) was an experienced aeronaut and an author on ballooning. His interest in ballooning started when he was a young boy and he went to see as many ascents as possible and admired the various aeronauts of the day. On 19 August 1844, at the age of 25 years, he made his first balloon ascent from Pentonville (now a part of Greater London) and just like other pilots of today, he became hooked on the experience and become a notable aeronaut himself. In the second half of the 19th century, he made many ascents in the British Isles and continental Europe and in 1848, he became a professional aeronaut. From 1848 to 1852, he made numerous ascents from Brussels and Antwerp in Belgium and also Cologne and Berlin in Germany including several other places in Europe. He returned to England in 1852 and continued flying balloons making a flight in 1863 when he piloted a balloon carrying Henry Negretti (1818-1874) a photographer, to make the first aerial photographs of England. Coxwell returned to Germany in 1870 to form two balloon companies for the German Army to use during the Franco-Prussian War.

Henry Coxwell's writing on aeronautics included publishing the *Aerostat Magazine* with around twelve copies produced from 1845 and from 1887 he also wrote his autobiography titled '*My Life and Balloon Experiences*'. After forty-one years as an aeronaut, he retired on 17 June 1885 at the age of 66 years and later moved to Seaford in Sussex where he owned a balloon factory. He died in 1900 at the age of 81 years.

Dr. James Glaisher FRS (1809-1903) was a fellow aeronaut, a meteorologist and astronomer. His claim to fame came on 5 September 1862 when he departed from the Wolverhampton Gas Works in the English Midlands with Henry Coxwell and climbed up to a record-making 29,000 feet (8,800 m) and possibly higher to an estimated 35-37,000 feet (10,700-13,000 m) in their coal-gas balloon. Their barometer stopped recording at 29,000 feet!

The purpose of the ascent was to enable Glaisher to make meteorological observations in the upper atmosphere on behalf of the British Association for the Advancement of Science. However, Glaisher fell unconscious from lack of oxygen and suffered frostbite from the cold air temperature. Coxwell had managed to release the valve to descend the balloon before he too lost consciousness; they were both lucky to survive their ordeal.

High-altitude flights were not made again until a suitable oxygen system became available. To this end, further aeromedicine research was made in France on the effects of high-altitude flight. A system was devised which contained oxygen and nitrogen combined, which was fed through tubes for the aeronauts to breath. However, in April 1875, three French aeronauts made a high-altitude ascent in *Le Zenith* and two were overcome and died of anoxia; the third member survived. It was not realized at the time that the oxygen supply should have been used continuously above 14,000 feet (4,250 m) altitude, now a legal requirement for all flights above that altitude.

Sir George Cayley

Aerostatics is the study of flight for hot air balloons and airships. It was Sir George Cayley (1773-1857) who turned to aerodynamics to describe the flight of heavier-than-air aircraft. He was an English physicist, designer, far-sighted inventor, aviation pioneer and a Member of Parliament.

As a young boy of thirteen years of age, George Cayley's interest turned to theoretical and practical experiments on airfoils. He tested his model airfoils on a five-feet long whirling arm at speeds from 10-fps up to 20-fps; his experiments revealed the importance of changes in the wing's angle of attack. He also discovered the effect of a wing's dihedral angle on lateral stability and that a cambered airfoil is more efficient than a flat plate. He is also noted for being the first to experiment, in 1808, on the location of the wing's centre of pressure and its movement and how it affects the aircraft's longitudinal stability.

Cayley was also the first to discover the four basic aerodynamic forces acting on an airplane and defined the terms of lift, weight, thrust and drag. He put forward the theory that the wing's lift and engine thrust be treated as two entirely different forces; that is, the lift equals the weight and thrust equals drag, now common knowledge to all pilots. He also stated the layout of an airplane should have a tail with an elevator and rudder at the rear end of a fuselage not at the front, and the biplane or triplane wings should be fixed rigidly to the structure, not flapping as found on ornithopters (man-powered flapping wings); the fixed-wing was the way to go.

It is claimed by some authorities, although unconfirmed, Cayley's young grandson John Cayley (1826-1878) was the first person to pilot the world's first flight in a heavier-than-air machine on 7 October 1849. He was launched from a hill in a glider towed by several people down the hillside. More reliable information points to George Cayley designing a man-carrying glider in June or July 1853, which was flown by an unconfirmed pilot, possibly his coachman John Appleby, near his home at Brompton Dale near the village of Brompton-by-Sawdon, in Yorkshire. John Appleby is claimed to be the world's first adult pilot of a heavier-than-air aircraft. A replica of Cayley's glider was built and flown at Brompton Dale in 1973 and is now displayed in the Yorkshire Air Museum.

In 1799, Cayley sketched on a silver disc a basic aircraft design with a separate rudder and elevator; the London Science Museum now holds the disc. In 1809-1810, he wrote his book *On Aerial Navigation,* in three parts. George Cayley's work became the basis for all aerodynamic studies to follow and since 1846, he is considered to be the 'Father of Aerial Navigation' and also the world's first aeronautical engineer. In 1974, he was inducted into the International Air & Space Hall of Fame at San Diego, California. The work of Sir George Cayley made him one of the greatest aeronautical pioneers who paved the way for the development of aircraft as we know them today.

This Cayley Glider replica in the Yorkshire Air Museum, York,
UK, was flown at Brompton Dale in Yorkshire in 1973.

Felix du Temple

Felix du Temple (1823-1890) was a French naval officer, inventor and pioneer aviator. He is noted, with his brother Louis, for building model flying machines powered first by clockwork and later by small steam-engines of his own design. It is claimed by some authorities, in 1857, he flew the first successful powered, model flying machine culminating in his historic *Monoplane* flight in 1874 at Brest in France. Du Temple built a full-size, steam-powered monoplane which was flown by a French sailor and became airborne after launching down a ramp and gliding a short distance (most likely in ground effect) before landing. Du Temple's monoplane was credited with being the first powered, heavier-than-air flying machine to become airborne and make a successful 'powered-glide' flight; this was before the Wright brother's first flight of 1903. Note: Cayley's flights were un-powered.

John Wise

The American, John Wise (1808-1879) became a successful aeronaut flying hot air balloons for over forty years; he was a true pioneer of balloon flight. He designed his first balloon in which he made his first ascent on 2 May 1835. He flew the world's first air mail flight, delivering 123 letters in his balloon named *The Jupiter* on 17 August 1859, for the US Postal Service flying from Lafayette to Crawfordsville in Indiana.

One night when flying at a very high altitude, he discovered what came to be known later as the jet stream, a long meandering tube of high-velocity airflow found near the tropopause in both hemispheres. His find was later confirmed by Wiley Post when flying his Lockheed Vega across the USA at high altitude in the 1930s. John Wise had plans to make a trans-Atlantic flight by making use of the jet stream but was forced down on a prior flight causing damage to his balloon on landing and thwarting any further ideas of an Atlantic crossing.

He disappeared during a flight over Lake Michigan, one of the Great Lakes, on 18 September 1879, with George Burr as his passenger. The balloon and John Wise have never been found although the body of George Burr was found in the lake. John Wise designed several balloons in which he made a total of 463 balloon flights over his 44 years as an active aeronaut until his death in 1879. He left us the term of 'aircraft' in 1850.

Henri Gifford

The French engineer, Baptiste Jules Henri Jacques Gifford (1825-1882) or Henri Gifford as he was known, invented the first powered and steerable (dirigible) airship in 1852. On 24 September 1852, his hydrogen-filled airship the *Gifford Dirigible* made its first flight covering a distance of about 19 miles (30 km) from Paris to Elancourt, in France. The dirigible airship was 144 feet (44 m) long and was powered by a three-horsepower steam-engine driving a single propeller of 11-feet (3.35 m) diameter and although it was underpowered as such, it was the first successful powered dirigible airship to carry passengers. Henri Gifford experimented with larger dirigibles but they were not as successful as his first airship and due to a lack of finance his experiments were terminated. It should be noted the first 'steerable airship' was flown in 1784, although it was not powered. Sadly, Henri Gifford chose suicide rather than facing the remainder of his life with deteriorating eye sight.

Charles Renard & Arthur Krebs

On 9 August 1884, two French Corps of Engineers officers, Captains Charles Renard (1847-1905) and Arthur Constantin Krebs (1850-1935) who was also an automotive pioneer, completed a full circular course of five miles (8 km) in the *La France*, an airship operated by the French Army. It was the first fully-controllable airship and powered by a nine-horsepower electric motor turning a four-blade propeller; it managed a speed of 6.7 mph. The *La France* was 170 feet (52 m) long with a capacity of 66,000 cubic feet (1,900 m3). Steam and electric motors were underpowered for airships and it was not until the advent of piston-engines that airships found favour with military and civilian operators as useful aircraft. A lack of funding curtailed any further attempts at flying airships for Renard and Krebs.

Frederick Marriott

Frederick Marriott (1805-1884) was an Englishman who worked in banking and newspaper publishing in England and later in San Francisco when he moved to live in 1866. Twenty or so years earlier in London, he was involved with John Stringfellow (1799-1883) and William Henson in the Aerial Transit Company, which was planning to fly passengers in their 'steam carriage' *Ariel*. The project only reached as far as a flying model glider without any further progress and the company was dissolved due to a lack of finance.

However, John Stringfellow had built a flying machine powered by his home-built steam engine driving two propellers. The craft flew straight for about thirty feet (9 m).

Frederick Marriott continued with his vision of air transport in San Francisco and in company with Andrew Hallidie, they established the Aerial Steam Navigation Company in 1866 with visions of flying passengers across the USA. An airship named *Avitor Hermes Junior* was designed and built under the direction of Marriott. It had a length of 37 feet (11.27 m) and a width of 14 feet (4.27 m) containing 1,360 cubic feet (38.51 m3) of hydrogen gas, which provided the majority of the lift required. On each side of the airship's envelope were two flat wings 18 feet (5.5 m) long providing the remainder of the lift-force. Twin, two-blade propellers at 4 feet (1.22 m) diameter each, were mounted on the wings powered by a 1-horsepower steam engine. Ailerons and a rudder provided some degree of control.

The *Avitor* was flight tested on 2 July 1869 making a tethered flight a few feet off the ground near the site of the present-day San Francisco International Airport. It was claimed to be the first unmanned, powered aircraft to fly in the USA. It never proceeded past its flight test stage due to the stock market crash in 1869; however, Marriott did pursue building a heavier-than-air triplane until his death in 1884. An attempt to revise the Aerial Steam Navigation Company was made in 1882 with refinancing. However, Marriott never found the success in aviation, which he had found in his publishing businesses.

The Avitor was the first unmanned, powered aircraft to fly in the USA. The replica shown here is displayed in the Hiller Aviation Museum, San Carlos, Ca.

Clement Ader

Clement Ader (1841-1925) was a French, self-taught electrical and mechanical engineer, inventor, aeronaut and aviation pioneer. He built a full-sized aircraft and introduced an early form of wing warping on his monoplane in 1890. The wing's inboard sections are fixed, with the trailing edge of the outer wing panels free to move up and down on each wing in opposition, having the same effect as ailerons to create a rolling moment and thus lateral control of the aircraft.

Clement Ader named his airplane the *Ader Eole* in which he claimed the first man-carrying, powered, heavier-than-air aircraft with a first uncontrolled flight of 164 feet (50 m) on 9 October 1890. The bat-shaped wings spanned 46 feet (14 m) and was propelled by a self-made 20-horsepower steam engine driving a four-blade propeller. This enabled Ader to make a powered take-off and to remain airborne briefly using ground effect to help support the plane's lift. He is recognised for almost being the first to achieve powered and sustained controlled flight. The name 'Eole' (Aeolus) is from the Greek 'god of the winds'.

In 1893, he built his second plane, the Ader Avion II. Some sources claim the Ader II was never completed, although Ader contradicts this statement claiming he made a flight of over 330 feet (100 m) in August 1892 near Paris. His next aircraft was the larger Ader Avion III powered by two steam engines. Ader claimed flying a distance of 900 feet (274 m) in 1897 witnessed by two people, although this has since proven to be incorrect. Other evidence points to control difficulty and failing to become airborne due to insufficient engine power. His Ader Avion III, was the world's first aircraft to receive government funding to develop it for military purposes; however, it was unsuccessful, failing to become airborne leading to the cancelation of the funding.

The French people consider Clement Ader to be the 'Father of French Aviation'.

Otto Lilienthal

At the same time that Clement Ader was aiming to achieve powered flight in France, an early pioneer of gliding flight was Otto Lilienthal (1848-1896) in Germany. He is recognised for achieving the first controlled flight in a glider in 1891.

He became interested in flight while attending grammar school and later qualified as a design engineer and formed his own engineering company in 1872. He became well-known from his exposure in newspapers and magazines for his many experimental gliding flights. He opined that flying machines (aircraft) would one day become a reality. In 1889, he published his book *Bird Flight as the Basis of Aviation*.

Lilienthal had a small artificial hill built close to his home in Lichterfelde, near Berlin from which he used to test his gliders by launching himself from the hilltop. In 1932, the hill was turned into a memorial to Lilienthal's glider flights. He also used other nearby natural hills. He designed and built sixteen different models of gliders; his first monoplane glider flew in 1891, which he named the *Derwitzer Glider*, for which he filed for a US Patent for his invention in 1894. Modern hang gliders flown by sport pilots today strongly resemble Lilienthal's design albeit with a Rogallo type wing. From 1891, Lilienthal made over 2,000 short-duration flights in his gliders logging about five hours of flight time. He also built a biplane type of glider and eventually covered a distance of 820 feet (250 m) using up-draughts and the wind to help keep him airborne. However, on 9 August 1896 his glider stalled from about fifty feet above the ground and crashed severely injuring Lilienthal. He died from his injuries the next day at Gollenberg, Germany.

Otto Lilienthal was one of the great aviation pioneers of that era, and his contribution to flight was very significant, which influenced other pioneers including the Wright brothers.

A replica of Otto Lilienthal's glider is displayed in the Science Museum in London.

Octave Chanute

The French-born American, Octave Chanute (1832-1910) was a civil engineer by trade working on the American railways and in his retirement, he turned to aviation studies to become one of the greatest pioneers of the theory of flight, although by then he was too old to attempt any flying himself.

He joined forces with other young pioneers and began designing and building hang gliders in the same year that Lilienthal died, in 1896. They experimented with several wings stacked one above the other, a method which Otto Lilienthal had tried. Chanute applied his bridge-construction knowledge to aviation with the use of Pratt struts using wires to brace the biplane wings, a method that was adopted by all biplane designers that followed over the coming years. His biplane glider-designs inspired the Wright brothers to pursue their dream of flight with a similar biplane design for their gliders and later, their powered aircraft starting with the Wright Flyer I.

Chanute provided advice freely to other aviation pioneers to help them towards gaining their goals of flight. In return, Chanute was a collector of information passed on to him about heavier-than-air flight with which he published his book *Progress in Flying Machines,* in 1894. Octave Chanute is considered to be the 'Father of Aviation' and is noted for his many experiments in glider flight.

Samuel Pierpont Langley

Professor Samuel Pierpont Langley (1834-1906) was born in Roxbury in Massachusetts, USA. He became a professor of astronomy, a physicist, a pioneer aviator and from 1887 to 1906, he was the third Secretary of the Smithsonian Institute. He almost beat the Wright brothers to become the first person to successfully fly a heavier-than-air powered aircraft, but his attempts were unsuccessful, as we shall see shortly.

In 1896, he became interested in aerodynamics and built two model aircraft. He also experimented with a steam catapult to launch his *Aerodrome No 5*, which maintained flight for about 3,300 feet (1,000 m); later models flew a distance of up to 5,000 feet (1,530 m), almost a mile. From his model design he constructed a full-size craft which he launched from a houseboat moored on the Potomac River near Washington, D.C. By that time petrol-powered engines were a new invention and his mechanic Charles Manly, built a fifty-horsepower engine for Langley's craft. The plane had tandem wings, not a biplane, but with one wing behind the other. Launched from the houseboat on 7 October 1903 it crashed into the Potomac River before any chance of flying some distance. It was repaired and a second attempt was made on the following day, which also failed, leading Langley to abandon any more attempts. Samuel Langley was the last of the early pioneers who tried and failed to complete a controlled flight in a heavier-than-air aircraft before the Wright brothers' famous first flight on 17 December 1903.

Pioneer aviators had varying success in those early days of manned flights. The French Army were the first to use airships in 1794 to observe the battle at Fleurus in Belgium, but after 1799 Napolean ceased using them. However, from the late 1800s into the early 1900s, ballooning became a very popular sport in America, England and Europe. Although balloons and airships continued to be flown and improved upon, including use by the military during both World Wars, the fixed-wing airplane was about to become a reality and eventually to evolve into the efficient and reliable aircraft that we know today. Man's quest to fly as free as the birds had finally come to fruition.

2 – Pioneers of the 20th Century

The Pioneering Age of Aviation

There were many aviation pioneers in the early 1900s, all vying to build and fly a workable and controllable aircraft. Just as there was with balloon and airship flights, there were many failures and a few successes with fixed-wing and later, rotary-wing aircraft for this new breed of pioneer aviators. The Pioneering Age of Aviation started in 1903 with the success of the Wright brothers and lasted until 1914, the start of WWI.

The Wright brothers

A day at the beach on a cold and windy, winter's day is not everyone's idea of a good day out. However, for the Wright brothers, the weather conditions suited them admirably; a fairly strong wind was blowing and the area was devoid of inquisitive people. The day was about to become a very significant day in aviation history, the 17 December 1903. The location, Kill Devil Hills just south of Kitty Hawk in North Carolina, USA.

The story of the Wright brothers' victorious achievement has been well documented many times and their endeavours are well-known to aviation enthusiasts and laymen alike. Therefore, a brief recap is all that is required here.

The Wright brothers were very scientific in their approach to flight, constructing their first wind tunnel in 1901 and testing many different shaped airfoils before settling on one that proved to suit their requirements. From 1895 to 1903, they had experimented with three different gliders before building the Wright Flyer, which was based on their third glider.

The Wright Flyer was an orthogonal biplane where the top wing was placed directly above the lower wing, typical of all early biplanes until it was discovered biplane wings work better when the top wing (usually) is placed forward of the lower wing to reduce what is known as biplane interference. The wings were muslin covered and single-surface, having no cambered lower surface, which was also typical for that era.

The Wright brothers' famous Wright Flyer of 1903 gathers much attention from daily visitors to the National Air & Space Museum in Washington, D.C. Note the absence of a fuselage and also ailerons; wing warping was used to keep the wings level. The front of the plane has canard stabilisers, seen on the right of the photograph. The pilot lay prone on the lower wing.

The wind tunnel designed by Orville Wright in 1916 for research work in his Dayton, Ohio laboratory. Seen here on display in the NMUSAF, Dayton, Ohio.

The Flyer used wing warping to keep the wings laterally level with no attempt to make turns; ailerons came later for manoeuvring. Wing warping moved the wing's trailing edges up or down operated by the pilot lying in the prone position by moving his hips from side-to-side on the cradle he was lying on. Moving the cradle also operated the rudder to control yaw. The horizontal elevator placed forward of the main wing as a canard surface, was controlled by a hand-operated lever being moved forward and aft to control pitch in the longitudinal axis.

The Flyer had no fuselage as such, except for a bracing structure at the rear of the main wings to support twin vertical rudders (no fins), for yaw control. The pilot's prone-position balanced the weight of the single-engine, which was placed off-centre on the lower wing. The twelve-horsepower engine turned a pair of contra-rotating pusher propellers by chain-drive.

On their first attempts to fly the Wright Flyer they were unsuccessful and the plane was damaged, which required repair work to be done. Wilbur Wright (1867-1912) had made the last attempted flight on the previous day and sharing the flights called for Orville Wright (1871-1948) to make the first flight of the day on the 17 December 1903. The flight was successful and history was made as the world's first controlled, heavier-than-air aircraft made its first successful flight with a controlled take-off and landing.

The Flyer was launched from a dolly running on a track laid out facing into the wind; the landings were made on the beach using the plane's skids. The first flight of the day covered a distance of 120 feet (37 m), a distance shorter than the wingspan of a Boeing 747. Three more flights were made that day, each flight increasing in length until a maximum distance of 852 feet (260 m) was covered with the Flyer remaining airborne for almost one-minute on the fourth and final flight of the day. Taking words from Neil Armstrong's quote, "One small step for the Flyer, one giant leap for the Wright brothers", describes the success achieved for the two brothers! Surprisingly, the Wright Flyer never flew again and the Wright brothers kept their success a secret until sometime well after their historic flight.

The Wright Flyer was followed by the Flyer II which made its first flight at Huffman Prairie near their hometown of Dayton, Ohio on 23 May 1904. Later that year on 20 September, Orville flew the Flyer II in four circles covering a total distance of 4,080 feet (1,240 m) to become the first person in the world to demonstrate controlled manoeuvring flight was possible. Although the Flyer II had several mishaps and repairs, it was eventually scrapped and replaced by their next aircraft, the Flyer III in 1905. The two brothers had a short absence from flying until 1908 when they went to France and gave demonstration flights.

Some authorities claim the flight in 1906 by Santos Dumont as the first official powered flight, because Dumont took-off in his wheel-equipped plane as opposed to the Wright brothers who used a track and dolly to launch their Flyer I. Disregarding the take-off method used, the Wright brothers' flights were made first and has been officially recognised for several decades by most authorities.

The Wright brothers now have forever-lasting fame for their exploits with their early aircraft. One bit of fame they didn't want, occurred on 17 September 1908 when Orville was flying with a passenger, Thomas Etholen Selfridge (1882-1908). Orville's aircraft crashed killing Thomas Selfridge who had the unwanted distinction of being the first person to be killed in a powered airplane accident. Orville was severely injured and was in hospital recovering for seven weeks.

Although the Wright brothers are associated with their flights in the Wright Flyer, where they had alternate turns at the controls, they only ever actually flew together in the same plane once and that was at Huffman Prairie, Dayton on 25 May 1910.

The Richard Pearce memorial consists of a reduced-size replica of the aircraft he built and attempted to fly circa 1903. The memorial is located near the small farming town of Waitohi in South Canterbury, New Zealand.

In 1910, the Smithsonian Institution initially declined the Wright brother's offer to exhibit the Wright Flyer. Charles Walcott, the Smithsonian's secretary at the time, gave credit to the previous secretary, Samuel Langley, for his flight as being the world's first powered flight. It was not until 1942 that the Smithsonian Institute reversed their decision in favour of the Wright brothers for being the first to make a successful, controlled flight.

The Wright Flyer was sent to England for display in the Science Museum in London until it was placed in safe storage during the Second World War. In 1948, it was shipped back to America on board the *Mauritania* and placed on display in the Smithsonian's Arts & Industry Museum. Since 1976, the Wright Flyer has been on display in the Smithsonian National Air & Space Museum in Washington, D.C. It now sits on a rotating turn-table and captures much attention from daily visitors from all over the world who come to see this iconic aircraft, the father of all aircraft that have followed, ever since that cold and windy day back in December 1903.

The two brothers were always very close throughout their childhood and adult life (they also had a sister, Katherine). However, Wilbur succumbed to typhoid fever and died on 30 May 1912; Orville lived on until 30 January 1948 when a heart attack took his life. He would have seen many advances in aviation over the forty-five years since those famous first flights with his brother, including jet and rocket powered flight and Chuck Yeager's flight through Mach one, on 14 Oct 1947, just a few short weeks before Orville died.

From hot air balloons to dirigible airships to gliders and finally to successful powered and controlled flight, the airplane had finally arrived with the Wright brothers' success.

Richard Pearce

New Zealand's Richard Pearce (1877-1953) was an eccentric South Island farmer, inventor and pioneer aviator who attempted to make several flights. He obtained a patent for his own airplane, engine and two-blade propeller, which he had designed and built himself. It is believed he made his first flight attempts at Waitohi on 31 March 1903; however, other information points to him making his flights in 1902, leading some people to claim he flew before the Wright brothers. Richard Pearce himself never made any claims of flying first, but he did claim his more successful flights were made in 1904. All the flights included a powered take-off with a short hop, but ended in crash-landings and were thus deemed to be uncontrolled flights. He made no further attempts to fly after 1904, knowing the Wright brothers had achieved controlled flight.

Henri & Maurice Farman

Pioneer aviator, Henri Farman (1874-1958) was born in Paris, France to English parents and became a French national in 1937. In his early days, he was a keen sportsman entering cycling and motor racing competitions. He trained to be a painter before his interest turned to mechanics and aviation. In 1907, he built model aircraft and then a home-made glider practicing his flying skills on the sand dunes at Le Tourquet in the Pas-de-Calais region of northern France.

In June 1907, he bought a Voisin II biplane in which he made several record making flights, each increasing in distance measured in metres, until he covered a distance of 2,529 feet (771 metres) to claim the world's longest flight, made on 27 October 1907, at Issy-les-Moulineaux in France, which lasted for more than one minute. He received the Ernest Archdeacon Cup for this record flight. He also received the credit for the first cross-country flight in Europe when he flew a distance of 17 miles (27 km) from Camp de Chalons at Bouy to Reims on 30 October 1908. On 13 January 1908, Farman exceeded his previous year's record when he remained airborne for nearly one and half minutes and covered a circular distance of over 1.65 miles (1 km). For his efforts he won the Archdeacon Grand Prix d'Aviation worth 50,000 francs.

Frenchman, Ferdinand Leon Delagrange (1872-1910), was the world's first fixed-wing aircraft passenger to fly, in 1908, when he was taken aloft by Henri Farman, near Paris. Delagrange must have been quite impressed with his flight; he later become another early French pioneer making several record flights himself.

The following year, Henri's brother Maurice Alain Farman (1877-1964) bought a Voisin Model 4 biplane and made several record-breaking flights reaching as far as 144 miles (232 km) on 3 November 1909. Also in 1909, he flew his first aircraft design, the Farman III biplane, to make the first circular flight in Europe, (to recall, the Wright brothers had made the world's first circular flight on 20 September 1904, in America). The Farman III was the first Farman-built model and in 1909, it was the world's first aircraft to be powered by a rotary engine; the first and second Farman-designed models were built by Voisin. He also won the Grand Prix d'Aviation on 13 January 1908. The same year, Henri Farman opened a flying school and later formed his own aircraft manufacturing business, the Farman Aircraft Company with his two brothers, Maurice and Richard.

The Maurice Farman Shorthorn was a well-known early World War I aircraft from the Farman factory. This one is exhibited in the Canada Aviation and Space Museum, Ottawa, Canada.

The military made good use of the Farman 1914 model during World War One and the Maurice Farman MF.II Shorthorn was another popular World War One aircraft. In 1918, the Farman Goliath was built. It was initially designed as a bomber but was too late for war-time service and the design was changed to become a passenger aircraft. This was the world's first long-haul airliner, long-haul in this instance, refers to the Paris to London route, which started on 8 February 1919. The Goliath was a twin-engine biplane with the pilot sitting in an open cockpit on top of the fuselage. A Farman Goliath is featured with a photograph in section 18 – Aircraft of the Fledgling Airlines.

Henri Farman and his brother Maurice both retired from aircraft manufacturing in 1937 when the French Government nationalised the French aircraft industry. Henri Farman was inducted into the San Diego Air & Space Museum's Hall of Fame in 1988.

Samuel Franklyn Cody

Samuel Franklyn Cody (1861-1913) was a Wild West showman back in his home country of North America before he moved to England and became a British citizen. He worked on war kites, balloons and later airplanes for the British Army at the Army Balloon Factory in Farnborough, later known as the Royal Aircraft Factory from 1912 when it built WWI aircraft for the

Royal Flying Corps/RAF and from 1918 it was known as the Royal Aircraft Establishment, or simply as Farnborough.

Samuel Cody is noted for being the first man to successfully design and fly a heavier-than-air airplane in England, achieving this milestone on 16 October 1908. He flew his British Army Aeroplane No 1, (also known as the Cody Flyer) which was built by the Army Balloon Factory at Farnborough and was a typical design for that era as an orthogonal biplane (with non-staggered wings) and powered by a French-built Antoinette engine.

The plane was quite large for an early attempt at powered flight, having a length of 37 feet 9 inches (11.51 m) and a large wingspan of over 43 feet (13.11 m) giving a wing area of 430 ft2 (in comparison, a Cessna 172's wing area is 174 ft2). An elevator was mounted forward of the top wing for pitch control and a rudder at the rear for directional stability and yaw control. It had a maximum speed of 72 mph (116 km/h). Like most early aircraft of that time, its layout was almost identical to the Wright Flyer.

Cody covered a short distance before his plane was damaged at the end of the flight and required repair work and modifications before his next flight, which he made on 16 October 1908. Several short flights were attempted before he managed to stay airborne long enough to cover a distance of 1,378 feet (420 m) to claim the first official controlled flight in Great Britain.

A replica of Britain's first successful airplane the Cody Flyer or British Army Aeroplane 1, housed in the Farnborough Air Science Trust Museum, Farnborough, England.

The second Cody V biplane has been on display in the Science Museum in London since 1913. Note the large canard stabiliser at the front of the plane just above the single nose-wheel. The pusher prop can just be seen to the right in the photo.

In mid-World War I, the British War office issued a requirement for a two-seat aircraft to carry a pilot and observer for the Royal Flying Corps. A competition was held to determine who would receive the prize of £4,000 and a contract to supply the required aircraft. The winner was announced on 1 August 1912. Samuel Cody had planned to enter two aircraft in the competition; however, both aircraft met with a mishap (read crashed). From the remains of both aircraft, Cody built a new pusher biplane with four-seats in an open cockpit and powered by the 120 horsepower Austro-Daimler engine from his wrecked monoplane. As the new rebuild, it made its first flight on 23 July 1912 at Salisbury, England. The War Office subsequently purchased this aircraft and ordered a second Cody V biplane. The first Cody V entered service with the Royal Flying Corps No 4 Squadron on 30 November 1912. It flew for the next five months before suffering an in-flight structural failure resulting in a fatal accident. The second Cody V first flew in January 1913 and also received damage from an accident and was waiting to be repaired. It was never flown again; instead, it was donated to the London Science Museum where it can be seen suspended from the ceiling in the Flight Gallery, as pictured above.

Samuel Cody died in an aviation accident in 1913.

Sir Alliott Verdon-Roe

Edwin Alliott Verdon-Roe (1877-1958) was a pioneer pilot and aircraft manufacturer and formed his own company known as the A.V. Roe Aircraft Company on 1 January 1910, in Manchester. He later renamed it to Avro Aircraft. It became a major British aircraft company building many different types of aircraft including the World War I Avro 504 training aircraft, World War II Lancaster bomber, the Avro Vulcan bomber, Avro Tudor airliner and Avro/BAe 748 turboprop transport, to name just a few types.

Verdon-Roe's interest in building a flying machine stemmed from his observations of the albatross birds while serving in the British Merchant Navy as a ship's engineer. After leaving the sea, he built several flying models, one of which won a £75 prize from the Daily Mail newspaper. He built his first aircraft, the Avro 1, which is historically significant as the first all-British built aircraft and engine, to fly in England making its first flight in 1909. Not forgetting, Samuel Cody had flown the previous year in 1908, in his aircraft which was powered by a French-built engine.

The prototype of the Avro 1 Triplane now displayed suspended from the ceiling in the Science Museum, London, UK. It was one of the first aircraft designs to employ a tractor propeller (mounted at the front of the fuselage).

In 1929, Verdon-Roe (he had changed his name slightly from Verdon Roe by deed poll) received a knighthood for his significant contribution to aviation during his pioneering days. His company stayed in business through to the mid-1900s. He died in 1958 and was inducted into the International Air & Space Museum Hall of Fame in San Diego, California in 1980.

The Avro I was an early experimental airplane with a tractor engine/propeller, orthogonal triplane main wings spanning 20 feet (6.1 m) and an unusual triplane tailplane. Unlike a modern aircraft's tailplane which normally produces a down-force for longitudinal stability, the Avro's tailplane was a second lifting surface providing a third of the total lift force; therefore, the Avro I was in fact, a tandem wing triplane. The wings were all single-surface airfoils, typical for that era. The fuselage was open frame-work with a triangular cross-section, with the pilot sitting in the open and unprotected from the elements. Roll control was handled by wing warping and pitch control by changes to the main wing's angle of incidence (the angle between the wing's chord line and the plane's longitudinal axis). The undercarriage consisted of two main wheels looking very much like bicycle wheels with a tail-skid at the rear. The single JAP V-twin, air-cooled, nine-horsepower engine drove a four-blade tractor propeller pulling the aircraft along at a maximum speed of 25 mph (40 km/h). The four-blade propeller was also unusual for that time as most were two-blade props; it may have been one of the first four-blade propellers to be made.

A.V. Roe made the first flight in his Avro 1, on 5 June 1909 and flew his last flight in it at Blackpool before he donated it to the London Science Museum. In 2008, the Brooklands Museum in Weybridge, Surrey built a replica Avro 1 Biplane, which they claimed "in theory it could make short hops like the original". The project was funded by Eric Verdon Roe, the grandson of Sir Alliott Verdon-Roe.

The Aerial Experiment Association

The Aerial Experiment Association (1907-1909) was formed in Canada with Frederick W. Baldwin (1882-1948) as the association's chief engineer in company with two well-known characters, Alexander Graham Bell as financier and pioneer pilot Glen Curtiss (1878-1930) as the director of experiments, who later formed his own aircraft manufacturing company, the Curtiss Aeroplane and Motor Company, in 1909.

The AEA built three aircraft of note, the Red Wing which first flew on 12 March 1909 flown by Frederick Baldwin to become the first powered aircraft to fly in Canada. However, it only flew for about twenty seconds before crashing and therefore did not qualify as the first controlled flight in Canada. It was not rebuilt. This was followed in 1908 with the second aircraft, the White Wing and a year later by the Silver Dart, the aircraft of interest here.

The Silver Dart's first flight was made in 1908 at Hammondsport, New York before it was shipped to Baddeck Bay in Nova Scotia, where it made the first officially recognised controlled and powered airplane flight in Canada on 23 February 1909 in the hands of its co-designer and pilot, John McCurdy. On the 2 August 1909, the Silver Dart made history again with the first flight in Canada carrying a passenger. A flight later that day ended with the Silver Dart being written-off while attempting a take-off and was damaged beyond repair.

The Silver Dart was powered by a fifty horsepower Curtiss V-8 engine, with a wingspan of 44 feet (12.22 m) and a length of 30 feet (9.14 m). A replica of the Silver Dart was built by the Royal Canadian Air Force with a sixty-five horsepower Continental engine for the 50th anniversary in 1959 of the Silver Dart's first flight. It is now displayed in the Canada Aviation & Space Museum in Ottawa, Canada.

The Silver Dart replica is displayed on a slowly rotating platform in the Canada Aviation & Space Museum in Ottawa, Canada.

Alberto Santos-Dumont

Two other pioneers also laid claim to have successfully flown before the Wright brothers' pioneering flight. They were the Brazilian, Alberto Santos-Dumont (1873-1932) inventor and aeronautical pioneer and the Frenchman, Louis Bleriot (1872-1936).

Alberto Santos-Dumont lived in Paris from the 1890s and was noted for his numerous pioneering flights in hot air balloons, airships and fixed-wing aircraft. He made the first practical routine flights in his non-rigid, dirigible airships (commonly known as 'Blimps'). He designed a total of eighteen balloons and dirigibles before turning to designing and building heavier-than-air airplanes. He made the first flight in his airship, the *Santos Dumont No 1*, powered by an internal combustion engine on 18 September 1898. He also made the first flight from Parc de Saint-Cloud to the Eiffel Tower and return in less than thirty minutes on 19 October 1901 in his dirigible airship *Number 6*, to claim the 50,000-franc Deutsch de la Meurthe Prize. The prize was offered by Frenchman, Henri Deutsch de la Meurthe (1846-1919) an oil businessman, to the first person to fly any type of flying machine from Parc de Saint Cloud to the Eiffel Tower and return, a distance of 6.8 miles (11 km) within a time of 30 minutes.

A replica Demoiselle Type 20 designed by Santos-Dumont. This one is displayed in the Brooklands Museum, Weybridge in England.

On 23 October 1906, Santos-Dumont flew his 14-bis (Little 14) biplane named as the *Oiseau de Proie (Bird of Prey)* over a distance of 197 feet (60 m) at a height of 18 feet (5.5 m) after a self-powered take-off from the grounds of the Chateau de Bagatelle, Paris. This flight was claimed to be the first official public flight-demonstration in Europe for a heavier-than-air aircraft after taking-off under its own power; it was witnessed by a large crowd of local people. The flight was historically significant for bringing controlled, powered flight to the public's attention and also for the first aviation accomplishment to be certified by the Aero-Club de France. For this flight, Santos-Dumont won the Deutsch-Archdeacon Prize for being officially observed to have exceeded 82 feet (25 m). The following month on 12 November 1906, Santos-Dumont flew a distance of over 722 feet (220 m) to claim the world's first distance-record to be certified by the newly formed Federation Aéronautique Internationale (FAI), the governing body which records all world-wide aviation-related records. Dumont also has the distinction of being the first pioneer aviator to be filmed while flying an airplane.

Dumont's 14-bis biplane appears to fly backwards having a forward canard stabiliser. The box-kite type, main wings had a span of 37 feet 7 inches and were set well back on the fuselage, which itself measures a length of 31 feet 6 inches. The craft had a maximum weight of 639 lb (290 kg) and was powered by an Antoinette V-8 engine of 50 hp driving a pusher propeller. From old photographs, it appears the plane was flown from a standing position or an unusually high seat, with Dumont's upper body well-exposed to the slipstream. Dumont built only one example of the 14-bis; it was destroyed on 4 April 1907. The box-kite wing structure was introduced in 1893 by the Australian, Lawrence Hargrave (1850-1915) in 1893, and was used by some early pioneer aviators.

From 1906 onwards, Santos-Dumont built several single-seat aircraft known as the Demoiselle (Dragonfly). The Demoiselle had a cruciform tailplane with an elevator and rudder and used wing warping for roll control, with the unusual feature of the wing warping only downwards to lift the wing. Later versions of the Demoiselle had the wing warping replaced with more effective ailerons. The last versions from series 19 to 22, managed a cruise speed of 75 mph (120 km/h) and could be constructed in fifteen days; they became the world's first mass-produced aircraft.

The first aircraft to be powered by a tractor engine/propeller (a front-mounted engine and propeller) was the Goupy II, designed in 1909 by a little-known French aviation pioneer, Ambroise Goupy (1876-1951), at Louis Bleriot's factory at Buc in France. It was also the first aircraft to use staggered biplane wings, which reduces airflow interference between the top and bottom wings on biplanes, mentioned previously. All biplanes are now built with staggered wings for increased efficiency. Wing warping was gradually replaced by ailerons and on the Goupy II, it had ailerons that were unique in their design; they were placed at the wing tips and stretched full chord (from leading edge to trailing edge).

It is interesting to note, the world's first powered monoplane was designed and flown by the Romanian, Trajan Vuia (1872-1950) a pioneer aviator and inventor; it flew a distance of 36 feet (11 m)) on 18 March 1906 and shortly after, he doubled this distance. Vuia's design introduced the monoplane and the wheeled undercarriage complete with pneumatic tyres to the world. Taking note, Albert Santos Dumont used wheels on his aircraft and Bleriot chose the monoplane design.

The Wright brothers' airframe layout, pusher engines and the box-wing structure were common to the very early pioneer aviators; however, the design gradually morphed into the more practical style of a monoplane layout with a tractor engine/propeller that we know today.

Louis Bleriot

Louis Charles Bleriot (1872-1936) was an early French pioneer aviator and probably the most well-known pioneer after the Wright brothers. His claim to fame occurred on 25 July 1909 after he made the first successful crossing of the English Channel in a powered, heavier-than-air airplane. He flew his Bleriot Type XI monoplane from France to England to win the £1,000 prize offered by the *Daily Mail* newspaper.

Louis Bleriot was drawn to aviation during his time at the Ecole Centrale in Paris (an engineering and science school). After visiting the 1900 Paris Exposition Universelle (a world fair to showcase the previous year's achievements) Bleriot saw Clement Ader (1841-1925) demonstrate his Avion III (Eole III) aircraft; Bleriot's interest in aviation matters was firmly established. He started performing experiments with flying machines, first with ornithopters before moving on to experimental gliders and powered aircraft.

After a period of trial and error, with a few mishaps along the way with several powered aircraft, Bleriot eventually developed his Antoinette IV monoplane in 1908, which became the world's first successful monoplane. Bleriot had pioneered the use of monoplane aircraft, as a departure from the biplane, then the most common type to be used in those early days of flying.

This Bleriot XI is the type Louis Bleriot used to make the first airplane crossing of the English Channel in 1909. This aircraft is an original Bleriot XI powered by an original Anzani W3 engine. It is the world's oldest aircraft still in flying condition and is owned and flown by the Shuttleworth Collection Museum at Old Warden in England.

Bleriot was also instrumental in developing the flight control system which later became the accepted standard for all aircraft where a control stick (or joy stick) was used to operate the ailerons and elevator and a foot-operated control bar operated the rudder.

In 1905, Bleriot entered into a business partnership with the Voisin brothers, Gabriel (1880-1973) and Charles (1882-1912). The two brothers soon parted company with Bleriot and established their own aircraft company, the *Appareils d'Aviation Les Freres Voisin* (Voison Brothers Flying Machines) who built their first successful airplane in 1905. One of their designs was a floatplane, which Bleriot filmed in flight, to become the first movie film of an aircraft flying.

Meantime, Louis Bleriot founded his own aircraft manufacturing company, the Bleriot Aeronautique. In 1910, Leon Lemartin (1883-1911) was employed by Bleriot's company as the world's first test pilot. Bleriot already had a successful car headlamp manufacturing company, which had financed his early aeronautical experiments. From 1909 to 1914, Bleriot's company built about nine-hundred aircraft, mostly various versions of his Model XI which held world records for range, endurance, speed and altitude. The Model XI was built between July 1909 to the start of WWI and was used by several of the various early air forces and later, by aero clubs.

Louis Bleriot also became president of the SPAD company from 1913, giving the company a small change in its name to Societe Pour L'Aviation et ses Derives (SPAD). In England, he set up a flying school and in May 1918 he established a new company, the Air Navigation & Engineering Company (ANEC), which made a few light aircraft, motor bikes and cars until its closure in 1926.

Aiming to claim the *Daily Mail* prize of £1,000, Louis Bleriot had three competitors, Hubert Latham flying an Antoinette IV, a Russian, Charles de Lambert and Arthur Seymour from England flying a Voisin biplane. Hubert Latham was the only competitor who actually made an attempt on the crossing. He departed Calais on 19 July 1909 but was forced to ditch in the sea due to engine failure, just six miles short of the Dover coastline to be picked up by the French Navy escort ship, the *Harpon*. His unwanted experience gave him the distinction of being the first pilot to ditch an aircraft on water.

Latham had a second Antoinette delivered from the factory ready for a second attempt; however, Bleriot was next to make the attempt on the crossing.

On the 25 July 1909, Louis Bleriot set off from Calais at sunrise to cross the English Channel to Dover 23 miles (37 km) away. He flew his Bleriot XI at about 250 feet high (77 m) and cruised at 45 mph (72 km/h). He flew overhead his escort ship to get a heading to fly towards Dover with the visibility deteriorating en route. He landed on the cliff-top close to Dover Castle thirty-six minutes after take-off to win the Daily Mail prize and to enter the aeronautical history books and become a famous celebrity. He had achieved the first Channel crossing in an airplane. His Bleriot XI was powered by a 3-cylinder Anzani engine developing a rather low 25-horsepower; the Anzani engine was designed by the Italian Alessandro Anzani (1877-1956).

Along with Henri Farman (1874-1958) and Gabriel Voisin, Bleriot was one of the major producers of aircraft in the early 1900s. Eventually, Louis Bleriot withdrew from flying planes but remained working in his aviation business until his death in 1936. He was buried at Versailles near Paris.

The Aero-Club de France issued the first pilot licence to Louis Bleriot on 7 January 1909. The FAI has awarded the Louis Bleriot medal to record-setters in the light aircraft class since 1936. He is remembered in the International Air & Space Hall of Fame at San Diego Air & Space Museum since 1967, a recognition he well-deserves as France's most productive and famous aviation pioneer.

Bleriot XI planes claimed several distance records. Apart from the aforementioned English Channel crossing, record flights included the first flight over the Alps Mountains in September 1910 and a non-stop London to Paris flight in 1911.

Gustave Whitehead

Across the Atlantic in Bridgeport, Connecticut, another pioneer also made claim to be the first to fly in his heavier-than-air machine on 14 August 1901. This was Gustave Whitehead (1874-1927), a German immigrant who claimed to have flown his plane over Bridgeport and nearby Fairfield at a height of 150 feet (45 m) for nearly two-miles. He also made claim to a 7-mile (11 km) flight over Long Island, New York, in 1901.

Both these claims are questionable. First, the Wright brothers claim their flight in 1903 was the first, three years before Santos-Dumont's 1906 flight. Secondly, the flight of Gustave Whitehead has no documentation to prove the fact; a blurred photograph was the only available evidence, which disappeared until it was rediscovered in Australia decades later!

However, in more recent years, March 2013 to be precise, 'Jane's, *All the World's Aircraft*' publication acknowledged Whitehead's flight as being the first in a heavier-than-air airplane. Opposing Whitehead's claim is the Smithsonian Institution's recognition of the Wright brothers as the first to fly a heavier-than-air machine.

Glen Curtiss

Glen Hammond Curtiss (1878-1930) was America's most influential aviation pioneer, active in many aviation exploits as a test pilot, competition pilot, flight instructor and record-setting pilot, including aircraft design and manufacturing; he gained many prizes and 'firsts' in the advancement of aviation.

One of his first ventures was his involvement with the Canadian Experimental Aircraft Association, mentioned above. He designed and flew the Aerodrome No 3 (June Bug) on 4 July 1908 at Hammondsport, New York, making a name for himself and bringing manned, powered flight to the public's attention. Curtiss flew the June Bug a distance of 5,360 feet (1,640 m) in one minute and 40 seconds to win the Scientific American Cup, the first aeronautical prize worth US$25,000 to be presented to any aviator who flew more than one 1 kilometre (3,280 feet).

The flight of the June Bug was the first to be filmed in America. Glen Curtiss also received the first pilots licence to be issued by the Aero Club of America.

Based on the AEA's June Bug, Curtiss built his first aircraft, the Curtiss No 1, which became the prototype for a series of pusher-propeller aircraft. It was the start of his Curtiss Aeroplane and Motor Company, the first licenced aircraft company to be established in America, starting business in January 1916. He went on to develop numerous types of aircraft over the following years supplying the US Army and the Navy with many of their aircraft. World War I was indeed a very profitable time for his aircraft manufacturing company. Glen Curtiss taught America's first woman pilot to fly, Blanch Scott in 1910. He also trained military pilots to fly in his flying training school (the first one in the USA) located in San Diego, now the Naval Air Station and known as the 'Birthplace of Naval Aviation'; Curtiss himself is known as the 'Father of Naval Aviation'.

The floatplane Fabre Hydravian named Le Canard (the Duck), was developed by Jean-Henri Fabre in which made the first successful flight operating from water on 28 March 1910. This was followed by the first successful flying boat, which was built in 1911-12 also by a Frenchman, Francois Denhaut (1877-1952) which made its first historic flight on 13 April 1912. Glen Curtiss further developed floatplanes, flying boats and amphibians and he became the first pilot to fly a floatplane in North America. His first successful floatplane was developed into his Curtiss Model D Headless Pusher in 1911.

A Curtiss D-III Headless Pusher replica built-up from original parts with a Curtiss V-8 engine. It was donated to the Smithsonian Institute in 1925 and is now displayed in the National Air & Space Museum in Washington, D.C.

The Curtiss N-9 was built for the US Navy as the floatplane version of the famous Curtiss Jenny. Note, the single float, more suitable for open water landings than twin floats. This N-9 can be seen in the Udvar-Hazy Center.

In February 1911, a long association between Glen Curtiss and the US Navy commenced when the Navy took delivery of their first aircraft, a Curtiss Hydroplane A-1 Triad from the Curtiss Aeroplane and Motor Company. It was the world's first amphibious aircraft with two main wheels and tail skid undercarriage with a single float for water operations. For this achievement, Curtiss received the first Collier Trophy to be presented in the USA. The example shown here is a replica displayed in the National Naval Aviation Museum in Pensacola, Florida.

In 1925, Glen Curtiss merged his company with the Wright Aeronautical Corporation to form the Curtiss-Wright Company, just five years before he died in 1930. He was inducted into the National Aviation Hall of Fame in 1964 and in 1990 to the Motorsports Hall of Fame of America; motor racing was one of his life-long interests.

His next step was to develop the Curtiss Models E and F and the now famous Curtiss JN-4 'Jenny', a light aircraft used to train US Army pilots for World War I service; the Curtiss N-9 was the seaplane version built for the US Navy. He also built the four-engine Curtis NC flying boats which were used by the US Navy to make the first powered airplane flight across the North Atlantic. [See 'Trans-Atlantic Pioneers; First Atlantic Crossing by Plane').

The Curtiss Hydroplane A-1 Triad replica in the National Naval Aviation Museum, NAS Pensacola in Florida. It was the US Navy's first aircraft.

Floatplanes, Seaplanes & Amphibians

The modern trend for floatplanes is to have a pair of floats mounted slightly outboard from the fuselage, which are quite suitable for operations on calmer inland waterways. However, the first floatplanes built for the US Navy were required to operate off the sea where conditions were much rougher. Therefore, the early floatplanes mostly had a single-float mounted directly below the fuselage with a pair of stabilising wing-tip floats, which better handled the sea conditions. Tip-floats are also used on flying boats; however, they can also be found on planes with twin floats, but are less common. Flying boats are generally, but not always, much larger than floatplanes and rely on their boat-shaped fuselage/hulls for water flotation. A few points of interest here:

- The terms seaplanes and floatplanes can be used interchangeably.

- An amphibious craft can operate from both land and water.

- Curtiss developed the stepped hull for flying boats and floats, used to help break free from smooth water on take-off.

- The Schneider Trophy air race was formed to promote floatplanes, which were lagging behind their land-based counterparts in regards to progress in their development.

- Helicopters can also operate off land and water with floats or boat-shaped hulls.

- The world's first airline service, the St. Petersburg-Tampa Airboat Line, in Florida, was operated by a pair of *Benoist XIV* flying boats in 1912.

To continue… During 1920, Elwood Wilson was a forestry worker employed by the Laurentide Company; he arranged to have two Curtiss HS-2L aircraft for use by the company on aerial mapping and forest fire-spotting. They became the first bush planes to operate in Canada's vast uninhabited northern regions. The Laurentide Air Services ceased trading in 1925.

The Curtiss HS-2L was originally built for the US Navy to spot submarines during the end of World War I from 1917 to 1919. It was built in Saint Maurice Valley, Quebec and was powered by a Liberty V-12 engine producing 369 horsepower.

Jean-Henri Fabre

Frenchman, Jean-Henri Fabre (1882-1984) was born in Marseilles in the south of France to wealthy ship-owner parents. He attended the Jesuit College

A Curtiss HS-2L flying boat (it has a boat-type hull) was Canada's first bush plane. It is displayed in the Canada Aviation & Space Museum in Ottawa, after a lengthy restoration program.

of Marseilles and became a marine engineer and pursued his interest in the study of aircraft and their propellers.

His claim to fame is for being the successful pioneer of floatplanes. He gained a patent for his float design and is credited for designing and building the first experimental floatplane, the Fabre Hydroplane *Le Canard* (mentioned above) in which he flew a distance of 1,650 feet (500 m) on 28 March 1910 at Lake Berre, Martigues near Marseilles. This flight was officially witnessed and recognised as the first aircraft to take-off and land on water under its own power.

The Fabre Hydroplane was powered by a seven-cylinder Gnome Omega rotary engine of fifty horsepower driving a pusher propeller. The aircraft was devoid of a wheeled undercarriage relying solely on three floats, having two main floats and one at the front of the plane. Henri Fabre designed and built floats for other pioneer pilots including Glen Curtiss and Frenchman, Gabriel Voisin. Henri Fabre died in 1984 at the age of 101 years; he was the last survivor of the Golden Age of aviation pioneers. However, his floatplane named *Hydravian* is now a museum exhibit in the National Air and Space Museum of France, Le Bourget, Paris, France.

The *Hydravian* was followed by the first successful flying boat, which was built in 1911-12 also by a Frenchman, Francois Denhaut (1877-1952) which made its first historic flight on 13 April 1912.

Gabriel Voisin

Gabriel Voisin, pioneer pilot and a First World War aircraft manufacturer, had previously attempted waterborne flight. On 6 June 1905 using a float-equipped glider, he was launched from the River Seine, flew about 450 feet (137 m) and landed back on the river; other successful glide flights followed. He later attempted flight with a powered floatplane built jointly with Louis Bleriot; however, that airplane was unsuccessful.

William Boeing

William (Bill) Edward Boeing (1881-1956) was a businessman with interests in the logging industry. He had attended Yale University to study engineering and he was also keen on boat and car racing. In 1914 or 1915, the year is questionable, Boeing experienced his first flight in an airplane, which was to change his life and eventually, the whole world forever.

He experienced his first airplane flight with pioneer pilot Terah T. Marony (1880-1929) in his plane when Boeing visited a flying exhibition near Seattle. His first flight experience led Bill Boeing to learn to fly at Los Angeles, the location of Glen Martin's Flying School and shortly after, Boeing bought his first float plane, a Martin TA trainer. Not satisfied with the design or performance of his Martin TA, Bill Boeing believed he could build a much better plane and he did. With the help of his friend, US Navy Lieutenant, George Conrad Westervelt who had graduated as an aeronautical engineer from the Massachusetts Institute of Technology, together they designed and built two float planes in a boathouse on the shores of Lake Union, near Seattle. Their result was the B & W Seaplane, named from the initials of Boeing and his business partner Westervelt.

Bill Boeing named his first aircraft, the *Bluebill, which* made its first flight on 15 June 1916; the second plane was named *Mallard,* which first flew in November of that year. The planes were first offered to the US Navy but they declined and instead, Bill Boeing made his first overseas sale to the Walsh Brother's Flying School, which operated from a beach on the Waitemata Harbour near Auckland from 1915 to 1924, training New Zealand pilots for the Royal Flying Corps. One of the B & W Seaplanes claimed a New Zealand altitude record when it climbed to 6,500 feet (1,981 m) on 25 June 1919. The two B & W's later made New Zealand history by flying the country's first air mail flight on 16 December 1919.

With the success of the Boeing B & W, Bill Boeing established his Pacific Aero Products Company on 15 July 1916 and the following year he changed the company's name to the Boeing Airplane Company, which has grown into the world's largest aircraft, defence and space manufacturing company and is still going strong over 100 years later.

A replica of Boeing's very first aircraft, the Boeing B & W, is on display in the Museum of Flight in Seattle, Washington, USA.

The fate of the two B & W Seaplanes is uncertain; rumours abound the aircraft were destroyed by intentional burning on an Auckland beach. Other people claim they are stored in tunnels somewhere near Auckland, but searchers have failed to find any trace or confirmation of their demise. A sad end to two very historic aircraft, with only a replica surviving and displayed in the Museum of Flight in Seattle, Washington State.

Eugen Ely

Pioneer aviator, Eugene Burton Ely (1886-1911) was born in Ohio where he graduated from the Davenport Grammar School in 1901. His early working life was involved with cars, being employed as a chauffeur, car salesman and racing car driver. In 1910 he learnt to fly, met Glen Curtiss and worked for him as a factory test pilot. Ely was the 17th person to receive a pilot licence from the Aero Club of America.

Eugene Ely made history for the first take-off from a ship on 14 November 1910 in a Curtiss Headless Pusher biplane. The ship, USS *Birmingham* was anchored off the Norfolk Navy base at Hampton Roads, Virginia in the USA. A special platform was built on the forward end of the ship for the aircraft's successful take-off run.

Eugene Ely also made the first landing on a ship, the cruiser USS *Pennsylvania* in San Francisco Bay on 18 January 1911. Again, a temporary wooden landing platform, 133 feet (40.5 m) in length was constructed on the ship's afterdeck above the gun turrets. A total of twenty-two weighted ropes were placed across the landing deck for the plane's arrester hook to latch on to and bring the plane to a stop, a similar method used on all aircraft carriers to this day.

The arrester hook on Ely's plane was, of course, the first one to be used and was designed by Hugh Robinson (1881-1963) an aviator and circus performer. The experiment demonstrated the possibility of aircraft carriers for the future, leading to the US Navy's first aircraft carrier, which was launched in 1922. The ship was named the USS *Langley,* named appropriately after Samuel Pierpont Langley, who the reader may recall, attempted to be the first to fly when he launched his plane off a houseboat on the Potomac River.

This is the original Curtiss Pusher that Eugene Ely used in 1910 to make the first take-off from a ship. Now exhibited in the Hiller Aviation Museum, San Carlos, Calif.

Eugene Ely had served in the US Navy before learning to fly and he became one of the world's first test pilots and flew for the Curtiss Aeroplane & Motor Company. While flying an air show routine at Macon, Georgia he crashed on 11 October 1911 and died of his injuries. He was returned to his home town of Davenport, Iowa for burial on his 25th birthday. In 1933, he was posthumously awarded the DFC for his pioneering work in Navy aircraft operations.

Charles Rumney Samson

Ely had made the first take-off and landing on a stationary ship; the next move was to launch a plane from a ship that was underway at sea.

This act was performed by newly promoted Royal Navy Commander (later Air Commodore) Charles Rumney Samson (1883-1931) on 9 May 1912 from the *HMS Hibernia*. A special platform was built on the forward deck of the ship to launch a Short Improved S.27, the first aircraft to take-off from a moving ship. Commander Sanson was one of the first of four Royal Navy officers to receive pilot training, in 1911. On 25 April 1911, he was issued his Royal Aero Club certificate after receiving only 71 minutes of dual flight instruction.

This is a replica of a Short S.27, the type used by Lieutenant C.R. Samson to depart from the ship HMS Hibernia while under-way on 9 May 1927. The replica is displayed in the Fleet Air Arm Museum at RNAS Yoevilton, England.

Samson served in the Royal Navy from 1897 until 1918 when he transferred to the recently formed Royal Air Force where he served until 1929, when he retired with the rank of Air Commodore or Group Captain.

Apart from his pioneering efforts to make the first take-off from a moving ship, he was also instrumental in developing night flying techniques and navigation lights, air navigation and communications, bombing and bomb sights, etc. For his various commands and contributions towards aviation progress, he was awarded several medals including the AFC and DSO & Bar.

Arthur Murray Longmore

The Australian, Lieutenant Arthur Murray Longmore (1911-1970) was an early British pioneer naval aviator. In fact, he was one of the first four along with Charles Rumney (mentioned above) to receive a pilot's license from the Royal Aero Club in April 1911. Following in the footsteps of his colleague Charles Rumney, Arthur Longmore made aviation history on 1 December 1911 for being the first British pilot to take-off from land and then successfully land on water, the first amphibious flight in England.

Naturally, his plane of choice was the same aircraft used by Charles Rumney, the Short Improved S.27, No. 38.

Arthur Longmore later transferred to the Royal Air Force and reached the high rank of Air Chief Marshal and received a knighthood with numerous awards. Between 1940-1941 he became the Commander-in-Chief of the Middle East Command.

The prototype of the Short S.27 made its maiden flight in 1910 and on 20 June pilot Cecil Stanley Grace (1880-1910) gained a British altitude record of 1,180 feet (360 m)! He went missing on a return flight across the English Channel.

Edwin Dunning

On 2 August 1917, Squadron Commander Edwin Dunning DFC (1892-1917) became the first pilot to land a plane on a ship underway when he landed his Sopwith Pup on *HMS Furious* in Scapa Flow, Orkney Islands to the north of Scotland. He attempted another ship-landing five days later but his engine failed just short of the ship resulting in a heavy landing. Dunning was knocked unconscious and the plane went over the side into the sea and he was drowned.

The Sopwith Pup was powered by an 80 hp Le Rhone rotary engine driving the Pup at a maximum speed of 112 mph (180 km/h).

The first landing on a ship underway at sea was achieved by Squadron Commander Edwin Dunning in a Sopwith Pup on HMS Furious in Scapa Flow. The photo shows a replica Sopwith Pup displayed in the FAA Museum at Yoevilton, UK.

Claude Graham-White

Claude Graham-White (1879-1959) was an English aviation pioneer, property developer in England and America and had substantial aviation business interests. He was well-educated having attended the Crondall House School and Bedford Grammar School until 1896. His working career started as an apprentice engineer and he later opened his own car maintenance company. Upon hearing of Louis Bleriot's flight across the English Chanel in 1909, his interest in aviation began. He went to France and met Bleriot and learned to fly in his school and became one of the first pioneer pilots in England to be issued with a pilot licence from the Royal Aero Club, in April 1910.

In the same year, he competed for the £10,000 prize offered by the Daily Mail newspaper company to the first pilot to fly from London to Manchester within a 24-hour period. He was competing against the Frenchman, Louis Paulhan who won the race. However, Graham-White's name was becoming well-known in those early days of pioneer aviators. He went on to win several other air races in England and also in North America, receiving several awards and prize money.

In 1911, Graham-White established his own aircraft manufacturing company along with his flying school at Hendon Airfield, near London where the RAF Museum Hendon is now located. He designed about thirty-five different aircraft and built about twenty of them on the original site when the factory first opened, along with licensed-built Morane-Saulnier and Breguet Bre.5 aircraft.

However, the history of the airfield goes back much further to August 1867, when Henry Coxwell (mentioned previously) was the first aeronaut to become airborne from the site that was later to become RAF Hendon. Coxwell launched from Hendon with some passengers in his hot air balloon but only managed to fly a short distance. The Hendon site was occupied by the Royal Flying Corps/RAF during WWI where many fighter pilots were trained at the flying school. The site was later bought by the Government to become RAF Hendon in 1927. During WWII, it was occupied by the RAF's Fighter Command flying Hurricanes during the Battle of Britain and throughout the war; the USAF also used the airfield as a base for its transport and communications aircraft. The airfield remained active until its closure in 1968 when London's urban sprawl encroached upon its boundaries and the land turned into a housing estate, known as Graham Park. All that remains of the original site, is one of Graham-White's original factory buildings that was dismantled brick-by-brick and re-built beside the main RAF Museum Hendon's buildings, which now holds the museum's large and interesting collection of military aircraft from both World Wars.

A rather strange-looking aircraft from the Graham-White factory at Hendon. This is a replica of the Graham White Type 20 Monoplane prototype, designed as an early scout plane. It is displayed in the Brooklands Museum, Weybridge, UK.

Writing was one of Graham-White's interests and he wrote and published fourteen books between 1910 and 1930 as well as articles for magazines and newspapers on military and civilian aviation topics. Following the demise of his aviation business at Hendon, he turned to the property market making his fortune before he retired and settled in Nice, Italy for the remainder of his life.

The Pioneer Sky Writers

Where and when did skywriting first start? In North America, Art Smith claims to have performed skywriting starting in 1915. From 1932, Sid Pike became the president of the Skywriting Corporation of America, with the Pepsi-Cola company becoming one of its first and biggest clients. In 1927, Andy Stinis was a barnstormer in America flying in his first plane, a Curtiss Jenny. He flew for the Pepsi company between 1931-1953. One of his early claims to fame, was when he used his skywriting skills to write the name *LaGuardia* above New York to resolve the dispute for the name for New York's new airport, after the mayor Fiorello LaGuardia, in the late 1930s.

The S.E.5a used by Major John Savage, which pioneered skywriting in England. In the background is the museum's large collection of aero engines. The S.E.5a has been owned by the Science Museum in London since its retirement in 1939.

Over in England, John Clifford Savage (1891-1945) received a US Patent in 1924 for his invention to 'make smoke in the air for advertising purposes'. Early in his flying career, he was a prentice to Claude Graham-White at Hendon Airfield near London. John Savage joined the Royal Navy Flying Service as a pilot during WWI where he rose to the rank of Lieutenant, before transferring to the RAF; he retired as a Major at the end of the war. With about 2,500 surplus RAF S.E.5's for sale at a cheap rate, he had the foresight to buy thirty-three of them for his new skywriting business and had them converted at Hendon. The armament was removed and to generate the smoke for writing, oil was injected into the two engine exhaust pipes installed each side of the fuselage and joined at the tail.

In 1922, he performed his first skywriting display, claiming to be the first person to do so. His first job was at the Epsom Derby, which attracted much attention from the visiting public when he wrote *Daily Mail* above the race course. He introduced skywriting to the USA when he and his business partner, ex-RAF pilot, Cyril Turner, took one of their planes to demonstrate their art over New York. From 1939, his fleet of planes diminished due to attrition.

The S.E.5a was built by the Royal Aircraft Factory (RAF) at Farnborough in England, where over 5,000 were built for combat in WWI. The aircraft of interest here was built too late to see any combat and it became one of the aircraft bought by Jack Savage, which he used for his skywriting business in England. The remaining plane (G-EBIB) is an original S.E.5 and was the last plane in his fleet; the Major gifted this aircraft to the London Science Museum on 1 June 1939, where it is now displayed in their Aviation Hall.

In America, the Travel Air Manufacturing Company in Wichita, was formed in 1925 by Clyde Cessna, Walter Beech and Lloyd Stearman who all went on to establish their own aircraft manufacturing companies, with Cessna and Beech aircraft all well-known by pilots and aviation enthusiasts; Stearman biplanes are still popular aircraft for the sport pilots but are no longer produced.

The aircraft of interest here is a Travelair Model D-4-D, which has an interesting past. It was originally flown with a Hispano-Suiza engine of 180 hp until that was replaced with its present engine, a Lycoming R-680-13 of 300 hp. With a 300 hp engine, it would be a nice, lively performer with its relatively light weight of 2,650 lb (1,200 kg) making it ideal for its role as a skywriting advertising plane for drink manufacturer, Pepsi. It was also used by American pilot Louise McPhetridge Thaden (1905-1979), to gain a women's endurance record when she remained aloft for twenty-two hours over Oakland, California, in 1929.

In 1931, the Skywriting Company of America bought the Travelair and it was frequently flown by Andy Stinis from Floyd Bennet Field in New York. He still owned the aircraft in 1973 when it was used again by Pepsi for further advertising across the USA. Jack Strayer, from Pepsi employed Peggy Davies in 1977 to fly the plane until she was replaced by Suzanne Asbury in 1980, to be joined by Steve Oliver in 1982 who she married, with a second Travelair added to their small fleet (but no children). By the year 2000, it was decided to retire the seventy-two-year-old Travelair and donate it to the Smithsonian's NASM. It can now be seen in the Hiller Aviation Museum at San Carlos, California.

Born in Oregon, Susanne Asbury Oliver was encouraged by her father to learn to fly gliders when she was only 14-year-old. Within four years she had earned her way up through the multi-engine and instrument flight instructor ratings. Susanne Oliver worked for Pepsi as their professional sky writer, one of a select few of professional female skywriter pilots employed in the USA. She was the last pilot to fly this plane before its retirement. Skywriting is rarely seen these days; however, formation aerobatic display teams use coloured smoke to highlight their aerobatic manoeuvres at air shows, the RAF's Red Arrows display team is a good example.

American pioneer pilot Louise Thaden learned to fly in 1928 to become Ohio's first licensed woman pilot. She met and worked for Walter Beech as his California aircraft sales person, with free flying lessons included. She worked her way up through the pilot ratings to be the fourth woman in the USA to gain an Airline Transport Pilots License.

On entering competition flying, Thaden was the first woman to hold altitude, endurance and speed records all at the same time for women pilots. Flying out of Oakland in California in the Travelair Model D-4-D featured here, she gained her altitude record when she climbed to 20,260 feet (6,275 m) in December 1928 and in March the following year, she gained her endurance record with a time of 22 hours aloft. On 18 August 1929, she won the *Women's Air Derby*, more commonly known as the *Powder Puff Air Derby*, an air race for women pilots only, flying from Santa Monica in California to Cleveland in Ohio, beating her eighteen rivals, which included her friend Amelia Earhart who came in third.

The colourful Travelair flown by Louise Thaden to a women's endurance record. It was also used by Pepsi for skywriting advertising. It can now be seen in the Hiller Aviation Museum in San Carlos, Ca.

The wrecked remains of the Thaden T-1, recovered from its crash site in Alaska, can now be seen in the Hiller Aviation Museum in San Carlos, Ca.

Together, Amelia Earhart and Louise Thaden founded the International Organization of Women Pilots in 1929, still going strong today and more commonly known as the *Ninety-Nines*. Louise Thaden won the New York to Los Angeles Bendix Trophy Transcontinental Race in 1936, taking just under fifteen hours to do so, when she also beat the male pilot competitors. It was the first year the race was open to female pilots.

Louise met her husband, Herbert von Thaden, who was also a pilot and engineer serving in the US Army Signal Corps. After leaving the service, Herbert Thaden established his own company, the Thaden Metal Aircraft Company in the late 1920s, to pioneer the production and introduce metal-built aircraft in the USA. Only one example of his first aircraft was built; the Thaden T-1 Argonaut, a high-wing, cabin monoplane with seating for eight occupants, all enclosed within the cabin. It was powered by a Pratt & Whitney Wasp radial engine of 425 horsepower, with which it made its first flight on 15 January 1928; however, it crashed in Alaska in 1933 and was abandoned until its recovery in 1986. All that remains of this historically significant aircraft is its battered fuselage displayed mounted on the wall in the Hiller Aviation Museum.

General Jimmy Doolittle

Harold James (Jimmy) Doolittle (1896-1993) was a pioneer aviator, an air race pilot winning several races, a long-distance flyer, US Army and Air Force officer, a WWI flying instructor, test pilot and pioneer of instrument flying and more.

His interest in aviation was stemmed from a school visit in 1910, to see the *Los Angeles International Air Meet*. There, he saw his first aircraft and his love of flying was born. In October 1917, he became an air cadet in the US Army Signal Corps reserve, where he learned to fly and graduated as a Second Lieutenant in 1918, spending the war years instructing new airmen at bases in Texas, California and Louisiana. In 1925, he was the first person in America to receive a doctorate in aeronautical engineering at the Massachusetts Institute of Technology, when he wrote his thesis on aircraft acceleration (during manoeuvring flight). He remained in the army until he transferred to the USAF until 1950. He saw active service during World War II when he commanded the 12th Air Force in North America, the 15th Air Force in the Mediterranean and the 8th Air Force in Europe.

He is best remembered for organizing and leading the Doolittle Raid on Japan in reprisal for the Japanese attack on Pearl Harbour. With a fleet of sixteen North American B-25 Mitchell medium bombers, they departed from the aircraft carrier *USS Hornet* in the Pacific Ocean on 18 April 1942, earlier than planned due to being spotted by the Japanese. Flying over Japan, they bombed several cities including Tokyo, then continued flying westward to mainland Asia intending to land in China or Russia, but the B-25 crews abandoned their planes when they ran out of fuel, due to bad weather and night-time preventing them from reaching and finding their safe recovery airfields. Not being able to find their destination airfields, General Doolittle considered his mission had failed. However, his superiors thought otherwise and promoted him to Brigadier General and presented him with the Congressional medal. The B-25 Mitchell bomber was the first twin-engine aircraft to operate off an aircraft carrier.

Jimmy Doolittle is also well-known for his early pioneering flights and work to develop instrument flying, now a common practice for professional pilots. In 1922, Lieutenant Doolittle flew solo across America from Florida to San Diego in a de Havilland DH-4. Further experiments with instrument flying were conducted by Doolittle on 24 September 1929, when he became the first pilot to take-off and return to land solely on the use of flight instruments and a radio navigation aid. He made the flight in a Consolidated NY-2, a single-engine biplane powered by a Wright R-760 Whirlwind radial engine to advance the use of flight instruments, for which he received the DFC, one of many medals he was to receive. As a result of his experiments, all professional pilots are now required to understand the physiological aspects of the body's sense of balance and be able to fly by reference to flight instruments without any outside visual reference points.

Elmer Ambrose Sperry (1860-1930) was an inventor and business man, famed for inventing gyroscopes to stabilize ship's rolling motions at sea and also for introducing gyro-stabilized flight instruments for aircraft. His inventions have been in use for over 100 years now and are familiar to pilots as the artificial horizon, gyro compass and the turn and bank indicator. Sperry is known as the 'father of air navigation technology'. Furthermore, when Sperry was developing his gyro flight instruments, it was Colonel William Charles Ocker (1880-1942) flying a Curtiss C-2 flying boat, who performed the flight testing of the new gyro instruments, in 1913. Jimmy Doolittle went on to make long-distance flights, for which he became famous, using the Sperry flight instruments without any outside reference, to prove the benefits to pilots. William Ocker received less publicity for his involvement in instrument flying, with most of the credit aimed towards Jimmy Doolittle.

∗

As an air racing pilot, one of his most notable race victories was winning the 1925 Schneider Trophy Air Race in Baltimore, flying a Curtiss R3C-2 Racer. The following day he claimed a world speed record of 245.7 mph (395.4 km/h). He also entered the Bendix race in 1931 flying a Laird Super Solution; the following year, he won the Thomson Race in the notoriously dangerous Gee Bee racer, before retiring from air racing claiming it was too dangerous.

On 25 May 1927, Doolittle was the first pilot to fly an 'outside loop' using a Curtiss P-1B Hawk. Unlike a normal loop where the pilot is on the inside experiencing positive acceleration, during the outside loop the pilot has to contend with negative acceleration, which is far more uncomfortable and is to be avoided if possible, in normal flying. All aircraft are built to withstand higher positive acceleration than negative acceleration.

A North American B-25 Mitchell, the same type used on the Doolittle Raid to attack Japanese targets. This one is displayed in the Navy Museum at NAS Pensacola in Florida.

While working as the Aviation Manager for the Shell Oil Company in 1935, he pushed for the development of 100-Octane aviation fuel for the more powerful engines being produced around that time. It turned out to be a very good investment for the company during the war-years from 1939.

Doolittle joined the US Army as a Private First Class on 10 November 1917; he progressed through the ranks receiving many promotions to eventually be honoured as a four-star General on 4 April 1985, twenty-six years after his retirement. His list of decorations, awards and honours is endless for all that he achieved in his life-time.

Sir Alan Cobham

Sir Alan Cobham (1894-1973) KBE, AFC, was a well-known English pioneer aviator devoted to many aspects of the burgeoning aviation industry, both in his civilian and military life when he flew as a pilot with the Royal Flying Corps in the First World War. After the war, he was a test pilot for the de Havilland Company and used de Havilland aircraft on his pioneering long-distance survey flights for the future British airlines.

He was especially well-known for his popular Cobham's Flying Circus, which he started in 1932. His varied fleet of aircraft and their crews toured around Britain visiting many airfields or farm fields, wherever they could land and take-off. They gave flight demonstrations, joy rides and introduced aviation to the visiting crowds, with many people enjoying their first flying experience with Cobham's Circus, until it ceased operation in 1935.

Another business venture for Alan Cobham saw him being appointed as one of the founding directors of Airspeed Limited, a small business in aircraft manufacturing co-founded by (Alfred) Hessel Tiltman (1891-1975) an aircraft designer and Nevil Shute Norway, the well-known author known as Neville Shute. Tiltman and Nevil Norway together had worked for the Vickers Company on the R100 airship project. The Airspeed Company had some success with manufacturing but was never a big player in the aircraft manufacturing field. Alan Cobham was the company's first customer ordering two, three-engine Airspeed Ferry aircraft for his Flying Circus company.

Always ready for a new experience, Cobham used a de Havilland DH-80 Puss Moth in an attempt to deliver the first airmail from the UK to New York on 25 November 1926. His plane equipped with floats, was launched from the trans-Atlantic liner, *RMS Homeric* when she was about 250 miles (400 km) away from New York. The plan was for Cobham to fly the remaining distance to deliver the mail before the ship arrived in port. However, the sea proved too rough for Cobham to take-off, the mission was aborted with Cobham and his plane being towed to New York by the ship. It was one of those 'good ideas' that didn't work. If it had worked, Cobham would have been the first person to deliver air mail across the Atlantic Ocean, but it was not to be. However, Cobham's unsuccessful attempt to deliver air mail from a ship at sea was later successfully performed on 26 July 1929, when a Heinkel HE-12 was launched from the German ship *SS Bremen* piloted by Jobst von Studnitz. He landed in New York a few hours before the ship docked.

Not to be daunted, Cobham started a new venture in 1935 with the Cobham Air Routes Ltd, a small airline connecting London and the Channel Islands. However, it was a short-lived operation for Cobham and he sold out to Olley Air Service Ltd, after he lost one of his pilots in an accident.

For his next venture, Cobham used a Handley Page Harrow for his air refuelling business, which he started in 1934 to refuel aircraft on long trans-Atlantic flights to increase their range. His trial flights were demonstrated publicly in 1935. The refuelling aircraft positioned above and forward of the recipient aircraft, trailing its connection cable for the recipient aircraft crew to manually haul in with the refuelling hose attached, to refuel via gravity feed. The trans-Atlantic Empire class flying boats were refuelled using Cobham's method from August to October 1939 on sixteen Atlantic flights. World War II interrupted his flight trials but they were continued after the war ended. Air refuelling (or in-flight refuelling as the Americans call it) is now a common procedure to enable military aircraft to extend their mission time or for deployment to distant airfields. Air refuelling was first trialled by the US Army Air Service in 1923 using an Airco DH.4B aircraft, as we shall see shortly.

Sir Alan Cobham was one of Britain's true aviation pioneers venturing into many aspects of the developing aviation industry. For his commitment to aviation, he received his knighthood in 1926 and also, he was awarded the Gold Medal by the Federation Aeronautique Internationale (FAI) in the same year. In 2016, he was inducted into the Airlift/Tanker Hall of Fame for his work in developing air refuelling.

Calbraith Perry Rodgers

Crossing the North American continent today on the airlines takes just a few hours of flying time. However, the first trans-America flight ever to be made lasted for nearly three-months!

Calbraith Perry Rodgers (1879-1912) became a pioneer aviator following in the footsteps of his naval aviator cousin, John Rodgers. Calbraith Rodgers was given ninety-minutes of flight instruction from Orville Wright to become the 49th pilot to be licenced by the FAI. He then bought himself a Wright EX to become one of the first civilian pilots to buy a plane and he promptly entered an endurance competition against more experienced pilots and won the $US11,000 prize.

The Wright EX was a biplane powered by a 35 horsepower Wright engine driving a pusher propeller to an average speed of 51 mph (82 km/h). The plane's length was 21 feet (6.4 m) with a wingspan of 32 feet (9.8 m) and a maximum weight of 900 pounds (410 kg), which by today's category classification, would be classed as an ultralight aircraft.

Rodgers entered the Randolph Hearst competition to be the first pilot to cross the USA within thirty-days to win the $US50,000 prize. He named his plane the Vin Fiz after his sponsor, Armour & Co's soft drink.

The Wright EX 'Vin Fiz' was the first plane to cross the USA, which required multiple stops along the way. Seen here displayed in the National Air & Space Museum, Washington, D.C.

The *Vin Fiz* departed Brooklyn, Long Island, New York on 17 September 1911 and after 69 landings along the way due to planned stops, engine failures and nineteen crashes, Rodgers arrived in California three months later on the 10 December 1911. He flew an approximate distance of 3,200 miles to 4,231 miles (5,200-6,800 km) in 82 hours 4 minutes flying time to complete the first coast-to-coast flight; the route flown has never been confirmed. The top speed of his plane was a mere 55 mph (88 km/h). His arrival at Long Beach in California was welcomed by a large crowd of 50,000 people. However, he failed to meet the deadline of 30 days to win the Hearst prize, but he did receive the fame he deserved for his trans-Continental USA pioneering flight.

Sadly, he was killed in a crash a few months later when he was flying a different aircraft in an exhibition at Long Beach on 3 April 1912. Flying into a flock of birds was the cause of his accident near to the location where his pioneering trans-America flight had ended. The *Vin Fiz* was donated to the National Air and Space Museum by his widow in 1934, where it has been on display since 1960 as a very iconic aircraft from the pioneering days of aviation. Was the *Vin Fiz* the first aircraft of many to suffer a bird strike?

Robert G. Fowler

Robert George Fowler (1884-1966) was the first man to fly across the USA from the west to east coast in an attempt to win the $US50,000 Hearst prize for a coast-to-coast flight. Powered by a Cole car engine, Fowler flew his Wright Model B *Cole Flyer* departing from San Francisco on 11 September 1911 and flying in stages to Jacksonville, Florida, he arrived there on 8 February. He also was too late to win the Hearst Prize which had expired at the end of 1911.

A year later in 1912, Fowler bought a Gage biplane, now known as the Fowler-Gage biplane which he used for barnstorming and joy-ride flights. In 1913, he made the first pioneering flight across the Panama isthmus in his plane equipped with floats. He flew from the Pacific end of the canal across the 52 miles (84 km) of land to the Caribbean side in fifty-seven minutes. His passenger/cameraman Ray E. Duhem filmed the Panama Canal and its fortifications then under construction, which opened in 1914. Publishing his photographic work of the canal put Duhem and Fowler in deep trouble with the authorities for filming military fortifications with a threatened court case, but that was eventually dropped.

The Fowler-Gage biplane was initially powered by a 60-hp Hall-Scott engine. The upper wing had a span of 42 ft 8 in (13 m) while the lower wing spanned 30 ft (9.1 m). The length was 25 feet (7.6 m) and a weight of 800 lb (363 kg) without the engine. The plane was retired in 1915 and donated by Fowler in 1950 to the Smithsonian Institution where it was restored. It is now on display in the Udvar-Hazy Center with a Curtiss OX engine until a Hall-Scott engine is found to replace the OX engine.

The Fowler-Gage, pictured here, was the first plane to fly across the Panama isthmus following the ship canal. It is now a museum exhibit in the Udvar-Hazy Center.

This Fokker T-2 made the first non-stop flight across the USA in 1923. It has been owned by the National Air & Space Museum in Washington, D.C, since 1924.

Oackley Kelly & John MacCready

The first plane to cross the USA non-stop was a Fokker T-2 piloted by two US Army Air Service pilots, Lieutenant Oackley G. Kelly (1891-1966) and Lieutenant John A. MacCready (1887-1979). On the 2 May 1923, the flight departed from Roosevelt Field on Long Island, New York and after nearly 27 hours of non-stop flying landed at Rockwell Field in San Diego, California. They covered a distance of 2,470 miles (3,950 km) flying at an average speed of 108 mph (174 km/h). The flight was not without hazards along the way having to fly at night, through storms and over unknown routes for half the flight. The purpose of the flight was to prove the practicality of aircraft making long-distance flights, the reliability of the Liberty engine and the ability of the two pilots to fly for an extended period of time. For this flight, Kelly and MacCready received the 1923 MacKay Trophy.

The Army Air Service bought the Fokker T-2 which was designed and built in Holland as a conversion from the Fokker F.IV ten-seat transport. The main wing's span was increased to 82 feet (25 m) and was fully cantilevered (without struts) and made entirely from wood. Power was provided by the 420 horsepower Liberty engine driving a two-blade propeller. To extend the plane's endurance, extra fuel tanks were installed within the fuselage and wings.

The non-stop flight across the USA was not the first long-endurance flight for Macready and Kelly. They had set a world-endurance record in the previous year, on 5 October 1922, staying aloft for 35 hours, 18 minutes, 30 seconds in the Fokker T-2 over San Diego in California. For this flight, they were given the 1922 Mackay Trophy.

Lieutenant Macready was also a test pilot at McCook Field at Dayton in Ohio, where he flew the first experimental flights in crop spraying in 1918. He also claimed an altitude record of 34,509 feet (10,500 m) in 1921 in a modified Le Pere biplane, for which he received his first Mackay Trophy in 1931. As a recipient of the trophy for the trans-America flight and also for the endurance flight, he is the only recipient to receive the Mackay Trophy in three consecutive years.

Smith and Richter went on to complete a record endurance flight of over 37 hours and made 16 new records for time and distance flights.

Macready also has the distinction of being the first pilot to parachute from an aircraft at night time. When returning to McCook Field at Dayton, Ohio

An Airco DH.4 in The Omaka Aviation Heritage Centre in Blenheim, New Zealand, similar to the DH.4B's used for the air-refueling experiments.

on the night of 13 June 1924, his engine failed and he elected to bail out rather than risk a crash-landing in the dark. Although he landed in trees and required assistance to reach the ground, he was saved by his parachute.

MacCready died in 1979 and was inducted into the National Aviation Hall of Fame in 1968 and the International Air & Space Hall of Fame in 1976.

Virgil Hine & Frank Seifert

The method to conduct in-flight refuelling was pioneered by US Army Air Services pilots Lieutenant Virgil Hine and Frank W. Seifert at San Diego when fuel was transferred through a hose between their Airco DH.4B aircraft to another DH.4B flying below them piloted by Lt Lowell H. Smith and John P. Richter, on 27 June 1923. [Note the DH.4 was first built by Airco in England before it became known as a de Havilland DH.4 after its designer]. During World War I they were built in America by Dayton-Wright & Fisher Body for the USAAC. Several DH.4B's became surplus aircraft at the end of World War I and were used for various experimental work including the aforementioned pioneer work in aerial refuelling and also for Air Mail flights around America.

Arnaiz & Calvo

The 1920s was the decade of many pioneering flights as aviation gradually grew to become one of the world's major industries. Pioneer aviators were venturing further afield to different parts of the world. In May 1926, the first flight was made from Madrid, Spain to the Philippines. That flight inspired Captain Juan Calvo (1898-1945) to make the first flight in the opposite direction from Manila, the capital of The Phillipines, to Madrid.

Captain Juan Calvo was born in Madrid but lived most of his life in The Philippins. He first learned to fly with the Curtiss School of Aviation at Paranaque in The Philippines in 1920. Later, in 1936 he gained his pilot licence from the Valeriano Flying School where he met fellow aviator Antonio Somoza Arnaiz (1912-1978); the two pilots became friends. Calvo suggested his idea of making a flight to Madrid together and between them they bought a used Fairchild Model 24 C8C, built in 1935 and powered by a single-engine Warner Super Scareb developing 145 hp. It was christened the *Commonwealth of the Philippines,* by local Mayor, Juan Posadas in May 1926. However, President Manuel Quezon was not in favour of the flight and refused government support on the grounds the flight was too dangerous to pursue. The newspaper *Manila Herald* stepped in to help finance the flight along with donations from other sponsors. The flight was named the *Arnacal Flight,* taken from the names of Arnaiz and Calvo.

The plane was equipped with a ferry tank to extend its range but lacked radio and seatbelts! With very little provisions for the two pilots, Calvo and Arnaiz departed on 28 May 1936 from Manila's Nielsen Field airport, now consumed by Manila's suburban sprawl. Their route crossed the South China Sea to Asia, Middle East and Europe with thirty-one stages to arrive in Madrid, Spain forty-four days later on 11 July 1936. The Spanish Air Force provided escort planes on the last stage of the flight between Barcelona and Madrid where they were met by a large crowd of spectators including Calvo's father, there to meet his son after thirteen years absence. Unfortunatly, they never met again. The Spanish Civil War had started, which soon became a problem for Calvo and Arnaiz.

Their Fairchild was place on board a German ship in Barcelona to be delivered back to the Philippines along with Calvo and Arnaiz. However, the ship was bombed in port by a Republican bomber (other authorities claim it was torpedoed by a submarine). However, the outcome of the attack, was the plane was a total loss and its two pilots had to escape from Spain via France and eventually make their way home to Manila.

On the 25th. anniversary of the flight in 1961, a commemoration stone was laid by Spanish Air Force officials at Cuatro Vientos Airport at Madrid, Spain, the destination of Calvo and Arnaiz. Antonio Arnaiz claimed the distinction for being the first Philippino to fly from The Philippines to Manila.

A Fairchild Model 24 C8C similar to this example was used by the pioneering Philippino pilots Arnaiz and Calvo on their pioneering flight from Manila to Madrid in 1936. The Fairchild pictured here is displayed in the Hiller Aviation Museum in San Carlos, California.

3 – Pioneers of Rotorcraft Flight

It was mentioned at the start of this work, the inventor, Leonardo da Vinci, designed a helical airscrew circa 1483 for a vertical lift machine, but it was never built. Going back in time even further to around 320 AD, in China and Japan, the Chines top or bamboo-copter was used as a toy, consisting of a shaft with rotor-type blades. It was spun by hand and rose into the air. Moving forward, a US patent was issued for a helicopter-design as early as 21 May 1861, but it too, never left the drawing board. The patent was obtained by its designer, Mortimer Nelson in New York, N.Y. He named his helicopter design as the *Aerial Car*. The word 'helicopter' was coined by the Frenchman, Viscount Gustave de Ponton d'Amecourt (1825-1888) on 24 September 1863, taking the Latin words of *helix* and *pteron*, for spiral and wing. The term rotary-wing was presented by Professor Alexander Klemin (1888-1950) much later in 1938.

The first successful helicopter flight is said to have occurred on 29 September 1907 in France. Louis Charles Breguet (1880-1955), his brother Jacques Eugene Breguet (1881-1939) and Charles Robert Richet (1850-1935), achieved the first vertical flight with a pilot at the controls in their Breguet-Richet Gyroplane No 1. It was very unstable and required assistance to hold it steady as it hovered just above the ground.

Another Frenchman, Paul Cornu (1881-1944) was one of thirteen children in the family. He became an engineer and like the Wright brothers, he manufactured bicycles. He first designed and built an unmanned helicopter powered by a two hp Buchet engine and later, he claimed to fly the world's first successful helicopter, getting airborne at Coquainvilliers near Lisieux in France, on 13 November 1907. It was powered by an Antoinette piston engine of 24 horsepower driving two counter-rotating transverse rotors and made a steady hover about four feet (1.5 metres) above the ground, although there is some doubt that his small engine was powerful enough to enable a hover to be made in the first place.

Paul Cornu was living in Lisieux in Normandy during the 1944 invasion; he died when his home was destroyed during the invasion fighting.

Raul Pateras Pescara

Another helicopter pioneer was the Argentine national, Marquis of Pateras-Pescara, Raul Pateras Pescara de Castelluccio (1890-1966). He was noted for being a lawyer, inventor, helicopter pioneer and an engineer of cars and piston engines. With his family, he moved to Europe where, in 1923, he received financial assistance from the French Government to proceed with his experimental Pescara Model 3. He had built and 'flight tested' two previous helicopters of his design before building the Pescara Model 3, featured here. His first two designs were underpowered.

The Pescara was an ambitious attempt at helicopter flight by Raul Pescara in 1924. Typical of all early helicopters it was unsuccessful at flight.

The Model 3 version, had four rotors, each in biplane configuration giving it a total of sixteen blades, which were mounted on a co-axial drive shaft turning in opposite directions to counteract rotor torque. Tail rotors were still in the future at this stage. The rotor system had a diameter of 23 ft 8 in (7.20 m) and were powered by a single Hispano-Suiza 8 radial piston engine developing a healthy 180 horsepower mounted in the helicopters nose. It had a maximum speed of 8 mph (13 km/h). Maybe if a propeller was mounted on the engine, autogyro-style, it could have flown faster? Pescara was one of the first pioneers to devise a form of cyclic stick to tilt the rotors system for control of direction and the blade pitch angle was adjusted by 'wing warping' of the rotor blades.

A world speed record for helicopters was claimed by Pescara on 18 April 1924 at Issy-les-of Moulineaux in France; he reached a speed of 8 mph (13 km/h) and claimed a distance record 2,415 feet (736 m) and at a height of 6 feet (1.8 m) to claim the first record issued by the Federation Aeronautique Internationale (FAI) for helicopters.

The Model 3 was Pescara's final attempt at helicopter design and building, before he went on to other engineering products. However, he did make one very important contribution to helicopter flying; it is claimed he developed the engine failure autorotation descent procedure familiar to all present-day helicopter pilots. But, from a height of 6 feet?

Raoul Hafner and Bruno Nagler

Another early attempt to produce a working rotorcraft was the Hafner Nagler Revoplane R.I introduced in 1931. It was designed by Austrians, Raoul Hafner (1905-1980) and Bruno Nagler in 1931 as an experimental helicopter.

Hafner's interest in rotary wing aircraft stemmed from his time studying at the technical college in Vienna, Austria. He became a pioneer of rotary wing aircraft after leaving his job with the Austrian Air traffic Control and teamed up with Bruno Nagler. Together, they designed and built the Revoplane I and II. Hafner went on to learn to fly the Cierva C.19 and C.30 autogyros and established his own company, the AR.III Construction Hafner Gyroplane Company where he designed and built the sole prototype experimental A.R. III Gyroplane and other models of autogyros. The Hafner Rotachute and Rotabuggy followed, neither of which passed the flight testing stage. In 1940 at the start of WWII, he was initially interned as an enemy alien but released on production of his naturalization papers. Post war, he was employed by the Bristol Aeroplane Company as a helicopter designer where he designed the successful Bristol Type 171 Sycamore and then the Type 173 which became the Belvedere tandem rotor helicopter.

The Haffner Revoplane was built in 1931 as an experimental helicopter. Just like other early helicopters it was a non-starter and only managed tethered hovering flight.

Hafner and Nagler's first helicopter version was unsuccessful and the second version, the Hafner Nagler Revoplane II featured here, didn't fare much better either; it only managed to become airborne under tethered flights. This second version was powered by a French-built Salmon 9 air-cooled radial engine developing 45 horsepower driving a three-blade rotor system. The radial engine was placed in the nose of the fuselage with the pilot sitting behind it and underneath the rotor system, exposed to the rotor downwash. The engine was started by a car-type hand crank. The Revoplane I and II were built in the days before tail rotors were invented to control rotor torque, instead two aerofoils looking like a pair of surf boards were mounted behind the pilot and sat in the rotor downwash. Tilting the boards side-to-side produce the aerodynamic force to control yaw.

The Revoplane II was moved from Austria to Great Britain when its sponsor, Scottish industrialist Major Jack A. Coates financed the project. After flight trials proved the Revoplane was a non-starter, it was placed in storage and forgotten. Rediscovered in 1961, it received a basic restoration before being displayed in various museums until its donation to the Helicopter Museum in England in 1979 who restored the helicopter for permanent exhibition.

It is now one of the world's few surviving helicopters from the helicopter pioneering days prior to world war II.

Getting airborne was one problem, the next problem was to make maneuvering flight. This proved very difficult for the early helicopter pioneers, until the Spanish aviator Juan de la Cierva (1895-1936) invented the autogyro, in which he made his first successful flight when he flew his Cierva C.4 Autogiro on 9 January 1923 in Madrid, Spain. It was his fully articulated rotor head invention that solved the problem of control for all future helicopters. The autogyro had limited success in the 1930s, mainly with military pilots, but with the helicopter emerging on the scene, autogyros were discontinued until after WWII when they were revived by sport pilots as the gyrocopter.

Heinrich Focke and Gerd Achgellis

In 1932, two Germans, Heinrich Focke (1890-1979) of Focke-Wulf fame, and Gerd Achgelis (1908-1991) developed their Focke-Achgellis FA-61 helicopter, which was first flown on 26 June 1936 with test pilot, Gerd Achgelis at the controls. It was claimed to be the world's first fully controllable helicopter, although it never went into production.

German pioneer pilot Heinrich Focke had served in the German Army during World War I spending time on the Eastern Front before joining the Imperial Army Air Service. Prior to the war, he attended the Leibniz University in Hannover and in 1911, he met Georg Wulf. They became firm friends and later business partners when they joined forces with Dr. Werner Naumann to form the Focke-Wulf Company Flugzeugbau GmbH in 1923, famed for its production of WWII fighter, bomber, reconnaissance and trainer aircraft and several other types too. In 1936, he parted from his company under pressure and joined with Gerd Achgelis to form his new company, Focke-Achgelis in April 1937. The company produced several designs of fixed-wing and rotary wing aircraft, including the development and flight testing of the FA-61.

Post war, Focke worked for the SNCASE, a French aircraft manufacturing company and other companies in Brazil and Europe. He died in Bremen, Germany in 1979 and was inducted into the International Air & Space Hall of Fame in San Diego.

The German, Gerd Achgelis (1908-1991) served an electrical apprenticeship and in 1928 turned his attention to aviation as an aerobatic pilot, a flight instructor from 1932 and test pilot for Focke-Wulf in Bremen, Germany in 1933. The 26 June 1936 was an auspicious day for Achgelis when he piloted the

FA-61 on its first flight. Many people consider the FA-61 as being the world's first practical helicopter; Igor Sikorsky would strongly disagree. Achgelis and Henrich Focke joined forces to establish the Focke-Achgelis Company to manufacture helicopters, in 1937. Achgelis flew as a test pilot until the end of the war before becoming a farmer on his family's farm; however, his interests in aviation remained, as it does with all of us.

The FA-61 helicopter was built-up from a Focke-Wulf Fw 44 Stieglitz biplane trainer fuselage minus its wings, with a Bramo Sh.14A 150 hp radial engine mounted in the nose, but differs from other helicopters by having twin rotors mounted on transverse outrigger arm each side of the fuselage. The FA-61 also claimed altitude, endurance and speed records in 1938 after reaching an altitude of 11,243 feet (3,427 m) and covering a distance of 143 miles (230 km). However, the FA-61's claim to fame can best be remembered when German test pilot Hanna Reitsch (1912-1979) flew it inside the Deutschlandhalle stadium in Berlin on a demonstration flight in 1938, to become the first pilot to fly a helicopters inside a building. To be precise, she was the first woman pilot to fly any helicopter.

A replica of the FA-61 is now displayed at the Hubschraubermuseum in Bückeburg in Germany.

Ken Watson

The almost unknown Weir W-6 was the world's first helicopter to carry a passenger. The helicopter was built in Thornliebank, Glasgow in Scotland by the G & J Weir Company with two sets of wooden rotors mounted on transverse outriggers similar to the FA-61 mentioned above. The fuselage had open framework, no covering. Power was provided by a de Havilland Gypsy Queen engine of 205 hp mounted in the helicopter's nose.

It was transported by road to Dalrymple in East Ayrshire where it made its maiden flight in October 1939, in the hands of test pilot Raymond Pullin, the son of the Weir's designer. Having three seats it later made history by carrying the world's first helicopter passenger namely, Ken Watson. Although Ken Watson received the credit for being the first helicopter passenger, it is recorded the Weir also carried Air Vice Marshall Arthur W. Tedder in company with Ken Watson.

Production of the Weir W-6 never proceeded beyond the prototype stage due to the advent of WWII.

Igor Sikorsky

Igor Ivanovich Sikorsky (1889-1972) was born in Kyiv/Kiev, Russia. He was a pioneer aviator and an aircraft designer and manufacturer in Russia and America of fixed and rotary-winged aircraft.

As a fourteen-year-old boy, Igor Sikorsky commenced studies in the Marine Cadet Corps but then gave that up and went to Paris to study engineering. In 1907, he returned to his home town of Kyiv to study at the Kyiv Polytechnic's Mechanical College. In 1908, he learned about the Wright brothers successful flights and the German Zeppelin airships, during a visit to Germany with his father. From then on, his attention was focused on aviation, leading him to attempt flight and to establish his first aircraft manufacturing company in Russia. In 1910, he built his first fixed-wing aircraft, the S-1. Powered by a French-built, 15-horsepower Anzani three-cylinder engine, it was too underpowered to become airborne. His next attempt at flight was made on 3 June 1910, in his S-2 with a 25-horsepower engine. It became airborne briefly before stalling and crashing to the ground. By trial and error, Sikorsky gained experience and knowledge of flight and found success in 1911 with his first practical aircraft, the S-5, a single-seat biplane. As a child, he had made a rubber-band-powered model helicopter and in May 1909, he made his first attempt to fly a helicopter of his own design, but it was underpowered and he abandoned any further attempts at helicopter flight until 1939.

Igor was employed by the Russian Baltic Railroad Car Works as their Chief Engineer, in St. Petersburg, where he built his first four-engine airliner, the S-21 Russky Vityaz (Russian Knight). It first flew on 10 May 1913 and was the world's first four-engine aircraft. He continued designing and building aircraft including fighters and bombers during World War One. In 1911, he gained his pilot licence, number 64, from the Imperial Aero Club of Russia.

Looking for better opportunities to design and build aircraft, he immigrated to the USA in 1919, where he first worked as a school teacher and university lecturer before establishing his Sikorsky Aero Engineering Corporation at Roosevelt Field, New York on 5 March 1923. The company name was later changed to Sikorsky Aviation Corporation and moved to a new location in Stratford, Connecticut, in 1925. He had built his first American aircraft in 1924, the S-29-A, a twin-engine passenger biplane for the airlines. With the advent of the flying boat era, he moved into building amphibious flying boats with his successful S-42 Clipper flying in 1934, used by Pan American World Airways and the smaller, two-engine version S-43 Baby Clipper was also built in 1934. [These aircraft are featured in section 18 – Aircraft of the Fledgling Airlines].

In 1939, he merged his company with Vought Aircraft and turned his attention again to building helicopters and developed his experimental VS-300 helicopter (Vought-Sikorsky), claimed to be the world's first practical and controllable helicopter. Its first flights were tethered leading to its first free-flight on 14 September 1939. It should be remembered Heinrich Focke and Gerd Achgellis claimed their FA-61 was also the world's first helicopter. However, Sikorsky's helicopters went into production as opposed to Focke and Achgellis who only produced their prototype; the answer is debateable.

Sikorsky continued his helicopter research and trials resulting in the Sikorsky R-4 helicopter, which made its maiden flight on 14 January 1942. It has the distinction of being the world's first mass-produced helicopter, from 1942 onwards and was the only helicopter to be used during the Second World War, flown by the US military which they designated as the HNS-1 and the British who named it the Hoverfly. The Sikorsky Company continues to build helicopters to this day both for military and civilian use. All of Sikorsky's aircraft and most of his helicopter designs have the designation 'S-' for Sikorsky, followed by a number and some with names.

Igor Sikorsky was one of the great pioneers of helicopter and aircraft production; he was inducted into the International Air & Space Hall of Fame in 1966. He was buried in his home town of Easton, Connecticut.

Colonel H. Frank Gregory

The first take-off and landings by fixed wing aircraft from ships were made in 1910 and 1927 respectively as mentioned earlier. It was several years later, before a helicopter made the first landing and take-off from a ship at sea. US Army Air Force helicopter pilot, Colonel H. Frank Gregory gained the distinction of becoming the first pioneer helicopter pilot to be credited with shipboard helicopter operations from a ship at sea. He also makes claim to being the first military helicopter pilot. On 7 May 1943, Colonel Gregory made twenty-three take-offs and landings in this Sikorsky XR-4C (41-18874) equipped with a float undercarriage, on the oil tanker *Bunker Hill* in Long Island Sound, New York. He proved the viability of helicopter operations from ships, which of course, is now a common practice, particularly for navy anti-submarine, anti-shipping warfare and other utility duties.

The Sikorsky XR-4C 4C (41-18874) in question, also made aviation history when it was flown by Igor Sikorsky and his Chief Test Pilot, Charles Lester Morris (1908-1991) from the Sikorsky factory at Bridgeport, Connecticut to Wright Field Air Base in Ohio. This flight was the first long-distance flight

In this Sikorsky XR-4C, US Army Colonel H. Frank Gregory made the first ever helicopter take-off and landing from a ship at sea, pioneering the way for all future ship-borne helicopter operations. This was also the first helicopter to make a cross-country flight, flown by Igor Sikorsky and Charles Lester Morris. Note, the uncovered fuselage side to expose the engine and framework to museum visitors.

made by a helicopter covering a distance of 761 miles (1,225 km). The flight was made over a five-day period in May 1942 in sixteen short hops logging a total flying time of 16 hours and 10 minutes in the air for an average ground speed of 47 mph (76 kmh).

This XR-4C also made history as the world's first helicopter to be delivered to a military unit for evaluation; in this instance it was taken on strength by the US Army Air Corps at Dayton, Ohio. The Udvar-Hazy Center, Chantilly, VA, now displays this very historic helicopter.

Bell Helicopters

Another major airplane and helicopter manufacturer was the Bell Aircraft Corporation, which started out in 1935. They turned to building helicopters in 1942, when two engineers, Arthur Young and Bartram Kelly designed the Bell Model 30 *Genevieve*. It was developed into the Bell 47, a very popular helicopter for its era. It was the start of a long list of Bell helicopter types, still in production today.

Marie Marvingt

Marie Marvingt (1875-1963) was a very talented French woman who entered aviation, first as a balloon pilot then as a fixed wing aircraft pilot and later in life, she gained her helicopter pilot licence.

Having made her first passenger flight in a balloon in 1901, she went on to gain a balloon pilot licence in 1910, the second woman to do so after Marie Surcouf (1863-1928). Marvingt was a woman with many interests including several different sports, gaining success as an aeronaut winning balloon flying competitions during 1909-10. Record breaking was also included in her ballooning experiences to become the first woman to fly a balloon across the English Channel to England on 26 October 1909.

A month earlier in September 1909, saw Marie Marvingt making her first flight as a passenger in a fixed-wing aircraft. The following year, she met Hubert Latham (one of Louis Bleriot's unsuccessful competitors to become the first pilot to fly across the English Channel) and she commenced flight training with him. She became the first woman to fly an Antoinette and the third woman to gain her pilots licence on 8 November 1910, issued by the Aero Club of France. Flying fixed-wing airplanes, she was present at several air meets and succeeded in flying over 900 accident free flights, a record in itself back then. Record flying was originally the domain of male pilots only, however, a change in the rules allowed Marie Marvingt to become the first woman pilot recognised with achieving aviation records for range and endurance flights, the first on 27 November 1910. She also has the distinction of becoming the first unofficial female combat pilot, having twice bombed a German air base during the First World War; she also flew reconnaissance flights in North Africa.

Marie Marvingt participated in many activities both within and outside of aviation. However, it was as a qualified nurse that she envisioned the use of aircraft for use as air ambulances, going as far as designing and raising sufficient money for an air ambulance to be built by Deperdussin back in 1910. However, the company went bankrupt, but Marvingt for many years pursued her air ambulance idea for casualty evacuation (Casevac), the transport of injured military personal from the battlefield. She was the pioneer of the air ambulance services now used worldwide. Through Marvingt's efforts, one of the world's first air ambulance services was Africa's first Medevac service established in Morocco as early as 1934.

Dr. Valérie Andre

It is due to Marie Marvingt's efforts we can now introduce another pioneer aviatrix, Dr. Valérie Andre (1922-202?), 100 years old at the time of this writing, who further advanced the air ambulance service. Dr. Valérie Andre, was also no stranger to warfare having served as a member of the French resistance during the Second World War. While serving in the Indochina war (pre-Vietnam war) she worked as an Army neurosurgeon with the rank of Medical Captain from 1948. Realising the difficulty of recovering injured soldiers from the jungle fighting, she returned to France and gained her helicopter pilot licence. Flying the helicopter herself, she was able to recover wounded soldiers from the jungle battlefields and fly them back to safety and give them the medical aid they required to help save their lives. She logged some 129 flights in the helicopter to rescue 165 injured soldiers during 1952-53. Her first flight into the jungle was made on 11 December 1951 giving her the distinction of being the first woman to fly a helicopter in a war zone, while coming under enemy fire. Using her experience as a certified parachutist, she also made two jumps to give immediate medical treatment to seriously injured soldiers in the jungle. Truly a pioneer aviatrix of great courage.

The Bell H-13 Sioux helicopters were a welcome sight for many injured soldiers during the Korean War. The H-13D Sioux was the most common version used in the Korean war. It was the world's first dedicated Casevac helicopter.

An air ambulance flight was first performed as early as 1917 by the British in Turkey to transport an injured soldier to hospital. From then on, the air ambulance service has grown to become a world-wide service operating in numerous countries around the world. Known as Casevac for casualty evacuation and Medivac for medical evacuation of injured or sick civilians. The service has saved many lives in war and in peace, all thanks to two pioneer women, Marie Marvingt and Dr. Valérie Andre who were both instrumental in establishing the air ambulance service that we have today.

Jean Boulet

Jean Boulet (1920-2011) was a French helicopter pioneer born near Paris, France. He graduated from the Ecole Polytechnique and in 1947 he joined the Societe Nationale des Constructions Aéronautiques du Sud Est (SNCASE) which was later renamed first as Sud Aviation and then as Aerospatiale.

Jean Boulet claimed his altitude and autorotation records
in an Aerospatiale Lama, similar to this one.

74

Boulet joined the French Air Force after receiving flight training in North America as a military pilot, gaining the distinction of being one of the first group of foreign pilots to gain a helicopter licence in the USAF. He went on to become a notable helicopter pioneer claiming several records for altitude, speed and distance. One of his most notable records was claimed in an Aerospatiale SA-315B Lama. On 21 June 1972, he claimed an absolute altitude record in the Lama when he reached 40,814 feet (12,442 m) after climbing out from Aerodrome d'Istres, to the north-west of Marseilles in the south of France. Then the unexpected happened. His engine flamed out and an autorotation commenced all the way back down to ground level resulting in a second record for Boulet for the longest and highest autorotation descent, which has yet to be broken.

He received the Aeronautical Medal in 1957 and in 1983 he was one of the founding members of the French National Air and Space Academy in Toulouse in the south of France.

Reginald (Reggie) Brie

RAF Flying Officer, Alfred Reginald Brie (1895-1988) was an early pioneer of rotary flight with experience on both autogyros and helicopters. He is noted for becoming the first British pilot to land a rotorcraft (a Pitcairn PA-39 autogyro) on the deck of a British Merchant Navy ship, in May 1942. He was also a rotorcraft test and exhibition pilot, an RAF pilot Commanding No. 5 Radio Maintenance Unit at RAF Duxford in 1940.

Reggie Brie was born in Egham, in Surrey and commenced his electrical engineering apprenticeship in nearby Southall. He became the test pilot for the Cierva Autogiro Company in 1930 and the following year he was promoted to the Company's Chief Pilot and Flight Manager. His duties included demonstrating Cierva's autogyros and sales, making record attempts to promote Cierva's craft and giving passengers their flight experience in an autogyro. It was in 1942 he made the first autogyro landing on a ship.

During the war years he flew autogyros for the RAF based at Duxford, flying on calibration flights of Britain's coastal radar network, amongst other flying duties. He also had the privilege to fly the Sikorsky R-4 prototype helicopter in America, being the only British pilot to so. The R-4 was the only helicopter to be used by Britain during the war and Reggie Brie was also involved in performing the deck trials for operating helicopters on board ships in 1944. By the time he retired from the RAF in 1945, he had reached the rank of Wing Commander.

This Cierva C-30A Rota Mk.1 was used for radar calibration work during WWII when it was based at RAF Duxford. It was withdrawn from RAF use in 1946. Post-war, it was placed on the UK register as G-ACUU and flew privately until its final retirement in 1960. However, it returned to Duxford, now the second home to the Imperial War Museum, where it is exhibited in its original RAF colours.

This Avro 671 Rota (K4232) is another example built initially for the RAF's School of Army Co-operation based at Old Sarum in Wiltshire. In September 1940 it was relocated to RAF Duxford and later used on radar calibration work. After the war it was placed on the civilian register and spent time in Sweden on test flying work until 1978 when it returned to the UK and eventually placed on display in the RAF Hendon Museum, London.

He was awarded the British Silver Medal for Aeronautics in 1954. He also received the first Helicopter Aviator's Certificate and what must be one of the UK's first Commercial Helicopter Pilots Licence. Furthermore, he became a founding member of the American Helicopter Society and also the Helicopter Association of Great Britain. He was truly a pioneer of helicopter flying and deserved his awards in recognition for his promotion of rotorcraft flying.

Stanley Hiller

American, Stanley Hiller Jr. (1924-2006) was a pioneer builder of civilian and military helicopters. At 17 years of age, he bult his first helicopter while attending the University of California. He established his first company in

1942, known as Hiller Industries, in Berkeley, California, just across the bay from San Francisco; however, in 1945, after teaming-up with Henry Kaiser, the company name was changed to United Helicopters. The year 1948 saw another name change to Hiller Helicopters.

Young Stanley Hiller designed and bult his first helicopter, the experimental Hiller XH-44 Hiller-copter in which he taught himself how to fly it. It was the first helicopter to be built on America's west coast and the start of Hiller's very successful helicopter manufacturing company. In 1944, Stanley was the first pioneer pilot to fly a helicopter across America, from California to New York, flying one of his later designs, the Hiller 360 of which, over 3,000 were built. The Hiller 360 was also the first helicopter to enter the Swiss civil aircraft register, in 1949.

A museum dedicated to Hiller's helicopters was opened in 1998 known as the Hiller Aviation Museum in San Carlos in California, where the attached photos of two of hiller's helicopters were captured.

The Hiller H-23 Raven was flown in the Korean War from 1950 to 1953, on Medivac and observation duties; the H-23 featured in the TV series 'MASH' based on the its Medivac duties in Korea.

Stanley Hiller's first helicopter design was the Hiller XH-44 Hiller-copter. The example shown here on display in the Hiller Aviation Museum is a replica; the original is in the Udvar-Hazy Museum near Washington, DC.

An early Hiller 360 (UH-12) surrounded by other exhibits in the Hiller Aviation Museum. Note, the open cockpit with only a windshield to protect the occupants. A Hiller 360 made the first trans-America helicopter flight.

4 – South America

South America Welcomes Aviation

The first recorded flight within South America was made on 7 January 1910, by Dimitri Sensaud de Lavaud (1882-1947) flying a plane assembled by Lavaud and his friend Lourenco Pellagatti. The flight was made near Sao Paulo in Brazil and covered a distance of 344 ft (105 m). Across the Andes Mountains, the first flight in Chile was made in August 1910, as we shall see shortly. Following these flights, aviation gradually progressed as it did in Europe and North America with pioneer pilots eventually crossing the South Atlantic Ocean to Brazil and with the establishment of the Postal Service to and around the South American continent.

Dr. Alexander Rice

The Curtiss Seagull in the attached photograph was the first of eighty Curtiss MF flying boats to be built at the Naval Aircraft Factory for the US Navy who used it from 1919 until 1922, when it was then transferred to civilian use. It was an up-graded version with a more powerful engine and an extra seat installed for a third person. As civilian aircraft, they were used in the Canadian outback to transport fishermen and forestry survey-workers, etc.

Dr. Alexander Hamilton Rice (1875-1956) was a man with many titles. He was a geologist, geographer, physician and a lecturer and professor of geography and the founder and director at the Harvard's Institute of Geographical Exploration from 1929 to 1952. He was involved with several organisations, some of which he participated in and also made substantial donations towards their cause. In return, he was awarded several medals, honours and recognition for work in his various specialised fields.

This Curtiss Seagull was used on the Amazon River expedition of 1924-25 by Dr. Alexander Rice. Now on show in the Canada Air & Space Museum in Ottawa, Canada.

He is specially noted for his survey work of large tracts of the Amazon Basin covering over 500,000 square miles of previously unexplored land and rivers reaching as far up-river as Colombia and Venezuela. His Amazon expeditions were detailed in the *Geographical Journal* of the Royal Geographical Society in London in the years 1914, 1918, 1921 and 1928.

The Curtis Seagull in the attached photograph was used by Dr. Alexander Rice in his 1924-25 survey expeditions of the upper reaches of the Amazon River in Brazil. It was one of the first aircraft to be used for aerial photographic survey work and map-making when it covered 2,000 miles (3,200 km) of the Amazon River. It was also the first aircraft of any type to visit the area.

This aircraft last flew in 1936 and was then placed in storage until about 1960 when it was bought by the US Navy. It was restored to its present condition at the site where it was first built by the Naval Aircraft Factory in Philadelphia. It is now on display in the Canada Aviation & Space Museum in Ottawa.

Pan American Goodwill Flight

To further improve relations and friendship between the USA and South America in 1926-27, the Pan American Goodwill Tour was organised with a small fleet of five Loening OA-1A amphibious aircraft touring Mexico, Central and South America.

The five Loenings had two crew members each, all volunteers who were accomplished pilots and mechanics, able to perform their own maintenance en route. Route finding throughout Latin America for future commercial airlines was also part of their job and introducing aviation as a commercially viable method of transport for the public and government officials of the countries they travelled through.

This is the 'San Francisco' one of the five Loening OA-1A's to fly the Pan American Goodwill Tour. Seen here in the Udvar-Hazy Center.

An advance party of Air Corps officers laid a supply-chain of fuel and oil for the Loening fleet during their tour and arranged meetings between the flight crew and officials along the way. The five aircraft departed from Kelly Field in Texas on 21 December 1926 and returned to Bolling Field near Washington, D.C., on 2 May 1927.

Their flight was not without mishap however. During the landing approach to Palomar near Buenos Aires in Argentina, the Detroit and the New York had a mid-air collision and locked together spinning to the ground. The two crew of the Detroit were killed but the New York crew bailed out to safety. The tour continued with the remaining three aircraft, the St. Louis, the San Antonio and the San Francisco.

The Loening OA-1A amphibious aircraft were designed by Grover Loening and the prototype of 165 built, made its maiden flight in 1923. They were built of wood with fabric-covered biplane wings and aluminium covered fuselage with a relatively small tail fin area. Power was provided by a modified, inverted Liberty engine to raise the propeller clear of the water line. The type was used by the US Navy, Army and the Air Corps.

The San Francisco, crewed by US Military pilots, Captain Ira Eaker (1896-1987) and Lieutenant Muir Fairchild (1894-1950) was the only aircraft to fly the Goodwill Tour relatively trouble free. It was donated to the Smithsonian Museum, restored in 1964-65 and is now exhibited in the Udvar-Hazy Center.

The Pan American crew were awarded the newly created Distinguished Flying Cross and the Mackay Trophy for their successful goodwill tour.

First Flight in Chile

The Voisin Tipu Cellular featured here was custom-built in France based on the 1907 Voisin II biplane. It has a conventional tail-dragger undercarriage with a small tail wheel, plus a nose wheel the same size as the main wheels to prevent tipping on its nose. It was a single-surface, orthogonal biplane with a forward canard stabilizer and conventional rear tailplane.

This Voisin Tipo Cellular replica represents the first flight of an aircraft in Chile, South America. It flew so slowly a dog could keep up with it, as shown in the bottom of the photograph, captured in the National Aeronautics & Space Museum in Santiago, Chile.

A 50 horsepower Gnome rotary engine powered the pusher propeller. The French-built Voisin Tipu Cellular made aviation history by becoming the first aircraft to fly in Chile on 21 August 1910. The pilot selected for the historic first flight was a Frenchman, Don Cesar Copetta Brosio. After the first flight, he was soon airborne again with Don David Echeverria as his passenger, the second person to fly in Chile. He was the part-owner of the Voisin Tipu with his brother, Miguel Coverrubias Valdez; it is not recorded if they were pilots or not. The original Voisin Tipu was lost in an accident; the date and details of which, are unknown. The replica was built locally by the National Aeronautic & Space Museum staff with help from the Andres Bello National University. It is now on display in their museum in Santiago, Chile.

The pilot of the Voisin's first flight, Don Brosio died on 27 October 1940 in a plane accident in Los Cerrillos, now a suburb of Santiago, Chile.

First Flights over the Andes Mountains

The first airplane to cross the Andes Mountains was a parasol monoplane, a Morane-Saulnier Type L flown by Luis Candelaria from Zapala in Argentina to Cunco in Chile on 13 April 1918. He crossed the mountains at 13,000 feet (4,000 m). Later that same year on 12 December 1918, Teniente Dagoberto Godoy flew a Bristol M.1C at 20,700 feet (6,300 m) over some of the highest of the Andes peaks from Chile to Argentina, risking the adverse effects of anoxia due to flying without any supplemental oxygen supply and in an open cockpit plane exposed to the cold temperatures. Godoy won the prize of 50,000 pesos presented by the National Congress of Chile to the first pilot to successfully fly across the Andes Mountains between the latitudes of 31° and 35° South. This region includes the 22,838 feet (6,961 m) Mt. Aconcagua at 33° South, the highest mountain in the Andes, which is also the highest mountain outside of the Himalayas.

The engine used was a Le Rhone 9J rotary piston engine driving a two-blade propeller with what must be the largest prop spinner ever to be used on a plane. The prototype Bristol M.1C was first flown on 14 July 1916. It had a high-mounted wing, open cockpit with gaps in each wing root to allow the pilot to see below the aircraft. The Bristol Aeroplane Company built a total of 130 M.1C's for the Royal Flying Corps/RAF and the Chilean Air Force.

The first pioneer female pilot to fly over the Andes was Adrienne Bolland (1895-1975) when she flew from Mendoza in Argentina to Santiago the capital of Chile, in her Caudron G.3 on 1 April 1921.

A replica Bristol M.1C similar to the Bristol used by Luis Candelaria to fly over the Andes Mountains in South America. This example is on show in the RAF Museum Cosford, UK.

A Caudron G.3, was the plane of choice for Adrienne Bolland when she flew over the Andes on 1 April 1921. This G.3 is displayed in the RAF Museum Hendon.

She was a French demonstration and test pilot working for Rene Caudron after gaining her pilot licence with his company, located at Le Crotoy in north-west France near the English Channel. Caudron sent her to South America to demonstrate his aircraft where he successfully made several sales.

It was during her time in Argentina that she made her attempt to fly across the Andes in her Caudron G.3. Her plane had insufficient power to climb over the highest mountains, having a service ceiling of 14,100 feet (4,300 m) and so she had to make her way between the mountain peaks. With no maps of the area, she received advice from a medium on the route to follow, which worked for her. She eventually arrived in Chile's capital, Santiago to become the first woman pilot to fly over the Andes. The flight was a great achievement for Adrienne, considering she only had forty-hours flying time in her log book. For her success on the Andes flight, she was awarded the Knight of the Legion of Honour in 1924.

Adrienne also entered a 2,300 mile (2,100 km) air race in France as the only female pilot competing against ten male pilots; she finished with an equal score. Furthermore, she flew 212 consecutive loops to claim the most loops for female pilots. One of seven children in the family, she grew up with a very determined attitude to life, which gave her the push to go out and achieve her ambitions.

The Caudron G3 was an early pilot trainer and reconnaissance plane, which first flew in 1913 and was flown in WWI by various military units in Europe, South America and Japan. In military service, it was armed with a machine gun and light weight bombs, which were dropped by hand. It had a maximum take-off weight of 1,565 lb (710 kg) and was powered by a single 80 hp Le Rhone 9C rotary engine producing a cruise speed of 66 mph (106 km/h).

5 – Trans-Atlantic Pioneers

Conquering the Atlantic

By 1910, advances in aviation and airplane technology were slowly increasing on both sides of the Atlantic, which allowed the early pioneer aviators to make flights over ever-increasing distances and at higher speeds. An increase in aeronautical technology boosted by World War One helped to produce aircraft of relatively higher performance compared to aircraft from just a few years earlier.

Louis Bleriot had crossed the English Channel in 1909 and the attention of early pioneer aviators turned to thoughts of attempting to cross the North Atlantic Ocean. It was a formidable challenge for any pilot of that period to undertake, considering the early engine technology, although improved, still had a very long way to go and become reliable.

With aircraft engines of doubtful performance and the slow speed of their aircraft, it would require many hours of flying over the open sea to cover the distance across the Atlantic, a distance considerably greater than the range of any of those early aircraft. They were truly a breed of pioneer aviators of great courage and determination to even consider such a challenge.

Walter Wellman

In 1909, Walter Wellman (1858-1934) had already attempted to cross the Atlantic from America in his dirigible airship, the *America*, without success. Flying into a storm and with his engine failing forced him to ditch before reaching as far as Bermuda; the five-crew were rescued by the British merchant ship *RMS Trent*.

First Atlantic Crossing by Plane

The US Navy had at their disposal a small fleet of long-range Curtiss NC flying boats intended for submarine hunting during the First World War. They were built by the Curtiss Aeroplane & Motor Company with the prototype making its first flight in April 1918. Too late to see war service, they served the US Navy briefly in 1919 and 1920.

The Curtiss NC flying boats were relatively large aircraft with biplane wings spanning 126 feet (38.4 m) and a fuselage length of 68 feet 5 inches (20.8 m). Power was provided by four Liberty V-12 engines delivering 400 horsepower each. From an inspection of the enclosed photograph, one could be excused for assuming the plane had only three engines. However, the centre engine is actually two engines mounted back-to-back with the front centre engine and the two outboard engines driving two blade, wooden, tractor propellers and the rear engine driving a four-blade pusher prop, just visible; hence, four engines.

This Curtiss NC-4 was the very first aircraft to fly across the Atlantic Ocean. Now on loan from the Smithsonian, it is presented here in the National Naval Aviation Museum, NAS Pensacola, Florida.

It was an opportunity for the US Navy to take up the challenge and to test the capability of their Curtiss NC flying boats in long-range operations. To this end, the US Navy went to great effort to ensure a successful outcome. Four Curtiss NC flying boats were made available for the challenge, these being the NC-1, NC-3 and the NC-4; the Curtiss NC-5 acting as a support plane. The NC-2 had suffered an accident prior to the Atlantic flight and was cannibalised to provide parts for the remaining four flying boats. Furthermore, a fleet of US Navy ships were strung out across the Atlantic from Newfoundland to the Azores Islands to act as markers along the route to be taken by the flying boats and to assist where required.

The three Curtiss flying boats departed the naval air station at Rockaway Beach, New York on 8 May 1919 making stops at Nova Scotia in Newfoundland, Horta in the Azores and Lisbon in Portugal to end the Atlantic crossing at Plymouth in England on 31 May 1919. The Curtiss NC-4 was the only one to complete the entire trip. A total flying time of 53 hours and 58 minutes over 24 days was required to cover the distance of 4,526 miles (7,284 km). The Curtiss NC-1 was damaged when it ditched in the sea and the other aircraft, NC-3 also ditched but managed to taxi the remaining 205 miles (330 km) to Ponta Delgado in the Azores.

The Curtiss NC-4 commanded by US Navy Lieutenant Commander Albert Cushing Read and his crew, made aviation history for the first trans-Atlantic flight by airplane from the USA to England. Although a great achievement in its own right, they failed to gain the Daily Mail prize because the flight time was longer than the stipulated seventy-two consecutive hours allowed and also, more than one aircraft was used for the attempt.

The US Navy's Admiral Richard Byrd was instrumental in the flight planning for the US Navy's attempt at the Atlantic crossing.

The Daily Mail Prize

Prior to World War I in 1913, Lord Alfred Northcliffe, the owner of the Daily Mail newspaper had offered a £10,000 prize to the first aviator(s) to cross the Atlantic Ocean by plane; however, the competition was suspended until after the war had ended. Interest in attempting the Atlantic crossing was rekindled and by May 1919 four teams of British pioneer aviators had set-up camp in Newfoundland ready to attempt the 1,800-mile Atlantic crossing to Ireland, the shortest distance across with the prevailing westerly winds to help them along their way. However, they also had competition from an American team – the US Navy's three Curtiss NC-4 flying boats, as mentioned above.

The first of the four teams assembled in Newfoundland ready to attempt the trans-Atlantic crossing was the Australian pioneer pilot, Harry George Hawker (1889-1921) of Hawker Aircraft fame (later the Hawker Siddeley Group) and designer of Sopwith Aircraft in WW 1. His navigator was Lieutenant Commander Kenneth Mackenzie Grieve (1880-1927). On hearing the news of the Curtiss flying boat's arrival in the Azores, Harry Hawker elected to depart Newfoundland immediately on 18 May 1919 in their modified Sopwith B1 Atlantic bomber, intending to make the first non-stop Atlantic crossing; however, they too ended up ditching in the sea (as Walter Wellman had done in 1909) and were picked-up by the SS Mary, a passing Danish steamship. There was no news of the two missing aviators until the ship arrived off Scotland several days later, due to the ship's radio being out of service. They were assumed to have been lost at sea and it was with great relief and jubilation when news of their survival reached England.

Frederick Raynham & C. Morgan

Frederick Raynham (1893-1954) with C.F.W. Morgan flying a Martinsyde single-engine aircraft, decided to take-off a few hours after Harry Hawker and Mackenzie had departed. However, during their take-off, they failed to get airborne due to their heavy fuel load and damaged their plane's undercarriage, preventing them from any further attempt on the Atlantic crossing.

Martinsyde aircraft were built at Woking, England between 1908 and 1922 and during the First World War the company was the third largest aircraft manufacturer in England. A factory fire in 1922 brought about its demise, with the company name now fading from memory.

Mark Kerr & Brackley

The fourth team consisted of Commander Vice Admiral Mark Kerr, pilot Major Brackley, chief mechanic Wyatt and Navigator Major Gwan, who planned to fly the Atlantic in a Handley-Page V/1500 bomber but Alcock and Brown were ready for their attempt at the crossing and departed before them on 14 June 1919. On learning of the arrival of Alcock and Brown in Ireland and their winning the Daily Mail prize for the first non-stop flight across the Atlantic, the Handley Page crew cancelled their Atlantic attempt and started their return flight to New York. A landing accident en route delayed their arrival due to waiting for a new fuselage to arrive from England to repair their damaged aircraft.

The Handley-Page V/1500 bomber they used was one of six built but none of them saw any active service, being too late for World War I. They were at the time, the largest aircraft to be built in Britain for the specific purpose of bombing Berlin.

Alcock & Brown

The US Navy's Curtiss NC-4 flying boat had completed the first airplane crossing of the Atlantic with multiple stops en route arriving on 31 May 1919. Failing to qualify for the Daily Mail prize for the first non-stop flight, it was still open to be won.

The aircraft manufacturer Vickers Limited, were considering to enter one of their Vickers Vimy bombers in the Atlantic competition and required a pilot. Also interested in flying the Atlantic was World War I pilot, Captain John Alcock (1883-1919) who approached Vickers looking for a plane in which he could enter the competition; he was quickly accepted by Vickers as their pilot. Lieutenant Arthur Whitten Brown (1886-1948) also approached Vickers looking for work and with his knowledge of long-range navigation was employed as navigator with Captain Alcock to fly the North Atlantic mission.

Consequently, the specially modified Vickers Vimy IV and the Vickers support team were shipped to Newfoundland to prepare for the Atlantic flight. Alcock and Brown crossed the Atlantic to Halifax on the SS *Mauritania* and then had a further two days of train and ferry travel to St. Johns in Newfoundland where they arrived a few days before their aircraft and support team. Their Vickers Vimy was assembled in due course and without any prior test flight, Alcock and Brown departed Lester's Field near St. Johns on the 14 June 1919. Getting safely airborne, they turned the Vimy on course for Ireland, 1,800 miles (2,900 km) away across the Atlantic Ocean.

They were the third team to depart and the only British team to have success, although the flight was far from easy for the two aviators. They had to contend with flying at night, in a cold open cockpit aircraft, with snow and fog obscuring visibility, and at one stage, causing Captain Alcock to suffer spatial disorientation resulting in a loss of control of the aircraft and nearly crashing into the sea. And of course, they had none of the modern radio navigation equipment used by pilots today.

However, after more than 16 hours of flying, they arrived near Clifden in County Galway, Ireland close to their planned landing place at 8.40 am the following day. Unfortunately, their chosen landing site turned out to be a bog, which caused minor damage to the aircraft on touch-down. But yes, they had completed the first non-stop flight across the North Atlantic Ocean, well within the allotted time of 72 hours to qualify for the £10,000 Daily Mail prize, which was presented to them by Winston Churchill, the Secretary of State for Air. They also received the KBE medal from King George V and also the fame and distinction of being the first two men to complete the first non-stop Atlantic crossing. John Alcock lost his life later that year in an aircraft accident.

The Vickers Vimy was a World War I biplane heavy bomber built for the Royal Flying Corps but arrived too late to see any combat, however, it became the mainstay for the RAF's heavy bomber fleet into the 1930s, along with its civilian counterpart, the Vimy Commercial.

It has a wingspan of 68 ft (20.7 m) and was powered by two, Rolls Royce Eagle VIII engines of 360 horsepower each, driving four blade propellers giving a maximum speed of 103 mph (166 km/h). The normal range for the Vimy was 900 miles (1,448 km) but with additional fuel tanks added, range was increased sufficiently for the trans-Atlantic flight to Ireland. The type was also used for other pioneering flights to Australia and South Africa.

The Vickers Vimy flown on the first Atlantic non-stop flight was donated to the London Science Museum in 1919, where it can be seen on permanent display as a very historic pioneer aircraft, now over 100 years old.

Alcock & Brown's Vickers Vimy in which they made the first non-stop trans-Atlantic flight on 14-15 June 1919, is now displayed in the Science Museum, London, UK.

The first non-stop Atlantic flight by Alcock and Brown having been successfully completed, inspired several other pioneer aviators over the following years, who also had ambitions of crossing the Atlantic. Not all aviators were successful in their attempt; some crashed on take-off and others disappeared forever after their departure from either North America or Europe.

A very recent trans-Atlantic flight was made by US pilot Steve Fossett and Mark Rebholz in a replica Vickers Vimy. They retraced the flight of Alcock and Brown from Newfoundland to Ireland taking 18 hours 25 minutes for the crossing, longer than the 16 hours taken by Alcock and Brown.

First Airship Double Crossing

Shortly after Alcock and Brown's successful flight, the British airship *HM Airship R-34* made history by successfully crossing the North Atlantic from RAF East Fortune, near Edinburgh to Mineola, New York, taking four and a half days from 2 July to 6 July 1919. The *R-34* airship had made the first west-bound North Atlantic crossing flying against the prevailing winds, arriving in New York with just an hour's worth of fuel remaining.

On their arrival in New York the *R-34* crew (and fare-paying passengers) received a warm welcome from the crowds and also from President Woodrow Wilson (1856-1924). Also onboard was William Ballantyne and Whoopsie his cat; they had boarded the *R-34* undetected to become the first stowaways on an Atlantic flight. They were not discovered until the airship was over the Atlantic; too late to be put off, they completed the trip to New York.

The *R-34* departed New York on the 10 July and made an uneventful return crossing to land at Royal Navy Air Station Pulham in England, arriving on the 13 July after about 75 hours flying time to complete the first double crossing of the Atlantic by airship. The purpose of the flight was to test the viability of commercial airship travel across the Atlantic. The *R-34* was flown under the command of Major George H. Scott (1888-1930).

The *R-34* was the largest airship built in England at the time and required five engines of 270 horsepower each to propel it through the sky at up to 62 mph (100 km/h). Its overall length was 643 feet (196 m) with a diameter of 79 feet (24.07 m). An accident in 1921 brought about the demise of the *R-34* and it was scrapped. The only part of the airship to remain is the nose cone, now housed in the Museum of Flight at East Fortune, near Edinburgh, from where the R-34 had departed to cross the Atlantic on its pioneering flight.

Rene Foncke

One of the early Atlantic attempts was made on 21 September 1926. French World War I ace, Rene Foncke (1894-1953) was provided with a Sikorsky S-35 plane, purpose-built for the flight with his crew consisting of his co-pilot Lieutenant Lawrence Curtin, the radio operator Charles Clarier and the mechanic Jacob Islamoff.

The take-off distance from Roosevelt Field on Long Island in New York, proved insufficient for the aircraft's weight which was 4,000 lb (1,814 kg) in excess of its maximum limit. It over-ran the runway end and careered down a slope damaging the undercarriage and bursting into flames. Foncke and his co-pilot Lt Lawrence Curtin survived the crash but the other two crew members perished.

The Sikorsky S-35 was a three-engine sesquiplane (a biplane with the lower wing of much shorter span than the upper wing). It was developed from a twin-engine transport and modified with an additional third engine, which were all Gnome-Rhone Jupiter 9A radial engines developing 425 horsepower each, driving two-blade propellers.

Noel Davis & Stanton Wooster

Another fateful flight involved two US Navy pilots, Lieutenant Commander Noel G. Davis (1891-1927) and Lieutenant Stanton H. Wooster (1895-1927) in the *American Legion,* a Keystone K-47 Pathfinder built by the Keystone Aircraft Corporation in 1927. The Pathfinder was a three-engine aircraft powered by Wright J-5 engines giving it a maximum speed of 115 mph (185 km/h); it had a wingspan of 66 feet (20.8 m), a maximum all up weight of 10,841 pounds (4,917 kg) and was designed to carry two crew and ten passengers. It was the first of only two examples built.

On the 26 April 1927, one week before its planned Atlantic departure date, it was flown on a test flight from Langley Field in Virginia in an over-loaded condition. It failed to become safely airborne and crash-landed in a marsh killing Noel Davis and Stanton Wooster. The aircraft was rebuilt and went on to serve West Indian Air Express before spending time with Pan Am.

Nungesser & Coli

The first aviators to attempt a west-bound Atlantic crossing from France to America were two French pilots, Charles Nungesser (1892-1927) and Francois

Coli (1881-1927). They departed Le Bourget Airport in Paris on 8 May 1927, to cross the Atlantic to New York in their Levasseur PL.8-1 biplane named the *L'Oiseau Blanc (White Bird)*. The aircraft was never seen again after crossing the French coastline heading out into the Atlantic, except for its undercarriage which had been jettisoned after take-off as planned. Less than two weeks later, Lindbergh safely arrived at their departure point, Le Bourget Airport, Paris.

The Levasseur PL.8-1 was one of two aircraft modified from the Levasseur PL.4, a French Navy reconnaissance aircraft. The two tandem cockpits were changed to a single cockpit with two, side-by-side seats and the wingspan was increased to 49 feet 3 inches (15 m). The main undercarriage was jettisonable after take-off to reduce the gross weight to 11,023 lb (5,000 kg). The fuselage was redesigned with a flying boat-type hull ready for a water landing on arrival in New York harbour. Two more fuel tanks were installed increasing the fuel capacity to 885 gallons (4,025 litres) sufficient to continually feed the single Lorraine-Dietrich W-12ED Courlis engine of 460 horsepower on the long Atlantic crossing.

Charles Nungesser was well-known as a flamboyant man with no fear of danger, a love of flying, fast cars and beautiful women, but he had no respect for authority. He received many injuries and wounds during his wartime flying and also from driving fast sport cars. He was the third highest-scoring ace in France with forty-three victories to his credit. His Nieuport 24 was painted with his *Knight of Death* emblem on the fuselage sides.

The Orteig Prize & Charles Lindbergh

New York hotel owner, Raymond Orteig (1870-1939) offered a prize of $US25,000 (nearly $370,000 in 2019 value) to the first Allied aviator(s) to fly non-stop across the Atlantic Ocean from New York to Paris, France or vice versa. Known as the Orteig Prize, it was first offered in 1922 and remained unclaimed until 1927.

In February 1927, Charles Lindbergh (1902-1974) went to San Diego to prepare his plane for the attempt on the Atlantic crossing. Lindbergh was taking a different approach to making the flight, flying solo instead of having a crew, and using a single-engine aircraft, not a multi-engine type. The plane he used is the now, well-known Ryan NY-P (New York-Paris), a one-off model based on Ryan Aircraft's 1926 design of the Ryan M-2 mail plane, with which Lindbergh would have been familiar with. Lindbergh named his plane, the *Spirit of St. Louis* after his backers (Earl Thomson, Albert Bond Lambert and others) from his hometown of St. Louis, Missouri.

One of aviation history's most famous planes is the 'Spirit of St. Louis', the plane flown by Charles Lindbergh on the first solo, non-stop flight across the Atlantic Ocean. A proud exhibit in the National Air & Space Museum, Washington, D.C.

On 20 May 1927, Charles Lindbergh departed Roosevelt Field, New York on the 3,600 mile (5,800 km) non-stop, solo flight to successfully land at Le Bourget Airport in Paris, France after 33 hours of continuous flying. He was welcomed by a large and enthusiastic crowd of Parisians and officials. Overnight, he became world famous for his Atlantic crossing; as a US Army Air Corps Reserve officer, he received the Medal of Honour, the highest US military medal and of course, he also received the Orteig Prize, which was presented to him on 16 June 1927. Lindbergh sold his Ryan NY-P to the Smithsonian Institute in Washington, D.C., for $1.00 in April 1928, where it is still proudly displayed in their aircraft museum next to other pioneering aircraft.

The Ryan NY-P was a single-seat, high wing monoplane with a wingspan of 46 ft (14 m), 10 feet longer than the Ryan M-2 and powered by a single Wright Whirlwind J-5C radial engine developing 223 horsepower. The Whirlwind engine used by Lindbergh was one of four specifically built for Lindbergh's flight. The cost of the aircraft was $US10,800 including the engine. An additional fuel tank increased the range to 4,100 miles (6,700 km) enabling it to safely cover the 3,600-mile (5,800 km) flight to Paris with reserve fuel; the flight was nearly 2,000 miles (3,200 km) longer than previous Atlantic flights. The extra fuel tank was placed in the cabin in front of Lindbergh's seat to reduce any change in the aircraft's centre of gravity as fuel was consumed. The tank blocked his forward view through the windscreen and a periscope was installed to allow forward view over the top of the fuel tank.

Douglas Corrigan (1907-1995) and his work-mate, Dan Burnett, were working for Ryan Aircraft and worked on Lindbergh's Ryan NY-P preparing it for the Atlantic flight. The success of Lindbergh's flight across the Atlantic instilled in Corrigan the idea to also fly the Atlantic, as we shall see shortly.

It is interesting to compare Lindbergh's flight to that of the US Navy's Curtiss NC-4 aircraft. The US Navy used three aircraft, each one having four engines and a crew of five plus a fleet of ships covering the 1,800 miles (2,900 km) across the Atlantic section of the flight. Then, along comes Lindbergh; one man, one plane, one engine and one flight to cover twice the distance of the US Navy's NC-4. One man versus the US Navy, job done!

However, there is more to Charles Lindbergh than his Atlantic flight; he was of course, a pioneer aviator, barn stormer, wing walker, parachutist, military officer, author, explorer, activist and inventor. He was known by his nick-names of Slim for his height, Lone Eagle for his Atlantic flight and Lucky Lindy for his four parachute jumps from stricken aircraft. He was born in Detroit, Michigan and lived in several different states around North America. He attended the College of Engineering in Wisconsin and in May 1923, he made his first solo flight at Americus, Georgia a year after starting flight lessons. He bought a war-surplus Curtiss JN-4 Jenny for US$500 and turned to barnstorming as 'Daredevil Lindbergh'. He entered further flight training with the US Army Air Service on 19 March 1924, spending one year at Brooks Field where he graduated top of the class as a commissioned officer with the rank of 2nd Lieutenant in the Air Service Reserve Corps. He was not required for service so he returned to barnstorming and flight instructing. He was awarded the rank of Captain in July 1926.

In April 1926, he joined Robertson Air Service at St. Louis in Missouri, to become their well-known, chief pilot flying their new air mail contract on the CAM 2 route, between St. Louis and Chicago via Springfield and Peoria in Illinois, a distance of 278 miles (447 km). With three other pilots, they flew a fleet of four, war-surplus DH.4 biplanes.

Moving away from aviation for a while, Lindbergh went to France in 1931 to work with French surgeon, Dr. Alexis Carrel. Lindbergh was instrumental in inventing a glass perfusion pump (basically, to keep human organs alive during transplant). He discovered Pyrex glass worked where different metals had an adverse effect on the organs. Decades later, heart surgery became possible due to Lindbergh's invention, leading to the first heart and lung machines, which help prolong human life.

Back in America, he had married Anne Morrow in 1929 and with her, they flew together from 1931 to 1933 on exploration route-finding flights for Pan American Airways and other airlines, covering polar air routes from North America to Asia and Europe. Together, they both made their first flight across the South Atlantic in 1933 from Africa to South America and along the Amazon River, before returning to the USA.

In 1944, Lindbergh saw wartime service when he flew fifty missions from the Solomon Islands in the Pacific, flying the Vought F4U Corsair fighter aircraft. He introduced the fuel-leaning technique to fellow pilots to increase the range of the Lockheed P-38 Lightnings, an engine operating technique used by all pilots today flying piston-engine aircraft. He also served in the Korean and Vietnam wars. He became a Brigadier General during his time with the USAAC, USAAF, USAF and gained the DFC and Congressional Gold Medal to add to his Medal of Honour.

With all the many exploits that Charles Lindbergh achieved throughout his life time, he will always be remembered for making the first solo flight across the North Atlantic Ocean. He is a pioneer of air mail flying and international air transport.

Seventy-five years after his Atlantic flight, Charles Lindbergh's grandson Erik Lindbergh, re-enacted the historic flight in his Lancair Columbia 200 on 2 May 2002. He flew the same route solo, from Long Island, New York to Paris in 17 hours and 7 minutes taking just half as long Charles Lindbergh's famous flight.

Admiral Richard Byrd

The US Navy's Admiral Richard Evelyn Byrd Jr., (1888-1957) a pioneer aviator and polar explorer, was another candidate preparing to cross the Atlantic in a Fokker C-2 Trimotor, named the *America*. His chosen crew were to be Floyd Bennett (1890-1928) as his chief pilot, with Norwegian Bernt Balchen (1899-1973), Bert Acosta (1895-1954) and Lieutenant George Noville. They were almost ready to depart on their Atlantic crossing when Lindbergh found success. However, they were struck with an unfortunate accident which delayed their departure.

The Fokker C-2 was taken on a test flight from Teterboro in New Jersey, with Anthony Fokker (1890-1939) as chief pilot, Floyd Bennett as co-pilot and with Richard Byrd and a radioman on board. Returning for a landing, the Fokker's tail kept rising on touch-down until the plane nosed over ending on its back. Anthony Fokker was thrown clear but Richard Byrd had an arm broken, Floyd Bennett received serious injuries as did the radio man.

According to this author's research, the accident was attributed to the aircraft being nose-heavy and Anthony Fokker was unable to get the tail down. However, this author doubts that reason. With the centre of gravity further forward than it should be, it would increase the lever arm between the centre of gravity and the elevator making it more responsive to control inputs, not less. Heavy braking on landing was more likely the cause of the tail rising causing the nose-over. The aircraft was repaired but not before Charles Lindbergh's successful Atlantic solo crossing.

Shortly after Lindbergh's success, Admiral Byrd made a successful flight in the Fokker C-2 from Roosevelt Field, New York to France on 29 June-1 July 1927. His flight crew consisted of his new chief pilot Bernt Balchen replacing Floyd Bennett who was still recovering from the crash and Bert Acosta and Lieutenant George Noville (1890-1963).

Aiming to land in Paris on the 1 July 1927 as Lindbergh had done, they found the airport was closed due to low cloud. A diversion was made to land near a Normandy beach with another crash-landing, fortunately without injuries on this occasion. Byrd and his crew received a hero's welcome in Paris and again on their return home to New York. They had flown the first official trans-Atlantic air mail flight from the USA to France. Byrd and Noville received the DFC for their flight, but Balchen and Acosta not being military men did not receive it.

Clarence Chamberlin & Charles Levine

Clarence D. Chamberlin (1893-1976) was a pioneer pilot and barnstormer and he became the second man to fly across the Atlantic in a fixed-wing airplane and the first to carry a passenger, Charles A. Levine, from New York to the European mainland. His aircraft of choice was the Wright-Bellanca WB-2 named *Columbia*.

In preparation for his planned attempt, Chamberlin made an endurance record flight over Long Island, New York, staying aloft for 51 hours 11 minutes, ensuring he would have sufficient endurance for an Atlantic flight.

However, a court case dispute on who would be the first passenger to cross the Atlantic with him, either Bernt Acosta or Charles Levine, kept his plane grounded until the court case was resolved. As a result, his plan to be the first person to cross the Atlantic by plane and gain the Orteig Prize was thwarted by Lindbergh's success when he completed his flight before Chamberlin was allowed to depart. Bernt Acosta missed out on the flight and his place taken by Charles Levine who boarded the plane at the last minute as Chamberlin was about to depart on 4 June 1927.

Chamberlin and Levine successfully crossed the Atlantic and arrived over Germany after a 42-hour flight; however, they failed to find Berlin, exhausted their fuel supply and landed at Eisleban 62 miles (100 km) south-west of Berlin. Acquiring some fuel, they continued to Berlin arriving on 7 June 1927, claiming the purpose of the flight was to prove regular trans-Atlantic flights were feasible. The sole Bellanca WB-2 was destroyed in 1934 in a hanger fire.

Charles Levine owned a successful car sales business and he bought the Bellanca Aircraft Company with its head office in New York, the company which had built the *Columbia* used for his trans-Atlantic flight.

Minchin, Hamilton & Princess Anne

The second attempt to be the first people to cross the Atlantic on a west-bound crossing from Europe to North America was made by RAF pilot, Lieutenant Colonel Frederick F.R. Minchin (1890-1927) with Captain Leslie Hamilton and their passenger, Princess Anne (1864-1927) of Lowenstein-Wertheim-Freudenberg of Germany. She was a British socialite, aircraft enthusiast and the widow of the German, Prince Ludwig of Lowenstein. The Princess provided the aircraft and finance for the flight in an attempt to become the first woman to fly the Atlantic Ocean.

Frederick Minchin served with the RFC/RAF and in 1923, he became one of the first British airline pilots when he joined Instone Air Line. Leslie Hamilton was a WWI 'ace' with six kills and after the war, he formed his own charter company in Switzerland flying a Vickers Viking amphibian aircraft.

The crew and Princess Ann departed from Upavon Airfield in Wiltshire, UK in their single-engine Fokker F.VIIa named *St. Raphael* (G-EBTQ) on 31 August 1927, bound for Ottawa in Ontario. They were spotted by an oil tanker, the SS *Josiah Macy* mid-way across the Atlantic and possibly by the SS *Blijdendijik* 420 miles (680 km) south-east of New York, way off track with a further distance than planned to fly to reach the North American mainland. However, just like Nungesser and Coli, they were never to be seen again.

James DeWitt & Lloyd Bertaud

A second failure occurred on an east-bound flight which resulted in the loss of James DeWitt Hill and Lloyd W. Bertaud when they departed Maine, USA heading for Rome, Italy on 6 September 1927. They too, were flying a Fokker F.VIIa named *Old Glory*; they were never seen again.

Walter Hinchliffe

The third failure involved Captain Walter Hinchliffe DFC (1893-1928) who was a Royal Navy Air Service and RAF pilot. He was chosen to accompany Elsie Mackay (1893-1928) a pilot and actress, who also wanted to be the first woman to cross the Atlantic Ocean by plane. They departed RAF Cranwell in England on 13 March 1928 in a Stinson SM-1 Detroiter named *Endeavour*. They made a stop at Crookhaven on the south-west tip of Ireland bound for Newfoundland. They were seen crossing the coast of Ireland heading out to cross the Atlantic and shortly after, were seen for the last time by the crew of a ship. Elsie Mackay was the second female to be lost on an Atlantic crossing attempt, after Princess Ann, mentioned previously.

First Non-stop Westbound

Success came on 12-13 April 1928 with the first Atlantic non-stop, east to west flight from Baldonnell in Ireland to Greenly Island in Quebec, Canada. The pilot was a German, Hermann Kohl (1888-1938) with co-pilot James Fitzmaurice (1898-1965) an Irishman and RAF pilot, accompanied by a German passenger, Baron Ehrenfried von Hunefeld (1892-1929). They flew the west-bound flight of 2,070 miles (3,330 km) in a time of 36½ hours in their plane, a Junkers W.33, which they named the *Bremen* after the German city. A landing on the remote Greenly Island was not part of the plan and they were way-off course.

The *Bremen* crew were stranded on Greenly Island and were rescued by Floyd Bennett and Bernt Balchen in their Ford Trimotor. However, on the return flight to New York on 25 April 1928, Bennett still affected by his injuries received in the crash with Anthony Fokker and having caught pneumonia while on an Arctic expedition with Admiral Byrd, died on the return flight. Bernt Balchen continued the return flight flying for eight hours to New York and received the sum of $US10,000 for his efforts, which he promptly gave to Floyd Bennett's widow.

*The Junkers W.33 had an in-line engine as used by Kohl and Fitzmaurice.
The W.33 was followed by the W.34 powered by a variety of radial engines
as shown here, otherwise the two models were similar. This Junkers W.34 is
on display in the Canada Air & Space Museum in Ottawa, Canada.*

All three men on the *Bremen* were the first foreign nationals to receive the DFC, presented to them by President Coolidge. They also received the award, 'Freedom of the City of Dublin'.

The prototype Junkers W.33 had made its first flight on 17 June 1926 and for its day, it was of a relatively advanced aerodynamic design of a low-wing monoplane, with a wingspan of 34 feet 5 inches (10.5 m). Its all-metal construction was also an advancement from the earlier wood-built aircraft. It was powered by a single Junkers L-5 inline engine of 306 horsepower giving a cruise speed of 93 mph (150 km/h). The *Bremen* is now displayed in the Bremen Airport Terminal building.

Paris to New York Non-stop

The two French aviators, Dieudonne Costes (1892-1973) and Maurice Bellonte (1896-1984) flew the reverse route flown by Charles Lindbergh flying non-stop from Paris to New York. They were the first to achieve the non-stop flight on the 1-2 September 1930. They were airborne for a total flight time of 37 hours 18 minutes to cover the distance of 3,850 miles (6,196 km) across the Atlantic Ocean from Paris. After their arrival in New York, Costes and Bellonte flew their Breguet Super Bidon on a tour around the USA before flying back across the Atlantic to Paris on 25 October 1930. Listed on the side of the fuselage are the names of all the US cities visited during the tour.

Dieudonne Costes was a French Air Force pilot ace, a mail pilot, a test pilot for Breguet and a long-distance and record-setting pilot. Maurice Bellonte was also a French pioneer pilot, air navigator, flight mechanic, radio operator and is best remembered for his long-range flight records in the 1920s, to far-off destinations including Siberia and the trans-Atlantic flight with his fellow pilot Costes.

Their aircraft was a Breguet Br.19 GR Super Bidon biplane named the *Point d'Interrogation (Question Mark)*. The Breguet Br.19 was based on the French military bomber/reconnaissance aircraft and was built specifically for the trans-Atlantic attempt with additional fuel tanks installed to extend its range. Power was provided by a Hispano-Suiza 12 LB 650 horsepower engine. The wingspan was 48 feet 8 inches (14.8 m) with a length of 31 feet 3 inches (9.5 m).

Other Breguet 19's was used to make long-distance flights, including an around-the-world flight by Dieudonne Costes with Maurice Bellonte in 1928 in their Breguet 19 named *Nungesser-Coli*, in honour of their colleagues who were lost on their Atlantic attempt.

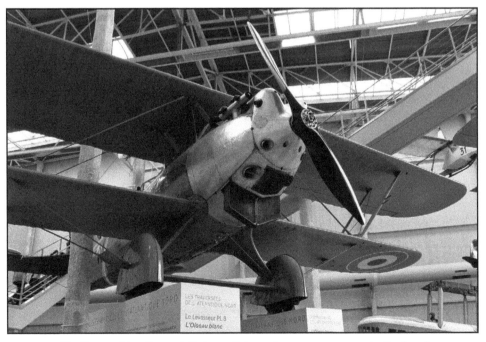

The far-reaching Breguet, its long-distance journeys now over, is displayed in the National Air & Space Museum of France, in Paris.

Amelia Earhart

Amelia Mary Earhart (1897-1937) is the world's most famous pioneer aviatrix with several long-distance flights to her credit. She became the first woman passenger to fly across the North Atlantic on the 17 June 1928 with pilots Wilmer Stultz and Louis Gordon at the controls of the Fokker F.VII. They flew from Trepassey in Newfoundland to Burry Port, near Swansea in Wales.

Four years later on 20 May 1932 at the age of 35 years, Amelia Earhart became the first female aviator to fly the North Atlantic solo from Harbour Grace in Newfoundland to Culmore, Ireland in her Lockheed Vega 5B single engine aircraft. Earhart was aiming to land in Paris as Charles Lindbergh had done but terminated her flight in a paddock at Culmore near Derry in North Ireland. Her flight time across the Atlantic Ocean was nearly fifteen hours. She was awarded the US Distinguished Flying Cross for her accomplishment.

Amelia had been attracted to aviation as a young woman and learned to fly in her twenty's. She became a record setting pilot and authored several books on her aviation experiences. In 1929, she was involved in the formation of the women pilot's organisation known as the *Ninety-Nines* (the number of women present at the inception of the organisation). She went missing on a world flight on 2 July 1937; this will be covered in more detail in section 12 – The Circumnavigators.

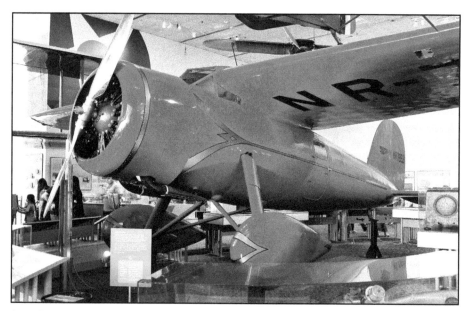

The red Vega used by Amelia Earhart for her record-breaking flights, including her solo flight across the Atlantic in 1932 and the first solo flight from Honolulu to Oakland in California. The Vega is on display in the National Air & Space Museum in Washington, D.C.

The Lockheed Vega was designed jointly by John Northrop (1895-1981) and Gerald Vultee (1900-1938); they both later, formed their own separate aircraft manufacturing companies. The Vega was powered by a Pratt & Whitney R-1340 Wasp 450 horsepower radial engine driving a two-blade fixed-pitch propeller. In the early 1930s, variable-pitch propellers were still in their development stage; constant-speed propellers came later still. Hence, the Vega used a fixed-pitch prop, giving the plane a maximum speed of 185 mph (298 km/h). The wingspan stretched out to 41 feet (12.5 m) with a length of 27 feet 6 inches (8.4 m).

Jim Mollison

Scottish pilot, Jim Allan Mollison MBE (1905-1959) became the first person to fly the Atlantic solo and non-stop on a west-bound flight, from Portmarnoc in Ireland to Pennfield in New Brunswick, Canada on 18-19 August 1932.

What makes this flight even more remarkable is the plane he flew, a de Havilland DH-80 Puss Moth, the lightest aircraft at that time to cross the Atlantic, with a maximum all up weight of 2,050 lb (930 kg). It was powered by a single DH Gipsy III in-line, inverted engine giving 120 horsepower, enabling a maximum speed of 128 mph (206 km/h). The normal range of the Puss Moth was a mere 300 miles (480 km) requiring a considerably greater fuel load to cross the Atlantic.

The following year, from 6-9 February 1933, Jim Mollison flew solo across the South Atlantic via Africa to Brazil in the same DH-80 Puss Moth, claiming the distinction of being the first person to fly both the North and South Atlantic Oceans solo. He is also noted for many other pioneering flights with his aviatrix wife Amy Johnson, a pioneer pilot in her own right, as we shall see later within this work.

Jim Mollison turned to aviation at the early age of 18 years to become the youngest officer to receive his Short Service Commission with the RAF and became a flight instructor at 22 years of age at the Central Flying School. He was also a civilian pilot instructor and airline pilot in Australia and then went on to fly record-breaking flights across the world from Australia to England and England to South Africa. Jim Mollison with his wife Amy Johnson both participated in the MacRobertson Air Race from England to Australia in October 1934 and they both served with the RAF Air Transport Auxiliary (ATA) in the Second World War. For his war-time ATA services, Jim Mollison was awarded the MBE. The couple were divorced in 1938.

Ulbrich & Newcomer

The Bellanca CH-400 Skyrocket *Miss Veedol* was later bought by Dr. Leon Piscili and renamed *The American Nurse* and was repainted from red to white. With his pilot William Ulbrich, co-pilot Edna Newcomer they departed Floyd Bennett Field, New York on 13 September 1932, intending to make a non-stop flight to Rome, Italy. The purpose of the flight was for Dr. Piscili to research the effects of long endurance flights and carbon monoxide poisoning (from the engine exhaust gas) on pilots of that era. Crossing the Atlantic they were about 400 miles (650 km) from their planned landfall at Cape Finisterre, Spain when they were last seen by the crew of an oil tanker, the *SS France*. They were never seen again.

The Experimental Aircraft Association's 424 Chapter built a replica of the *Miss Veedol*, which is now based in East Wenatchee in Washington State, where Clyde Pangborn and Hugh Herndon crash-landed at the end of their trans-Pacific flight.

Idzekowski & Kubala

Another Atlantic west-bound crossing was attempted on 13 July 1928 from Paris to the United States in an Amiot 123 biplane flown by Ludwick Idzekowski (1891-19?) and Kazimierz Kubala (1893-1976). They made it as far as the Azores Islands where they crashed putting an end to their hopes of making a non-stop Atlantic flight. The Amiott 123 was a biplane built by SECM-Amiott as a long-range, single-engine version of the Amiott bombers used by the French Air Force.

Darius & Girenas

One other flight of interest that nearly achieved a non-stop east-bound flight, departed from New York bound for Kaunas in Lithuania on 15-17 July 1933. Two Lithuanian-American pilots, Steponas Darius (1896-1933) and Stasys Girenas (1893-1933) flying a Bellanca CH-300 Pacemaker named *Lituania*, had covered over 3,983 miles (6,411 km) of their route with only 403 miles (650 km) to run when they crashed in a German forest after 37 hours 11 minutes of flying time. They had crossed the Atlantic and reached Europe but their flight was not recognised as a successful crossing. In comparison, the Junkers W.33 on the westbound flight (mentioned above) was considered to be a successful flight even though they were off course, way short of their destination and had to be rescued!

The Bellanca used by Darius and Girenas named Lituania and the Miss Veedol/The American Nurse, mentioned above, no longer exist. The Bellanca CH-300 shown here, is the world's sole remaining example.

The Bellanca used by Darius and Girenas was similar to the Bellanca CH-300 pictured here. This Bellanca was built in 1929 and is displayed as it was used for 33-years as a Canadian bush plane. It is now an exhibit in the Canada Aviation & Space Museum in Ottawa, Canada.

Beryl Markham

Flying a Percival Gull named *The Messenger* from Abingdon in England and heading for New York, Beryl Markham (1902-1986) became the first woman to fly the west-bound North Atlantic route solo on 4-5 September 1936. However, her destination of New York was cut short after twenty hours of flying and she landed at Cape Breton Island in Nova Scotia in Canada due to fuel starvation when the fuel tank's vent iced over.

Beryl Markham was a Kenyan national born in England, with an adventuristic spirit becoming a pioneer aviator and bush pilot in Africa, racehorse trainer and a published writer of excellent works.

Wrong Way Corrigan

Douglas Corrigan (1907-1995) was born from Irish parents living in Galveston, Texas. He is best remembered for his North Atlantic crossing which he claimed was a navigational error.

In 1925, he had his first joy ride in a Curtiss JN-4 Jenny with a barnstorming pilot as his introduction to aviation. Within a week he was taking flying lessons and learning about aircraft maintenance from the local mechanics. He made his first solo flight on 25 March 1926 and gaining experience he moved through the advanced pilot levels and also qualified as a skilled aircraft mechanic. His life revolved around aircraft working as a pilot and aircraft mechanic at various places in America. In 1926, he was employed by the Ryan Aeronautical Company, where he worked on assembling Charles Lindbergh's plane, the Ryan NY-P.

Inspired by Lindbergh's successful Atlantic flight, he bought a four-year old Curtiss Robin OX-5 in 1933 and performed his own mechanical repairs to make it airworthy for his planned Atlantic flight. However, his permission to fly the Atlantic was denied by the Bureau of Air Commerce in 1935; his plane was considered to be un-airworthy and not fit to fly anywhere and was grounded. Undaunted, Corrigan spent more time and money to get his plane certified for a flight across America from his base at Long Beach in California to Floyd Bennett airfield in New York, in 1938.

A Curtiss Robin, the type used by Wrong Way Corrigan to fly the Atlantic Ocean to Ireland. This one is displayed in the Museum of Flight in Seattle, Washington.

Early in the morning of 17 July 1938, Douglas Corrigan departed from Floyd Bennett airfield, ostensibly on his return flight to California, according to his flight plan. Although he had been denied permission to fly the Atlantic, he turned the plane to head out across the Atlantic, later claiming a navigational error due to weather and an incorrect reading of his compass, which took him the wrong way, an error he 'discovered' after 26 hours of flying. The following day, 18 July saw him arrive at Baldonnel Airfield in Ireland. He had achieved his dream of flying the Atlantic Ocean, a flight that lasted for just over 28 hours. For his so-called error, he was nick-named 'Wrong Way Corrigan'.

After the flight, officials condemned his plane for its poor condition and cited Corrigan with a list of violations he had made. He was banned from any further flying for two weeks, the time he and his plane spent returning by ship to New York, where he received a hero's welcome.

During World War II, Corrigan was a production test-pilot flying bombers, a Ferry Command pilot and later an airline pilot. For the remainder of his life, he always maintained his Atlantic flight was a genuine error.

Douglas Corrigan's Curtiss Robin is now on display in the Planes of Fame Museum in Chino, California.

Jets Across the Atlantic

Leaving behind the great pioneer aviators who tackled the vast North Atlantic Ocean, we now move forward a mere ten years to the jet age of 1948.

The de Havilland Venom is very similar to the DH Vampire,
the first jet aircraft to cross the Atlantic.

On 14 July 1948, RAF Wing Commander D.S. Wilson-MacDonald (1912-1996) DSO, DFC, led a flight of six de Havilland Vampire F.3 jet fighters from 54 Squadron RAF across the North Atlantic via Stornoway, Iceland, Labrador and Montreal at the start of a goodwill tour of the USA and Canada. They made aviation history for the first jet aircraft to cross the North Atlantic Ocean.

Roland Beaumont

Roland Prosper Beaumont (1920-2001) OBE, DSO and bar, DFC and bar, was a Royal Air Force fighter pilot during WWII and served until 1947 before he turned to test flying. He flew for Hawkers and later Chief Test Pilot for English Electric Aviation/BAC where he flew the maiden flights of the TSR-2, the Lightning and the Canberra.

Roland Beaumont flew an English Electric Canberra on the first non-stop, un-refuelled jet flight across the North Atlantic to Gander in Newfoundland on 21 January 1951. The following year on 26 August 1952, he flew the first return crossing of the North Atlantic by a jet aircraft in one day when he flew the prototype English Electric Canberra B.5 (VX185) from Aldergrove (near Belfast) in Ireland to Gander and return to Aldergrove in a total time of 10 hours and 3 minutes.

A month later, another English Electric Canberra B Mk.2 made a trans-Atlantic flight on 21 February 1951 flown by Squadron Leader A. Callard from the Aeroplane & Armament Experimental Establishment at Boscombe Down in England. The 2,067 mile (3,326 km) flight was covered in 4 hours and 37 minutes from Aldergrove in Northern Ireland to Gander in Newfoundland. The Canberra was then delivered to the USA to be used as a pattern aircraft for the Martin B-57 bomber, which was built under licence by the Glen Martin Company in California.

Alcock & Brown Remembered

Alcock and Brown's Atlantic crossing was also remembered on 21 June 1979 when a McDonnell Douglas F-4K/M retraced their flight.

The Phantom XV424, was flown from Goose Bay in Labrador to Ireland by two other 'Alcock and Browns', Squadron Leader Anthony 'Tony' Alcock, the nephew of Sir John Alcock (the pilot of the original flight) and with his navigator Flight Lieutenant W. 'Norman' Brown. Their flight time was five hours and forty minutes flying sub-sonic all the way; they received five air-refuels from RAF Handley Page Victor tankers. Their Phantom is now a museum exhibit in the RAF Museum Hendon near London.

The McDonnell Phantom that re-enacted Alcock and Brown's flight sixty years later, on 21 June 1979. It is shown here in a well-preserved condition in the RAF Museum Hendon, London.

This chapter has covered many of the attempts to fly cross the North Atlantic Ocean, some flights were failures, others a great success, which paved the way for future regular passenger-carrying flights. The names of a few pioneer pilots who tackled the Atlantic will be remembered forever; other names are less familiar and almost forgotten. However, four names that have become synonymous for Atlantic pioneering solo flights are:

- Charles Lindbergh, the first man to fly the Atlantic solo when he flew eastbound to Europe on 20 May 1927

- Jim Mollison was the first man to fly solo westbound to North America on 19 August 1932

- Amelia Earhart made the first solo female to fly the eastbound Atlantic crossing to Ireland on 20 May 1932

- Beryl Markham was the first female to fly solo westbound across the Atlantic on 16 September 1936.

6 – The South Atlantic

The South Atlantic Beckons

Due to the number of ambitious pioneering aviators who resided in North America and Europe, the North Atlantic was the obvious first choice of ocean to conquer. Although the North Atlantic suffered from unpredictable bad weather such as the North Atlantic fogs, weather fronts, depressions and generally cloudier and colder weather, it was eventually crossed. The South Atlantic was a much easier ocean to cross due to the mostly calmer and warmer tropical weather. Alcock & Brown and other pioneer aviators had crossed the Atlantic as early as 1919, but it was to be another three years, in 1922, before the South Atlantic was first attempted and eventually crossed by several pioneer aviators. Regular South Atlantic services started in the 1930s flown by airlines from Italy, France and Germany, etc. However, it was the Portuguese Navy who was the first to tackle the South Atlantic Ocean.

Sacadura Cabral & Gago Coutinho

Departing Lisbon, Portugal on 30 March 1922 in a British-built Fairey III-D floatplane, were the Portuguese Navy aviators, Lieutenant Commander Sacadura Cabral (1881-1924) and Commander Gago Coutinho (1869-1959). They departed Lisbon on the first stage of their South Atlantic Ocean crossing heading for Rio de Janeiro in Brazil, 5,209 miles (8,383 km) away. Their flight took them nearly three months to complete, arriving in Rio de Janeiro on 17 June 1922. The flight was not without its hazards, twice ditching in the ocean required the use of three different Fairey III-D aircraft to complete the journey.

Sacadura Cabral chose a modified Fairey IIID for the flight based on its reliable Rolls Royce Eagle VIII engine, the type used on Alcock and Brown's

Vickers Vimy for the North Atlantic flight. The choice of the Fairey having floats was based on the lack of runways available and the fact ditching on the sea could happen, and it did; the floats were a wise choice.

Their plane was equipped with twin floats; a better choice would have been a single float which would have been more suitable for sea landings. The size of the twin floats with their increased drag, along with a higher engine fuel consumption and lower cruise speed all contributed to a decrease in performance adding to the difficulty of their long over-water flights.

Their flight was made, not just to be first across the South Atlantic Ocean, but also, to flight test a new type of bubble-sextant designed for use in aircraft which had an artificial horizon built-in to conduct Astro-navigation. They were the first pilots to pioneer the use of Astro-nav, which became a major navigation method before the advent of radio navigation and later, flight management computers. The second reason for the flight, was for Cabral and Coutinho to be the Portuguese representatives in Rio de Janeiro on 7 September 1922 for the 100th year anniversary of the Independence Day of Brazil celebrations; it was previously a colony of Portugal.

After preparations for the flight were completed, Sacadura Cabral and Gago Coutinho departed from Lisbon Naval Base on 30 March 1922, in their floatplane named the *Lusitania*. The first leg of their journey took them from Lisbon to Las Palmas in the Canary Islands and five days later on the 4 April they continued their journey with stops along the way at the Cape Verde Islands, Santiago Island and St. Peter & St. Paul Archipelago, with still some distance to run before reaching Recife on the coast of Brazil. However, on arrival at St. Peter & St. Paul their water landing was not their best; alighting on the rough water caused one of the plane's floats to break off and the plane sank. This is where a single-float plane would have fared far better. Fortunately for Cabral and Coutinho the Navy support ship *NRP Republic* was on hand to rescue them and put them ashore on the island of Fernando de Noronha in Brazil.

The Portuguese Navy decided to supply a second aircraft for them to continue the flight to Rio de Janeiro. The new Fairey III-D named the *Patria* was delivered to the aviators waiting on Fernando de Noronha. Following pre-flight preparations to continue their journey, they departed on 11 May 1922 returning to the island of St. Peter & St. Paul to pick up their route where they had previously landed and sank and then continued their journey to Rio. However, a second ditching in the ocean occurred a couple of hours later following an engine malfunction due to fuel starvation. They were rescued by a passing British ship the *Paris City* after nine hours adrift and returned once again to the island of Fernando de Noronha. Not to be beaten, the Navy supplied a third plane, the Fairey III-D named *Santa Cruz* and shipped it to the stranded aviators in Brazil. Their journey once again continued to Rio on 5 June 1922, via Recife, Salvador da Bahia, Vitoria and finally arriving in Rio de Janeiro on 17 June 1922 to a hero's welcome by the crowds. They also had the privilege to be greeted by pioneer aviator, Alberto Santos-Dumont.

Their flight covered a total of 79 days clocking up a total of 62½ hours of flying time. The South Atlantic had been successfully crossed by plane for the first time flown by the Portuguese Navy aviators Cabral and Coutinho. For achieving their successful flight, Cabral was promoted to Commander and Coutinho became a Rear Admiral, promotions they both earned and deserved.

The Portuguese Navy had bought three Fairey IIID as practice torpedo bomber trainers but they were never used for that purpose. The first two Fairey's were lost as mentioned above, but the third surviving Fairey, the *Santa Cruz,* saw further military service along with two other Fairey IIID aircraft in 1927 in the South China Sea. The *Santa Cruz* was luckily saved and is now a proud historic exhibit in the Navy Museum in Lisbon, Portugal.

Duran, Franco, Miqueleiz & Rado

There were to be no more attempts on the South Atlantic until January 1926. The four Spanish aviators Juan Duran, Ramon Franco (1896-1938), Julio Miqueleiz (1897-1936) and Pablo Rado made the first South Atlantic crossing in a single aircraft from Spain to South America in their Dornier Do J (Do 16) aircraft named *Plus Ultra*. Their route was similar to that taken by Cabral and Coutinho. They departed Spain on 22 January 1926 via the Grand Canary Island, Cape Verde, Pernambuco, Rio de Janeiro and Montevideo, arriving there on 26 January 1926 after flying a total distance of 6,381 miles (10,270 km).

The Dornier Do J was a monoplane with twin-engines mounted in tandem in the push-pull configuration on top of the parasol wing; the front engine powered a four-blade propeller, the rear engine had a two-blade pusher prop. The engines were Rolls Royce Eagle IX V-12's developing 355 horsepower each, giving the aircraft a cruise speed of 90 mph (145 km/h) and a normal range of 500 miles (800 km); it would have had extra fuel tanks installed for its Atlantic flight. The wingspan covered 72 feet 2 inches (22 m) with a length of 56 feet 7 inches (17.25 m). Large sponsons were mounted on the lower fuselage for stability when on the water, giving the impression of a biplane.

The normal take-off weight was 15,432 lbs (7,000 kg). Of German origin, the Do J prototype made its first flight on 6 November 1922 in Italy and most of the 250 Do J's that were built went to Spain.

The Dornier Do J used on the flight to South America is now displayed in the plane museum at Lujan in Buenos Aires, Argentina.

First South Atlantic Non-stop

Two famed French pioneer aviators, Dieudonne Costes (mentioned earlier) and Joseph LeBrix made the first non-stop South Atlantic crossing in their Breguet 19 named the *Nungesser-Coli*. Departing from Senegal in West Africa they crossed the South Atlantic on the 14-15 October 1927 to make their first landing in Brazil.

Their aircraft was the same type as used by Dieudonne Costes and Maurice Bellonte who flew from Paris to New York on the 1-2 September 1930. It was named in honour of the two Frenchmen, Nungesser and Coli, who disappeared on their attempt at crossing the North Atlantic on 8 May 1927.

Bert Hinkler

Herbert John Louis Hinkler AFC, DSM (1892-1933), was born in Bundaberg, Queensland, Australia. As a young boy he watched the ibis birds flying near his home, which instigated his interest in the theory of flight leading him to build and fly two gliders. In 1913, he found employment in England with the Sopwith Aviation Company, famed for producing WWI aircraft. This was the start of Hinkler's aviation career as a pioneer pilot, aircraft designer and builder. He flew as a gunner/observer with the Royal Naval Air Service during WWI and transferred to the RAF in 1918 as a pilot and was posted to Italy. After the war's end, he left the RAF and was employed by the A.V. Roe aircraft manufacturing company in Southampton as their test pilot.

He was the stand-by pilot for the Schneider Trophy Race in 1925; he also claimed many aviation records of his own for long-distance flights in the 1920s. He made the first solo crossing of the South Atlantic Ocean in 1931. Starting his journey in Canada, Hinkler flew the long route via New York, the West Indies, Venezuela and Guiana to Brazil. From Brazil he crossed the South Atlantic to become the first person to make an eastbound solo crossing on 27-28 November 1931. His aircraft of choice was a de Havilland DH-80 Puss Moth, a single-engine biplane, which was popular with other long-distance pioneer pilots.

Hinkler also made the first solo flight from England to Darwin, Australia to claim a new record of 15½ days for the flight, departing on 7 February 1928. For this flight he flew the prototype Avro Avian (G-EBOV) which is now on display in the Queensland Aviation Museum in Brisbane, Australia.

He died in a fatal crash on another solo record attempt in the Tucson Mountains near Florence, Italy in 1933, less than a year after marrying Catherine Rome.

Bert Hinkler was awarded several medals for his flying exploits including the Distinguished Service Medal in 1917, the Britannia Trophy in 1920, 1928 and again in 1931. In 1928 he won the Air Force Cross and the FAI Gold Medal and then the Segrave Trophy in 1931. The Royal Aero Club awarded him the Gold Medal and he also received the Johnston Memorial Prize plus four Oswald Watt Gold Medals.

Jim Mollison

Pioneer aviator, Jim Mollison (mentioned earlier) was the first pilot to make a South Atlantic solo westbound flight, crossing from Africa to Brazil on 6-9 February 1933. Having already crossed the North Atlantic westbound to Canada on 18-19 August 1932, he became the first person to cross both the North and South Atlantic Oceans solo, using the same de Havilland DH-80 Puss Moth aircraft on both flights.

Italo Balbo

The Italian, Italo Balbo (1896-1940) was an influential World War I veteran, a Fascist Party General, the Italian Minister of Aviation and pioneer aviator. He is best remembered for his leadership and development of aviation in Italy.

From 1930 to January 1931, he led a formation flight of twelve Savoia Marchetti S.55X flying boats on a flight from Rome, Italy to Rio de Janeiro, Brazil. The flight to Rio de Janeiro was the first mass formation flight to cross an ocean (the South Atlantic) and the formation flight was filmed as the first aviation documentary film to be made, the *Atlantic Flight (1931)*. In 1933, he led a flight of twenty-four Savoia *S.55X's* from Rome to Chicago.

Italo Balbo was later appointed as the governor-general of Libya in North Africa in 1933. In 1940, his plane was shot down by friendly-fire and he was killed in the crash at Tobruk in Libya.

Joao Barros

One flight of particular interest was made on 24 April 1927, when the Brazilian aviator Joao Barros crossed the Atlantic with his three crew members in a Savoia-Marchetti S.55 named *Jahu*. The aircraft is now the sole remaining S.55 example and was on show in the aircraft museum in Sao Paulo in Brazil.

The Savoia Marchetti S.55 flying boats were the largest aircraft to cross the Atlantic at that time and several other S.55's have since flown from Italy to South America and return. The Savoia-Marchetti S.55 was an unusual design; it was a flying boat with twin-hulls for accommodation (as found on a catamaran boat) and joined by a centre section between the two hulls which housed the cockpit. The wings spanned 78 feet 9 inches (24 m). The craft was powered by two Issotta Fraschini Asso V-12 engines of 500 horsepower each, mounted on pylons, on top of the wing and back-to-back driving a fixed-pitch, two-blade tractor propeller and a four-blade pusher prop. Twin tail-booms supported a horizontal tail with three fins and rudders. The stall speed was a relatively low 65 mph (105 km/h) for an aircraft with a maximum all up weight of 18,210 lb (8,260 kg). The type was also used as a passenger and freight aircraft by civilian operators and the military.

7 – Across the Pacific

Pacific Pioneers

Having conquered the North and South Atlantic Oceans, the pioneer aviator's next challenge was to cross the vast Pacific Ocean, the largest and deepest ocean on Earth covering 63,800,000 square miles. From the west coast of the USA to Hawaii was 2,400 miles across open water; at the time it was a vast distance for the planes of that era with their reduced endurance. However, several pioneer aviators took up the challenge to tackle the Pacific, some successfully, others were lost without trace.

Albert Hegenberger & Lester Maitland

The first flight from the USA mainland to Hawaii was made on 28-29 June 1927 by two US Army Air Corps pilots, Lieutenants Albert Francis Hegenberger (1895-1983) and Lester James Maitland (1899-1990). They departed from Oakland, California flying an Atlantic-Fokker C-2 named the *Bird of Paradise*. They covered the 2,400-mile (3,862 km) distance over the Pacific Ocean to Wheeler Field on Oahu Island in the Hawaii group in 25 hours and 2 minutes. They did not qualify to win the Dole Race because their flight and destination of Wheeler Field had been pre-planned before the Dole Race was announced. At the time, the route to Hawaii was the longest over-water route in the world, no land to be seen anywhere between the two points. Navigation was done mostly by celestial navigation with radio beacons giving only intermittent help from California and Hawaii.

The Fokker C-2 was built as a military version of the Fokker F.VIIa/3M by the Atlantic Aircraft Corporation in America under licence for the USAAC. It was used to flight test the experimental low frequency radio range beacons being developed at that time, preceding the non-directional beacons and the VOR navaids still used today. The *Bird of Paradise* was later destroyed intentionally at Wright Field at Dayton in Ohio, home to the US military flight-testing base.

Sir Charles Kingsford-Smith

The Australian pioneer aviator, Sir Charles Kingsford-Smith (1897-1935) was a World War One fighter pilot, a record-making pilot and also an owner/operator of his own fledgling airline in Australia. However, it is his trans-Pacific Ocean flight from the USA to Brisbane, Australia for which he is best remembered, accompanied by his crew of Charles Ulm (1898-1934), Harry Lyon (1885?-1963?) and James Warner (1901-1970).

Kingsford-Smith and his crew departed Oakland in California on 31 May 1928 in his Fokker F.VIIb Trimotor named the *Southern Cross* (after the Southern Cross asterism visible in the Southern Hemisphere). With 7,316 miles (11,773 km) of open-ocean to cross, they stopped to refuel and rest at Honolulu and Fiji and arrived at Brisbane on 9 June 1928 to become Australia's greatest heroes. The first aircraft had crossed the Pacific, under hazardous conditions. Severe tropical weather was a bane to the flight and their navigation gear failed to function correctly; there were times when they nearly didn't make it to Australia.

Kingsford-Smith's Fokker Trimotor was greeted by crowds of people on arrival at Blenheim, during its tour of New Zealand after its trans-Tasman flight from Australia. This original photograph was taken in 1928 and passed on to this author many years ago, by C.L. Woodgyer.

Kingsford-Smith, or Smithy as he was known, made several long-distance pioneering flights with his crew in the *Southern Cross* including the first flight across the Tasman Sea to New Zealand arriving in Christchurch on 31 May 1928. They also made the first New Zealand to Australia flight departing from Blenheim on 9 June 1928. The accompanying photograph is an original photo taken at Blenheim of the crowds who turned out to greet the *Southern Cross* on its arrival from Christchurch.

Kingsford-Smith went missing, never to be found, with his co-pilot John Thomson Pethybridge on 8 November 1935 in the Andaman Sea near Burma (now known as Myanmar). He was well known as a playboy who liked the ladies and the drink but was not as successful in his business deals, although as a pioneer pilot making new flight records, he excelled.

The Fokker F.VII was a popular single-engine aircraft designed by Walter Rethal in 1924 and built by the Fokker Aircraft Company in Holland for the Dutch KLM airline. It was redesigned by Reinhold Platz, Fokker's chief designer, with the addition of two wing-mounted Wright J-5 Whirlwind radial engines producing 220 horsepower each, which required an increase in the main wing's span to 71 feet 2 inches (21.7 m). It was given the new designation of Fokker F.VIIb/3m; the 3m signifies three motors. As such, it was capable of carrying two pilots and eight passengers for a total maximum weight of 11,470 lbs (5,200 kg). Its cruise speed was 106 mph (170 km/h).

The Fokker F.VIIb/3m Trimotor Southern Cross displayed in its purpose-built, glass-front hanger, in the Kingsford Smith Memorial Hangar, at Brisbane Airport, Australia.

120

The *Southern Cross* was previously owned by Sir Hubert Wilkins, an Australian Arctic polar explore before he sold it to Kingsford-Smith. This is Australia's most significant historical aircraft and has been preserved at Brisbane Airport in the specially designed glass-front hanger, designated as the *Kingsford-Smith Memorial Hangar.*

Clyde Pangborn & Hugh Herndon

Clyde Pangborn (1895-1958) was one of those true, American pioneering pilots from the first half of the 20th century. Brought up in Washington State, he later spent time at the University of Idaho where he studied engineering before working for a mining company. With the onset of World War I, he joined the US Air Service and became a flight instructor teaching new recruits how to fly. Using the Curtiss Jenny for his instructing he discovered how to fly the plane inverted (upside-down) and earned himself the nickname of 'Upside-Down Pangborn'. After the war he formed his Flying Circus business, barnstorming around the country giving flight demonstrations and taking people for joy rides in his plane.

In 1929, he turned to record-breaking flying and in company with Hugh Herndon (1899-1950) as his co-pilot he set out to make the first non-stop flight across the Pacific Ocean. They departed Aomori in Japan on 4 October 1931 flying over 5,500 miles (8,900 km) of the sparse open sea with little choice of landing en route. After flying for 41 hours 13 minutes, they landed at Wenatchee in Washington State in their Bellanca J-300 Long-distance Special named *Miss Veedol*. Their intention was to land at Seattle but the US North West was closed-in by fog giving them little choice of places to land. With their landing gear jettisoned to reduce drag they had to settle for a belly landing at Wenatchee air strip causing minor damage to their plane. But they landed victoriously having made the first non-stop Pacific flight in history. With their plane repaired and a new undercarriage, they continued on to New York to complete their world circumnavigation flight. Clyde Pangborn and Hugh Herndon were both awarded the Harman Trophy presented for the 'greatest achievement in flight' for that year.

Clyde Pangborn with Roscoe Turner, flew a Boeing 247 airliner in the 1934 MacRobertson Air Race from England to Australia, but more of this flight later. Pangborn was the Bellanca Aircraft Corporation's chief test pilot in the USA and also a test pilot in England for the Cunliffe-Owen Company testing military aircraft during the 1930s. Pangborn's long-distance flying experiences served him well during World War II. As an RAF pilot he flew with the RAF Ferry Command and the US military flying over 170 oceanic flights across the Atlantic and Pacific Oceans delivering aircraft.

Clyde Pangborn was a very experienced pilot accumulating over 24,000 hours in his log books on all types of aircraft including single engine light aircraft and multi-engine aircraft, having flown most World War II bombers and seaplanes. He was a true aviation pioneer having accomplished many things during his forty years in aviation. He is remembered in the National Hall of Fame since 1995.

Charles Ulm

Charles Ulm had crewed several flights with Sir Charles Kingsford-Smith including the first flight to cross the Pacific to Australia, mentioned above. On 3 December 1934, in company with G.M. Littlejohn as his co-pilot and J.S. Skilling as the radio operator and navigator, they were delivering an Airspeed Envoy, the *Stella Australis* across the Pacific to Australia. Having departed Oakland near San Francisco, they are believed to have arrived close to Hawaii, their refuelling stop, but they never arrived; possible fuel starvation or mechanical problems could have forced them into the Pacific.

Amelia Earhart

Amelia Earhart (1897-1937) became the first woman passenger to fly across the Atlantic on 17 June 1928 onboard the Fokker F.VII/3m *Friendship* flown by Wilmer Stultz and Louis Gordon and later she flew the North Atlantic solo in her Lockheed Vega, as we saw in section 5 – Trans-Atlantic Pioneers.

She went on to make other pioneering long-distance solo flights including the first solo flight from Honolulu across the Pacific to the US mainland landing at Oakland in California on 21 May 1932, achieving what other aviators had failed to do. The flight covered 2,400 miles (3,862 km) in a flying time of 18 hours. She made further record flights flying from Los Angeles to Mexico City and from Mexico City to Newark, New Jersey. However, her most famous flight was yet to come, which is covered in section 12 – The Circumnavigators.

Captain Patrick (Bill) Taylor

Captain Patrick Taylor (1896-1966) was born and brought up in northern New South Wales, Australia. He applied to join the Australian Flying Corps but was turned down. Not one to be easily put-off, like many other Australians he sailed to England in 1916 where he joined the Royal Flying Corps. As a pilot flying with 66 Squadron, he eventually received the Military Cross for his gallant actions in France. After his return to Australia, he continued his flying career instructing new pilots for the Australian Flying Corps. He also flew as a pilot for the de Havilland Company and later as a Captain with Australian National Airways in 1930-31.

During the 1930s, he teamed-up with Kingsford Smith and flew with him on several overseas pioneering and record-making flights, acting as his co-pilot or navigator. One notable flight was made in 1933, when he flew as navigator for Kingsford Smith on a flight from Australia to New Zealand in Smith's Fokker F.VII/3m Trimotor, the *Southern Cross*. Half way across the Tasman Sea, the starboard engine (No 3) failed forcing them to dump some fuel and the cargo to lighten the plane's load as they returned to Sydney. Taylor climbed out on the wing struts six times and used a thermos flask to transfer oil from the failed right engine to the port (No 1) engine which was overheating with the possibility of also failing. For his efforts, he received the George Cross.

A nicely presented, privately owned Consolidated PB-2 Catalina in full flying condition, similar to the plane flown across the South Pacific by Captain Taylor.

During the Second World War, he joined the Royal Australian Air Force before transferring to the RAF and flying as a ferry pilot for the Air Transport Auxiliary in 1943-44.

After the war, Captain Taylor became a captain with Australia's international airline, QANTAS. In 1951, he flew across the South Pacific from Sydney, Australia to South America and return on a route-proving flight for QANTAS. His aircraft of choice was a Consolidated PB-2 Catalina flying boat named *Frigate Bird II*. He made stops at several islands in the Pacific including Tahiti and Easter Island. He and his crew arrived at the Quintero Air Force Base near Valparaiso in Chile on 23 March 1951 after the first ever air-crossing over the South Pacific Ocean.

Captain Taylor flew seventy-one different types of aircraft and the Catalina was later presented to him, which he intended to use for his own company, but that never eventuated and the plane went into storage. It is now displayed in the Powerhouse Museum in Sydney.

8 – North to Alaska

Alaskan Bush Pilots

Alaska holds a unique place in the aviation world to this day. Located in the north-west corner of the North American continent, Alaska covers an area of 66,268 square miles with a sub-Arctic to Arctic climate, producing long, cold winters with short temperate summers. The land is covered by thousands of lakes, numerous glaciers in the mountainous areas and tundra on the North Slope with large areas of marshlands and wetlands. It is by far the largest, the most desolate, the most inhospitable and the least populated of all the US states. Many communities have no road or rail services, leaving aircraft the most popular mode of transport to move around this vast area.

Light aircraft operating on skis, floats or wheels with large tundra tyres, supply most of the services and goods required by those people living in the wilderness. The planes are also a lifeline to service the fish trade, gold mining, gas and crude oil reserves and to fly mail, tourists and mountain climbers, etc., to and from their destinations. The fleet of light aircraft have largely replaced the original dogsled teams that first supported the isolated places, ever since Carl Ben Eielson (1897-1929) became Alaska's first bush pilot when he made the first flight in Alaska in 1923, proving that aircraft are an essential part of daily life in Alaska.

Eielson & Wilkins

The polar explorer Roald Amundsen, made the first transpolar flight in the airship *Norge* in May 1926, and Admiral Byrd supposedly flew by plane to the North Pole and returned to his starting point.

Carl Ben Eielson (1897-1929) and Sir George Hubert Wilkins (1888-1958) MC and Bar, were also pioneer aviators and polar explorers. Their claim to fame could have been one of several events that both men accomplished in their life-time. But of interest to us here, is their claim for being the first two men to fly by plane across the Arctic Ocean via the North Pole. But, more of this shortly.

Carl Ben Eielson was a US aviator, bush pilot, mail pilot, polar explorer and was the first pioneer bush pilot to fly in Alaska. Born in the USA to Norwegian parents, he developed an interest in aviation at a very early age. In 1917, he joined the US Army Air Service as a pilot but was still under flight training when WWI ended. He returned home and went to university to complete his education in Law School and worked part-time as a policeman. He made his way to Alaska to work as a bush pilot for the *Farthest North Aviation Company*, which had been formed in 1923. The following year, he flew the first air mail flight between Fairbanks and McGrath and proved a three-hour flight could cover the distance where a dog-sled team required about thirty-days. He also flew the first air mail flight from Atlanta, Georgia to Jacksonville in Florida. Back in Alaska, Eielson established *Alaskan Airways* for its parent company, the Aviation Corporation of America.

A man of many talents, George Wilkins was born in South Australia to pioneer sheep farmers. His list of accomplishments include soldier, air navigator, pilot, aerial photographer, climatologist, author, journalist and more. In 1912, he took the first aerial photographs from above the frontline, during the Battle of the Balkans, fought between the Turks and Bulgarians. In September 1918, while working as an official war photographer he briefly took command of several American soldiers who became separated from their officers at the Battle of the Hindenburg Line in France. He had joined the Australia Flying Corps in 1917 as a Second Lieutenant after being inspired to learn to fly by Claude Graham-White. In July 1918, he received promotion to Captain and placed in command of the No 3 Photographic Section of the Australian war records unit. In 1919, he returned to flying and journalism.

In 1921-22, he accompanied Ernest Shackleton (1874-1922) and Rowett on their polar expedition to the Southern Ocean on the ship, the *Quest*, as their official ornithologist (one who studies birds) and during 1923, he worked for the British Museum as their ornithologist in North Australia. Back in America, he teamed-up with Carl Ben Eielson and together, they studied the drift ice in the Arctic Ocean north of Alaska by plane and made the first-ever plane landing on the frozen sea-ice.

Their first choice of aircraft to attempt the Arctic flight were two Fokker VII/3m Trimotors named the *Detroiter* and the *Alaskan*; The *Detroiter* was owned by their sponsor, the *Detroit News*; the *Alaskan* was the stand-by aircraft. Both aircraft crashed in the Arctic and the *Alaskan* was recovered and repaired to flying condition by George Wilkins. However, the aircraft proved too large for his requirements and he sold it to Kingsford-Smith who renamed it the *Southern Cross,* which Kingsford-Smith used to make his famous first flight across the Pacific to Australia and on other pioneering flights.

Wilkins bought a Lockheed Vega, the third Vega to be built and equipped for long-distance flying. On 15 April 1928, Carl Ben Eielson and Hubert Wilkins were the first men to fly in a fixed-wing aircraft across the Arctic from Point Barrow in Alaska to Spitzbergen in Northern Norway, via the North Pole. Remember, the airship *Norge* made the first transpolar flight on 12 May 1926. Eielson and Wilkins were airborne for 20 hours and 20 minutes on their flight covering 2,500 miles (4,000 km). During their journey, they landed on Grant Land on Ellesmere Island, Canada's third largest and most northerly island. Wilkins acted as the plane's navigator with Carl Eielson at the controls.

On his return, Wilkins was knighted by King George V for the Transpolar trip and his many other achievements. During celebrations in New York, he met his wife-to-be, Australian actress, Suzanne Evans (stage-name Bennet).

Wilkins and Eielson together, also explored part of the Antarctic continent. The expedition received $US40,000 finance by newspaper magnate, William Randolph Hearst (1863-1951) for press and radio rights on their Antarctic exploration, plus a promise of a further $US15,000 if they were the first to reach the South Pole by air. However, they failed to reach the Pole; Richard Byrd and his pilot Bernt Balchen were there first on 29 November 1929. As a way of thanks to Hearst, Wilkins named Hearst Island in his honour. In return, Hearst paid for Wilkins and his new bride to have a trip on the airship *Graf Zeppelin.*

Although Eielson and Wilkins failed to reach the Pole, they still claimed the distinction for making the first plane flight in Antarctica on 20 December 1928 and to become the first polar pioneers to fly in both polar regions in the same year. Their Antarctic flight departed from Deception Island in the South Shetland Islands and flew about 600 miles (970 km) across Graham Land at the top of the Antarctic Peninsula exploring uncharted territory.

Having earlier flown across the Arctic ice in 1931, Wilkins made the first attempt to reach the North Pole under the pack ice by sailing on a privately owned, ex-USA Navy submarine of WWI vintage. However, many mechanical problems with the submarine thwarted his expedition and he failed to complete the mission, but he did prove it was possible to reach the

North Pole by sub. The submarine was eventually scuttled in a Norwegian fjord being beyond economical repair.

The US Navy submarines *USS Skate* with the *USS Nautilus* were eventually the first subs to sail under the Arctic ice; the *USS Skate* was the first on the 11 August 1958. In his will, Hubert Wilkins requested his ashes to be scattered at the North Pole. This request was honoured by the US Navy when their submarine *USS Skate* returned under the Arctic sea-ice to the Pole and surfaced there on 17 March 1959. A great tribute to a man of many talents. It should be remembered, the Arctic region is covered by sea-ice as opposed to the Antarctic, which is a land-mass.

His fellow exploring partner, Carl Eielson was less fortunate. Eielson and his fellow plane mechanic, Earl Borland, were rescuing people from the ship *Nanuck* which had become trapped in the ice at North Cape in Siberia in 1929, when their plane crashed and they were both killed. Carl Ben Eielson received many awards for his life-time exploits and expeditions to the Polar regions.

Noel Wien

Noel Wien (1899-1977) was born in Minnesota where he learned to fly in the popular Curtiss Jenny JN-4 with the Curtiss Northwest Airplane Company's flying school. He gained his licence after eight hours of flight instruction and turned briefly to barnstorming in his Standard J-1 before heading to Anchorage in Alaska, in 1924.

Jimmy Rodebaugh formed his own company, the Alaska Aerial Transportation Company and required a pilot to fly his two Hisso Standard J-1 planes. Noel Wien was hired as his pilot, to become one of the first pioneer bush pilots in Alaska, where he made the first flight from Anchorage to Fairbanks on 6 July 1924. He is noted for his pioneering flights around the state and for introducing the usefulness of light aircraft as a more efficient and quicker form of transport to move around the vast, wild and largely thinly populated areas of Alaska. And to this day, Alaska has more aircraft per capita than any of the other contiguous states in the USA.

In 1927, he established his own business, Wien Air Alaska flying a Stinson Detroiter with passengers, freight and air mail. It was the first airline in Alaska. He achieved several first flights, including the first aviator to fly north of the Arctic Circle in February 1925 and the first to cross the Bering Strait to Siberia on 7 March 1929 with a return on the following day.

Wien Alaska Airways was sold in 1929 and with other companies formed Alaskan Airways, Inc. However, in August 1932, Noel Wien restarted his original company, Wien Airways of Alaska, flying a Bellanca CH-300 Pacemaker. His company moved into the jet-age flying the Boeing 737 and Douglas DC-8 before closing shop on 23 November 1984.

Noel Wiens had lost his right eye due to an infection in 1946, but was able to keep his pilot licence and continued to fly commercially, logging over eleven thousand hours before he stopped recording hours in his log books. He retired from flying in 1955.

Robert Campbell Reeve

Robert Campbell Reeve (1902-1980) was an American pioneer aviator paving the way in South America and later in Alaska where he was the founder of Reeve Aleutian Airways.

Robert Reeve was born in 1902 in Wisconsin, USA. He joined the US Army in 1917 at the early age of fifteen years and served until the end of World War I reaching the rank of sergeant. He spent time working in China and Russia before returning home to the USA and going back to High School and University.

A Ford 5-AT-B Trimotor similar to those flown by Robert Reeve in South America. The example shown here is in the colours of Pan American Airways System (Pan Am). It is displayed in the San Diego Air & Space Museum in California.

Aviation had been one of his interests from an early age and after moving to Texas, he worked for two barnstormers in exchange for flight instruction and eventually gained his Commercial Pilot Licence. He also received one of the first Aircraft and Engine Mechanics Licences to be issued, in 1926. Moving on, he flew air mail contracts for Panagra in Ford Trimotors from the USA to Lima in Peru and later, to Santiago in Chile and Montevideo in Uruguay after the route was extended. He chose to terminate his service with Panagra in 1932 before he had chance to be fired after crashing one of their Lockheed Vegas.

Leaving South America behind, he headed north to fly in Alaska, influenced by stories he heard about the advantages of Alaskan bush flying. Arriving at Valdez in Alaska, he worked on repairing a crashed Alexander Eaglerock for Owen Meals, which had been a spare aircraft for Sir Hubert Wilkins' Transpolar flight from Alaska to Norway. Reeve returned the plane to airworthy condition and used it for his introduction to his new flying career in Alaska, flying supplies to an airstrip at Chisana, eventually earning sufficient money to buy a Fairchild 51 and become a seasoned, Alaskan bush pilot.

A restored Alexander Eaglerock displayed in the Passenger Terminal at Seattle's Sea-Tac Airport in Washington State. The type Bob Reeve repaired and flew when he first arrived in Alaska.

Charter flying proved very profitable for Robert Reeve and in February 1946, he formed his own airline under the name of Reeve Aleutian Airways, based in Anchorage. His company flew charters and scheduled air routes throughout Alaska, western Canada and later to Honolulu, and Houston in Texas and across the Bering Sea to Russia.

His fleet of aircraft ranged in type from the Beech Twin Bonanza and the amphibians, Sikorsky S-39-C and the Grumman Goose. Moving up to larger aircraft as his airline expanded, he flew the NAMC YS-11A, Douglas DC-3, DC-4 and DC-6 through to the Lockheed L-188 Electra and the Boeing 727. The airline ceased operations on 5 December 2000. Robert Reeve will always be remembered as one of Alaska's pioneering pilots.

Joe & Marvel Crosson

It is fairly common for husband-and-wife teams to fly together, such as Charles Lindberg with his wife Anne and Jim Mollison and his wife Amy Johnson. But for a brother and sister to enter aviation together is relatively uncommon, but that is what happened with Joe Crosson and Marvel Crosson (1900-1929) two pioneer American aviators.

They both saw their first aircraft while visiting a state fair in Logan, Colorado, when Marvel Crosson was thirteen years old, which induced her and her brother to eventually become pilots. Marvel was to become the first female pilot to fly in Alaska and to make a name for herself across America as an aviatrix. Her brother Joe Crosson was the first to learn to fly and went solo in June 1924, with Marvel helping to provide him financial assistance. Together, they bought a dis-assembled and damaged ex-Navy Curtiss Jenny N-9, the navy's floatplane version of the Curtiss Jenny. The siblings reassembled and restored it to flying condition after finding an engine and converted it from floats to a wheeled undercarriage. Joe Crosson then taught his sister Marvel how to fly.

Joe moved to Alaska in 1926 to accept a flying job as a bush pilot for the Fairbanks Airplane Corporation after being advised of the vacancy for a pilot. He flew alongside pioneer bush pilots such as Noel Wien, Ben Eielson and Russ Merrill. Joe Crosson was the second pilot, in 1927 to fly into Barrow, Alaska to assist George Wilkins and Ben Eielson as they set-up their supply drops for an attempt to fly from Alaska across the North Pole to Spitsbergen, Norway, which they achieved in March 1927.

Joe later started his own bush flying business in Alaska and was eventually joined by his sister Marvel who flew for, and managed the company. After the loss of his sister, he had returned to continue flying in Alaska to become a well-known bush pilot, flying supplies and medication to isolated communities and gold mining sites and also mail and passengers throughout the rugged and desolate terrain. He also helped to pioneer new air routes around Alaska and over the mountain ranges allowing climbers access to new routes in the mountainous regions of Alaska. He was also the first bush pilot to land an aircraft on the 20,310 feet (6,190 m) Mount McKinley's (now Mt. Denali) Muldrow glacier.

It was mentioned above, Ben Eielson and Earl Borland, fatally crashed during rescue operations from the

trapped ship *Nanuck* at North Cape in Siberia. It was not until February 1930 before their bodies were recovered by Joe Crosson with his fellow pilot, Harold Gillam after a long search in the cold and dark winter before they found the crash site some ninety miles east of North Cape in desolate Siberian back country.

Another fatal crash rescue operation was performed by Joe Crosson in 1935, when he flew the bodies of Wiley Post and his passenger, Will Rogers back to the USA. They had crashed after take-off on 15 August 1935 near Point Barrow.

In 1949, mountaineer Bradford Washburn named the 12,352 feet (3,765 m) peak in the Alaska Range in memory of Joseph Crosson.

Joe's sister Marvel Crosson, gained flying experience and fame after winning the first Women's Air Race from Palo Alto to Oakland in California organised specifically for women by the National Aeronautic Association. She also gained an altitude record on 28 May 1929 when she flew to a new record height of 23,996 feet (7,314 m) which increased her fame across America. The Ryan Brougham was loaned to her from the manager of Union Oil, Earle Brewster. Marvel exceeded the altitude record of 20,260 feet (6,275 m) claimed by record-setting pilot, Louise Thaden in December 1928, flying an open-cockpit Travelair Model D-4-D biplane. The Ryan B-5 Brougham was a high-wing cabin monoplane similar to the plane used by Charles Lindbergh to fly the Atlantic.

While still living in California, she met her fiancé, Emory Bronte, who flew as the navigator for Ernie Smith on the first civilian flight from Oakland to Hawaii. Marvel gained her commercial pilot licence, which allowed her to fly mail and freight runs in Alaska in her brother's business, where she became the first female pilot to be licenced there and also the first female pilot to fly in Alaska. Truly a female, pioneer pilot of bush flying in Alaska.

Returning to California, she entered the first *Women's Air Derby* (also nick-named *'the Powder Puff Derby'*), the first air race that allowed women to enter a race organised solely for women pilots by race organiser, Cliff Henderson. The race departed Santa Monica in California on 18 August 1929 to Cleveland, Ohio, flying in stages. The race included such famous pilots as Amelia Earhart, Jessie Miller, 'Pancho' Barnes, Louise Thaden and Ruth Elder (also a record setting pilot) and several other contenders. Seven days later, Louise Thaden would be the first pilot into Cleveland, the finish line of the 2,700-mile race. However, disaster struck Marvel Crosson on 19 August 1929; she fatally crashed near Wellton on the race-leg through Arizona, with undetermined causes; possible engine failure, or carbon monoxide poisoning (not very likely in an open cockpit plane) and sabotage were all suspect, but nothing was proved. She was to have married her fiancé, Emory Bronte, after her arrival in Cleveland and return to flying in Alaska. But it was not to be, the life of a famous pioneer aviatrix ended far too soon. In 2011, she was enshrined in the Alaska Women's Hall of Fame.

9 – Arctic Aviators

Who Was First to the Pole?

Roald Amundsen (1872-1928) the Norwegian pilot and explorer, was the first person to reach the North Pole travelling overland across the ice in 1911. He had previously discovered the North-West Passage on his 1903-06 expedition by sea.

In 1925, Amundsen with Lincoln Ellsworth (1880-1951) and their pilot Hjalmar Riiser-Larson, made an attempt to be the first to reach the North Pole by plane, in an expedition funded by Ellsworth's father. They were flying in a Dornier Wal (N25) flying boat with an open cockpit for its three crew members accompanied by a second Dornier Wal (N24) also with a crew of three. However, on 21 May just 203 miles (325 km) short of the North Pole at latitude 87° 4' North, the Wal (N24) had an engine failure and made a forced landing on the ice incurring damage. The other Wal also landed and it took Amundsen and his men 26 days to prepare a suitable take-off path to return to Northern Svalbard with all six men cramped into the one airworthy plane, all thanks to Riiser-Larson saving the mission. This plane, the Dornier (N25) is now exhibited in the Dornier Museum in Friedrichshafen in Southern Germany.

Having failed his first attempt to reach the Pole by plane, Amundsen made a second attempt with his Amundson-Ellsworth-Nobile airship flight. On the 12 May 1926, he flew north from Spitsbergen, Norway in the airship *Norge* with Riiser-Larsen acting as navigator to claim the first flight across the North Pole. With Italian, Captain Umberto Nobile (1885-1978), Lincoln Ellsworth and the airship's crew, they continued flying over the Pole and then south to land in Teller in Alaska after a 72-hour non-stop flight. The *Norge* was designed and built by its captain, Umberto Nubile.

Roald Amundsen with Rene Guilbaud and Leif Dietrichson on 18 June 1928, went missing and were never found while they were searching for Captain Umberto in the Italian Air Force airship *Italia*, which was assumed to have crashed in the Barents Sea area. It is now believed the crash site was about seventy-five miles (120 km) north-east of Svalbard, a long way from the Barents Sea,

A few days prior to Amundsen's flight in the *Norge*, on 9 May 1926 to be precise, the US Navy's Richard Byrd and his Navy pilot Floyd Bennett claimed to be the first to fly to the North Pole in their Fokker F.VIIa/3m the *Josephine Ford*. They too departed from Spitsbergen in Norway, flew to the Pole and returned to Spitsbergen after flying 1,535-miles (2,470 km) on a flight lasting for 15 hours and 57 minutes. Admiral Byrd was given a hero's welcome on his return to the USA and was promoted to a Commander and Floyd Bennett was promoted to a Warrant Officer; both men were presented with the Medal of Honour by President Calvin Coolidge on 5 March 1927.

But, did Admiral Byrd actually reach the North Pole before Amundsen's flight? There is a certain amount of controversy surrounding his claim. It is believed that Byrd turned back to Spitsbergen before reaching the North Pole due to an engine problem, but claimed in his official report that he had reached the Pole. However, in his personal diary the actual sun-sites he made of his true position were erased but still legible and were changed to read the same as his official report. Based on the time he was airborne; it was claimed the plane could not have covered the entire route to the Pole and return. However, this was disputed, claiming an anti-cyclone gave him tail-winds on both the outbound and return legs of the flight increasing his ground speed in each direction. But anti-cyclones are generally slow moving and of light winds, so it is highly unlikely he would have had favourable winds in both directions. However, the time and distance given above for the flight, would have required an average ground speed of 100 mph (160 km/h) for the return trip, quite feasible for an aircraft with a given true air speed of 111 mph! The amount of fuel carried would be the determining factor.

Furthermore, Floyd Bennett is said to have confessed to Bernt Balchen that Byrd had made a false claim. Contradicting his statement, Bennett also gave interviews and wrote a magazine article claiming that Byrd had reached the Pole.

So, was Richard Byrd's claim to be first to the North Pole true, or not? Or was the Norwegian, Roald Amundsen the first to reach the Pole? I leave it to the reader to form his/her own conclusion.

Hjalmar Riiser-Larson

Hjalmar Riiser-Larson (1890-1965) was the son of a sea captain; he also went to sea and rose to become a captain himself in 1926. He made his first flight as a passenger in 1913 in a naval aircraft which encouraged him to learn to fly and become a pilot for the Norwegian Navy on flying boats. In 1921 he gained his airship pilot licence in England.

When Amundsen became bankrupt, Lincoln Ellsworth financed his next expedition with the help of Riiser-Larson's business connections in the aviation industry. In 1926, Riiser-Larsen was the second-in-command on Amundsen's airship flight to the North Pole and return. He also acted as navigator on the Amundson-Ellsworth-Nobile Trans-Arctic flight from Svalbard to Alaska, mentioned above.

In 1928, Riiser-Larsen conducted a search for Umberto Nobile after he disappeared in the Barents Sea in his airship *Italia* (also previously mentioned). Riiser-Larsen used two Hansa-Brandenburg aircraft for the search; the second one was flown by Finn Lutzow-Holm (1890-1950) a Norwegian military officer and aviation pioneer and together they made several search flights to no avail. Amundsen also disappeared during this same search. Later, Riiser-Larson also made two expeditions to the Antarctic, the first one in 1929-30 and the second in 1930-31. He was the founder of the Royal Norwegian Air Force, a military officer, polar explorer and businessman. He flew several route-finding trips for the newly established Scandinavian Airlines System (SAS) and became the company's director. He also instigated the transpolar air route for SAS from Scandinavia to Alaska over the polar route, which commenced routine flights after he retired in 1955.

Lindbergh's Route finding

Most people associate Charles Lindbergh with the Ryan NY-P, the plane with which he crossed the North Atlantic. But of course, he also flew other planes and one plane of interest was his Lockheed Model 8 Sirius.

The Lockheed Sirius was a single-engine, low-wing monoplane built initially with a wheeled undercarriage, which was later swapped for a pair of floats. The plane was designed in 1929 to the requirements put forward by Charles Lindbergh for his pioneering route-finding flights for Pan Am Airways. The plane was designed jointly by Jack Northrop and Gerard Vultee at Lockheed using the same basic fuselage as the Lockheed Vega. The Sirius had two seats in tandem with a sliding canopy over the cockpits; Charles

Lindbergh flew from the front seat with wife Anne, also an accomplished pilot, in the rear seat acting as navigator and radio operator. The plane had a 42 feet 10 inch (13.1 m) wingspan and a maximum weight of 7,099 lb (3,220 kg) with a wheeled undercarriage. The engine was a single Pratt & Whitney Wasp radial putting out 450 horsepower, which was later replaced for his second trip with a Wright Cyclone radial engine of 680 horsepower. With the Wasp engine and wheel undercarriage the maximum speed was 185 mph (298 km/h) with a range of 975 miles (1,569 km). For their next trips in 1931 and 1933, Edo floats were installed which would have added a tad more weight and reduced the maximum speed a shade due to their extra drag.

The first flight made by Charles Lindbergh with his wife in their floatplane was west to the Orient in 1931. Their plane capsized and was damaged while being off-loaded from the aircraft carrier HMS Hermes in Hankou Harbour in Shanghai, China and had to be returned to Lockheed for repair work before it could be flown again. Another important route-finding flight they made for Pan Am in 1933, was across the North Atlantic, not non-stop to Paris but via Greenland as one of the many countries they visited. When they were in Angmagssalik in Greenland, the local Inuit children gave the plane its name of Tingmissartoq meaning 'one who flies like a bird.' The aircraft has worn that name ever since.

The Lockheed Model 8 Sirius floatplane used by Charles Lindbergh and his wife on route-finding flights for Pan Am. Displayed in the National Air & Space Museum, Washington, D.C., close to his Atlantic-crossing Ryan NY-P.

From Greenland they continued across the North Atlantic to visit a total of 21 countries in Europe, Russia and Africa. On the return trip home to America, they flew across the South Atlantic to Brazil arriving back in the USA at the end of a 30,000 mile (48,280 km) trip.

Apart from Lindbergh's Sirius, the US Air Force took on strength a further fourteen Sirius aircraft, mostly built of metal with a retractable undercarriage, flown as utility airplanes.

Lindbergh's Sirius was first exhibited in New York's American Museum of Natural History. In 1955 it was moved to the National Museum of the USAF in Dayton, Ohio before being passed on in 1959 to the Smithsonian Institute where it is now displayed in their National Air & Space Museum in Washington D.C.

Clyde Pangborn

Pioneer aviator Clyde Pangborn (1895-1958) made a transpolar Arctic flight in 1936 flying a Vance Flying Wing from Dallas, Texas to Moscow. The lack of a visa to enter Latvia saw him detained by the authorities until he was released on 21 July1937 allowing him to continue on to Moscow.

First Transpolar Flight from Moscow

The first airplane to make a transpolar flight from Moscow to Vancouver in Canada was a Tupolev ANT-25RD. The pilot was Valery P. Chkalov, co-pilot Georgi F. Baidukov and navigator Alexander Belyakov. Departing from near Moscow on the 18 June 1937 they flew for 63 hours and 25 minutes to cover the 5,670 miles (9,130 km) to Vancouver in Canada. Some authorities claim the transpolar flight was a hoax, with the plane actually flying from Russia across to Alaska and then continuing on to Vancouver. The Russians claimed their aircraft had a range of 8,078 miles (13,000 km) more than sufficient for a transpolar flight. It is also claimed the ANT-25RD was a modified French, Dewoitine Trait d'Union D33, a single-engine, low-wing monoplane with a fixed undercarriage. The question remains, did it actually fly non-stop from Moscow?

Mustang Over the Pole

Captain Charles F. Blair Jr., (1909-1978) flew his North American Mustang D named *Excalibur III* across the Arctic via the North Pole from Bardufoss in

Norway to Fairbanks in Alaska on 29 May 1951, a total distance of 3,260 miles (5,246 km). The non-stop flight taking ten and a half hours was made possible by the long-range fuel tanks installed by its previous owner, Hollywood stunt pilot Paul Mantz (1903-1965), who had used the aircraft for air racing.

Crossing the frozen Arctic was quite a challenge due to the magnetic compass being affected by magnetic dip in the far north causing false readings. Radio navigation aids and radio communications and airfields were all non-existent in the Arctic, making navigation more difficult. After departing Norway, Captain Blair was totally on his own until arriving in Fairbanks, Alaska. To find his way across the Arctic, he had devised a system of celestial navigation using pre-planned 'sun sights' to confirm his position along the route. From Norway he flew north along the East 20° meridian, crossed over the pole continuing his flight south along the West 160° meridian and then turned south-east to his destination of Fairbanks in Alaska.

Captain Blair's initial plan was to make a world circling flight but his plans were thwarted by the outbreak of the Korean War; the polar flight became his new objective. Prior to the polar flight, Blair had broken the trans-Atlantic record time by crossing from New York to London in just under eight hours on 31 January 1951, a record which still stands for piston-powered aircraft. But Blair was not done yet; he set another non-stop record from Fairbanks back to New York in a time of 9½ hours.

One outcome of the polar flight made it obvious to the US military that North America could be attacked from a European enemy by flying over the Arctic. An early warning defence system was eventually put in place.

This Mustang flew across the North Pole from Scandinavia to Alaska in 1951. It can now be seen suspended from the roof of the Udvar-Hazy Center.

The record transpolar flight earned Captain Blair the Harmon International Trophy presented to him by President Truman in 1952. As a captain for Pan American Airways, Blair suggested they buy his plane and donate it to the Smithsonian's Aeronautical Collection; it has been a museum exhibit since 1953 and is now in their Udvar-Hazy Center, Chantilly, Va.

The Pole Revisited

This was not a pioneering flight as such, but a polar flight made in remembrance of the original flight of Eielson and Wilkins from Barrow in Alaska across the North Pole to Spitsbergen in Norway, back in 1928.

Two Antonov AN-2 Colt biplanes were used for the transpolar flight led by Captain Shane Lundgren flying his own Antonov named *Polar 1*. The two aircraft departed Anchorage on 9 April 1998 for Spitzbergen via Barrow and Eureka, a weather research station, on their 3,550 miles (5,700 km) flight with a forty-minute stop at the North Pole on 13 April 1998 before continuing their journey. Fourteen hours were spent crossing the Beaufort Sea, part of the Arctic Ocean, with a total flying time en route of seventeen hours.

The flight was sponsored by the Dublin plane leasing and finance company, Pembroke Capital Ltd., with company vice-president, Trevor Henderson, as part of the crew; there was three crew men per plane.

The Antonov AN-2 Colt named Polar 1 was flown by its owner Shane Lundgren who landed at the North Pole on 13 April 1998. After completing the flight, the Antonov Polar 1 was donated to the Museum of Flight in Seattle, Washington State, where it remains on display.

10 – Antarctic Pioneers

The Frozen Continent

Antarctica, the world's most southerly continent covers some 5,500,00 square miles making it the world's fifth largest continent, larger than Europe. Unlike the Arctic, which is an ocean covered in sea-ice and devoid of human habitation, Antarctica's inland plateau is an ice-covered land mass with its highest elevation at 9,383 feet (2,860 m) above sea level. The Vinson Massif peak in the Ellsworth Mountains towers up to 16,050 ft (4,892 m). The Earth's coldest recorded temperature was recorded at the Soviet Vostok Station, Antarctic on 21 July 1983 at -89.2 °C (-128.6 °F).

Despite its hostile environment, it was the last continent to become inhabited by a human population, with several research stations manned all-year round since they became established in the mid-20th century. The 1800s saw sea-going polar explorers venturing close to its coastline before man eventually set foot on the frozen continent, to become the pioneers of polar exploration, with names such as James Clark Ross, Douglas Mawson, Ernest Shackleton, Robert Falcon Scott, and the Norwegian with a name now familiar to us, Roald Amundsen. With the advancement of aviation in the 1900s, aircraft of different types were used by polar expeditions and today, are part of the vital support system moving supplies and personnel to and from the research stations.

The first use of aircraft in Antarctica to support the early expeditions now follows in this section of the book.

Byrd's Antarctic Expeditions

Richard Byrd became well-known as a pioneering pilot and polar explorer leading five expeditions to Antarctica and for setting up an early American base known as *Little America*. He was also instrumental in establishing the McMurdo Station on Ross Island for the 1955-56 *Operation Deep Freeze* base, which has been in continuous operation ever since, manned by staff who winter-over there through the very short daylight hours during the southern winter months.

Richard Byrd was an experienced pilot having allegedly flown to the North Pole and later to the South Pole to claim the distinction for being the first person to fly over both Poles. He made the first flight to the South Pole and return, from Little America, with his pilot Bernt Balchen (1899-1973) and his co-pilot Harold Junes. Ashley McKinley, the mission's photographer was also on the flight. They crossed over the Pole not long after midnight on the 28/29 November 1929; it would have been daylight with the Antarctic's summer-time, mid-night sun. They were airborne for 18 hours and 41 minutes in their Ford 4-AT-B Trimotor, named the *Floyd Bennett* for his previous pilot who died during the rescue flight of the *Bremen* from Greenly Island in Quebec.

Richard Byrd accomplished many things in his life-time for which he received numerous awards, including the Distinguished Flying Cross, Medal of Honour and the US Navy Distinguished Service Medal to name just a few. The original Ford Trimotor used by Richard Byrd is now a museum exhibit in the Henry Ford Museum in Dearborn, Michigan.

A Ford 5-AT-B Trimotor similar to that used by Admiral Byrd on his expeditions. This example was flown by American Airlines and is now housed in the National Air & Space Museum in Washington, D.C.

The Ford Trimotors were reliable and popular aircraft, entering service in 1928 with the early airlines in the USA. They were also favoured by pioneer aviators for long-distance flights having three engines and good load carrying ability. The Ford Motor Company's, Stout Metal Airplane Division built 199 Trimotors, the first of which made its maiden flight on 2 August 1926; they were the largest aircraft to be flown in America at that time. It had a wingspan of 77 feet 10 inches (23.7 m) and a maximum weight of 12,650 lb (5,638 kg). Power was provided by three Pratt & Whitney Wasp radial engines of 420 horsepower each giving a maximum speed of 135 mph (217 km/h).

The Ford Trimotor pictured here is on display at the Smithsonian National Air & Space Museum in Washington, D.C, following its restoration and gifting to the museum by American Airlines.

Another aircraft used on Richard Byrd's Antarctic expeditions was a Fairchild FC-2W2 built by the Fairchild Aircraft Corporation in New York in 1928 and it too is now almost a century-old aircraft. It was given the patriotic name of *Stars and Stripes* by Richard Byrd. Power was provided by a Pratt & Whitney Wasp-B radial engine of 410 horsepower, similar to the Wasps used on the Ford Trimotor. The wingspan stretched out to 44 feet (13.41 m) with a length of 31 feet (9.45 m) weighing in at its maximum weight was 3,600 lb (1,633 kg). It is now displayed in the Udvar-Hazy Center, with snow skis and unusual-shaped 'spats' on its undercarriage, as it was used in Antarctica.

This historic Fairchild FC-2W2 named 'Stars and Stripes' was used on Byrd's Antarctic Expeditions for survey and mapping work. Seen here in the Udvar-Hazy Center.

This Fairchild was used on Admiral Byrd's Antarctic expeditions during 1928-1930 and again in 1932 to 1935. After the first expedition ended, the Fairchild was left in Antarctica and after spending three years buried in the snow it was recovered and used on the second expedition for map making and pioneering survey work. At the end of the second expedition, it was brought back from Antarctica and used for photographic survey work in the USA and Guatemala. In 1961 it was gifted by the Fairchild Stratus Corporation to the Smithsonian Museum and restored by the Cradle of Aviation Museum and finally returned to rest in the Udvar-Hazy Center. This is a beautiful example of a pioneering aircraft.

A Kellet K-3 autogiro was used on Byrd's Antarctic Expedition in 1933-34. It made history for being the first rotorcraft to be flown in the Antarctic and it was also the first rotorcraft to crash there, on 28 September 1934; it was abandoned. The K-3 version differed from the K-2 only in its change of engine with a Kinner C-5 of 210 horsepower replacing the K-2's Continental engine.

A Kellet K-3 similar to this example was used by Byrd on his Antarctic Expedition in 1933-34. This rare example is displayed in the NMUSAF, Dayton, USA.

Lincoln Ellsworth

The American, Lincoln Ellsworth (1880-1951 and his Canadian pilot Herbert Hollick-Kenyon (1897-1975) made the first flight across the Antarctic continent in 1935.

Two abortive attempts were made to fly the *Polar Star* in Antarctica. The plane was damaged and nearly lost through the pack ice when off-loaded from the supply ship and was returned to Northrop in America for repairs. Back in the Antarctic again, a broken piston rod required a second trip back to Northrop for more repairs. Success came on its third visit down to the ice and on 23 November 1935, Ellsworth and his pilot departed Dundee Island on the Weddell Sea and flew across the vast frozen, unexplored area of the Western Antarctic continent which Ellsworth named after his father as Ellsworth Land.

They were heading for the base at Little America, which was established earlier by Richard Byrd, 2,400 miles (3,865 km) away and during one of their four stops crossing the Antarctic they were snowed-in by a blizzard and had to clear the snow out of the plane before they could continue on their way.

The Northrop 2B Gamma named 'Polar Star' was flown by Lincoln Ellsworth on exploration flights in the Antarctic. Note, the fully enclosed undercarriage legs. It was donated in April 1936 to the Smithsonian Museum, Washington, D.C.

They almost made it to their intended destination of Little America, but on 5 December 1935, they were forced down due to fuel exhaustion just 16 miles from the camp, a mere five minutes or so of flying time away. It took them six days to walk the remaining distance. They were both assumed to be missing, but were eventually rescued on 15 January 1936 by the research vessel *Discovery II*.

The *Polar Star* was also rescued from its forced landing site and was returned to America and can now be seen in the Smithsonian's National Air and Space Museum, in Washington, D.C.

The Northrop Corporation built the first Gamma in January 1932 as the next model after the Northrop Alpha as a single-seat mail plane. The Northrop Gamma 2B was chosen by Lincoln Ellsworth and named the *Polar Star* to use on his Antarctic expedition. The Gamma *Polar Star* was built as a two-seat, dual-control model to carry Ellsworth and his pilot Herbert Hollick-Kenyon within an enclosed cockpit having the luxury of heating, a requirement for its use in research into high-altitude flying or for flying in the cold Antarctic. The Bristol Aeroplane Company in England also used a Northrop Gamma for engine testing.

The Gamma's wingspan was 47 feet 9 inches (14.57 m) with an all-up weight of 7,350 lb (3,334 kg). It was powered by a single Wright R-1820 Cyclone 9-cylinder radial engine of 710 horsepower giving an excellent power/weight ratio. It had a very good rate of climb of 1,390 feet per minute and a service ceiling of 23,400 feet (7,100 m) which is relatively high for a piston-powered aircraft. It was relatively fast too, having a maximum speed of 223 mph (359 km/h) and a good range of 1,970 miles (3,170 km). It was suitable for operations on wheels, floats or skis as shown in the accompanying photograph where a ski is just visible at the bottom of the photograph.

Commonwealth Trans-Antarctic Expedition

The Trans-Antarctic Expedition started in 1955 and lasted until 1958; its purpose was to make the first overland crossing of the Antarctic continent. The expedition commenced on opposite sides of the Antarctic; the British expedition led by polar explorer Sir Vivian Fuchs, started from Vahsel Bay on the Weddell Sea where Shackleton Base was established.

Sir Vivian Fuchs and his party of twelve men departed in November 1957 heading for the South Pole and onwards across the frozen continent. They used Sno-cats and Weasel tractors for transport and performed scientific research projects along the way.

On the other side of Antarctica, the New Zealand party led by Sir Edmund Hillary (1919-2008) established Scott Base on Ross Island in McMurdo Sound, right next door to the American's McMurdo Station. Scott Base is used by New Zealand scientists who were initially part of the International Geophysical Year. It has remained in operation ever since as a permanent base to continue scientific work, as also is the McMurdo Station and both remain operational all-year round.

Edmund Hillary and his party departed from Scott Base on a route-finding and supply-drop mission for Vivian Fuchs' party to follow from the Pole to reach Scott Base, their final overland destination. However, Hillary and his party arrived at the South Pole a few days ahead of Vivian Fuchs' team, on 19 January 1958, to become the first overland expedition to reach the South Pole since Amundsen's 1911 expedition and Scott's expedition of 1912, 46 years previously. Hillary's party flew back to Scott Base leaving Vivian Fuchs' party to continue overland, arriving at Scott Base on 2 March 1958 at the end of their 2,158-mile (3,473 km) trek. The American's had established their permanent base at the Pole by air, known as the Amundsen-Scott South Pole Station in November 1956, where the elevation is 9,301 ft (2,935 m) above sea level. It is still in operation as a major research station to this day.

One of the two Auster T7 Antarctica's used on the Trans-Antarctic Expedition of 1956 based at Shackleton Base. It is now on show in the RAF Museum Cosford at Shifnal, UK.

The Trans-Antarctic Expedition had the use of two Auster aircraft. The aircraft pictured here was built in 1952 by Auster Aircraft Ltd, for the RAF as a two-seat, dual control Auster AOP.5 aircraft. Two examples were modified in January 1955 as the Auster T7 Antarctica for the Trans-Antarctic Expedition. Equipped with skis or floats, they carried extra radio gear, an extra fuel tank and an enlarged tail surface and were painted in a high-visibility bright orange. The Trans-Antarctic Expedition used them for reconnaissance work and to transport personnel in conjunction with a larger de Havilland DHC-3 Otter.

The first Auster was based at Scott Base on the Ross Sea for use by the New Zealand Air Force to support Sir Edmund Hillary's part of the expedition. The second Auster was used by Vivian Fuchs' party flying out of Shackleton Base by the Weddell Sea where the main Trans-Antarctic expedition began. In December 1957, the Auster was shipped back to England and arrived at RAF Cosford and placed as a museum exhibit in February 1989.

The first airplane to land at the South Pole was a Douglas R4D-5L Skytrain, the US Navy's version of the Douglas DC-3. The ski-equipped Douglas made the historic landing on 31 October 1956 flown by Lt Commander Gus Shinn and his crew.

A US Navy DHC-3 Otter smartly displayed in the National Naval Aviation Museum, NAS Pensacola, Florida. An Otter similar to this one was used in the Antarctic for a non-stop trans-Antarctic flight in December 1957.

The Douglas Skytrain is the US Navy version of the Douglas DC-3. This was the first aircraft to land at the South Pole, in 1956. It is now displayed in the National Naval Aviation Museum, NAS Pensacola, Florida.

The plane had an extended nose to house the radar antenna and also had jet-assisted take-off (JATO) bottles mounted underneath the fuselage for extra take-off thrust. It is now exhibited in the National Naval Aviation Museum in Pensacola with its JATO bottles and skis still attached and wearing its name below the cockpit windows of *'Que Sera Sera' (What will be, will be)*. After landing at the South Pole, Admiral George Dufek (1903-1977) had the historic privilege of being the first man to stand at the Pole since explorer Robert Falcon Scott had been there more than forty years earlier.

A de Havilland Canada DHC-3 Otter made a non-stop 1,430-mile (2,300 km) flight across the Antarctic continent from Shackleton Base via the South Pole to Scott Base in December 1957. The route closely followed that taken by Vivian Fuchs' overland route.

The Antarctic has been decreed as open to all nations for research purposes and several research stations are now established on the frozen continent operated by various countries. Christchurch Airport in New Zealand has been the jumping-off point for RNZAF and US military planes heading for the research bases in the Antarctic. The 'airport' at McMurdo has an ice runway built on the Ross ice-shelf which requires a new runway to be ploughed each year at the start of the summer season. The unpredictable and fast changing weather in the Antarctic causes many flights to turn back to Christchurch before reaching their 'point of no return'.

This is one of twelve Lockheed C-130D Hercules to be equipped with skis for operation in the Arctic and Antarctic regions. It was used by the USAF from 1960 to transport personnel and supplies from Christchurch, New Zealand to the US base in Antarctica in support of the Project Deep Freeze 60 research stations. This one is displayed at the Pima Air & Space Museum in Tucson, Arizona. All aircraft here are cocooned (all openings covered) for long-term storage.

11 – To the Antipodes

Venturing to Distant Horizons

The end of World War I saw a surplus of military aircraft available and although they were still in their primitive stages of development, they were far more advanced than pre-war examples. There was also an abundance of pilots and mechanics all eager to wander further afield from England to various countries of the British Commonwealth. Record setting and route finding became the new era of pioneering aviation, not only for the aviators but also for the aviatrix, as we shall see within this section of the book.

Amy Johnson

The de Havilland DH-60 Gipsy Moth was a relatively small aircraft designed for private flying in the years between the first and Second World Wars. It had a wingspan of only 30 feet (9.15 m) and a maximum all up weight of 1,650 lb (748 kg). The cruise speed was also a low 85 mph (136 km/h) as was the normal range at 320 miles (515 km). They were quite suitable for pleasure-flying around England, but not quite the statistics you would choose to make a long-distance flight from England to Australia; however, that was the aircraft chosen by the aviatrix Amy Johnson (1903-1941) for her first pioneering flight. Amy Johnson, who qualified as an aviatrix and ground engineer, was the first woman to make a solo flight from England to Australia in her Gipsy Moth which she named Jason. She departed from Croydon near London on 5 May 1930 to her first landing on Australian soil at Darwin in the Northern Territory on 24 May. She continued heading south east to Brisbane but damaged her plane when performing a downwind landing. She continued on to Sydney with Captain F. Follett while her plane was repaired and flown to Sydney by Captain Lester Brain.

A pioneer of long-distance flights in various aircraft, aviatrix Amy Johnson's Gipsy Moth named 'Jason' in which she flew to Australia is now displayed in the Science Museum in London.

Amy Johnson was married to Jim Mollison (also a pioneer aviator) in 1932 which lasted for just six years. With her husband and also alone she made several more pioneering flights, setting many records. After exchanging her Gipsy Moth for a de Havilland DH.80 Puss Moth, which she named *Jason II*, she flew with co-pilot Jack Humphreys to make the first flight in one day between London and Moscow in July 1931. From Moscow they continued their journey across Siberia to Japan in record time from England.

Her husband, Jim Morrison had claimed a London to Cape Town record flight, which Amy Johnson beat in July 1932 in her DH.80 Puss Moth named *Desert Cloud*. Her next flight was made with her husband in a DH.84 Dragon from Wales across the Atlantic to New York with the intention of making a long-distance record flight from New York to Baghdad.

However, their arrival in New York didn't go as planned, they ran out of fuel and crashed near to Stratford, Connecticut. They both survived the crash but suffered serious injuries and were later welcomed with a ticker tape parade in New York City.

In 1934, Amy and her husband Jim flew one of three built, specially-designed air-race plane, a de Havilland DH.88 Comet named *Black Magic* in the England to Australia MacRobertson Air Race. They arrived in India in record time but had to retire from the race due to having engine trouble.

Flying solo in May 1936, Amy Johnson regained her England to South Africa record flight in a Percival Gull Six. Her flight time to Cape Town was 7 days, 22 hours and 43 minutes. That was to become her last record-breaking flight. She received the Harmon Trophy and the CBE in 1930 and the Gold Medal from the Royal Aero Club in 1936. In 1938, she gained her divorce.

In World War II, she flew for the RAF's Air Transport Auxiliary delivering aircraft from the factories to the RAF air bases. She died in a plane accident on 5 January 1941; two versions of her cause of death are quoted. First, after flying into adverse weather conditions in an Airspeed Oxford, her plane ran out of fuel. She bailed out over the Thames estuary and was drowned before crew from the *HMS Haslemere* could rescue her. A second version of her death claims she was shot-down by friendly fire after failing to give the correct identification signals. Either way, it was a sad ending for a very famous pioneer aviatrix.

Moncrief & Hood

The first attempt to cross the Tasman Sea from Australia to New Zealand was made by John Robert Moncrief (1899-1928) and George Hood (1891-1928) on 10 January 1928. They had departed from Sydney in Australia on what should have been a 14-hour flight. However, the last radio signal was received about two hours before their planned arrival time at the Trentham race course near New Zealand's capital, Wellington. A large crowd waited for hours to greet them, but they never arrived. A long search along parts of New Zealand's west coastline failed to find any evidence of their demise. It was the first aircraft to go missing in, or near New Zealand.

Robert Moncrief emigrated from Scotland to New Zealand when he was sixteen years old and took his first job as a motor mechanic. He began flying training at Wigram Aerodrome near Christchurch and gained his pilot's licence in 1918, but was too late for WWI service and returned to a car mechanic's job. He instigated the Tasman Sea crossing accompanied by George Hood after hearing about Lindbergh and other pilots making long-distance flights.

A Brougham B-5 was used by Moncrief and Hood to fly the Tasman Sea. This is one of four remaining Brougham's in the world, shown here in the San Diego Air & Space Museum in San Diego, California.

George Hood was born in New Zealand and developed an early interest in aviation. He left New Zealand in 1914 as a Sergeant with the New Zealand Army to fight in WWI. In 1917, he transferred to the Royal Flying Corps as a pilot and lost his right leg shortly after in an accident, but continued to fly on his return home to New Zealand.

Moncrief and Hood were founding members of the New Zealand Air Force in 1923. In 1931, the airfield at Masterton in the North Island was named Hood Aerodrome in honour of Captain George Hood, who was born in Masterton.

The airplane specifically chosen by Moncrief and Hood to fly the Tasman Sea was a Ryan B-5 Brougham named *Aotearoa*, the Māori name for New Zealand; it was a similar plane to Lindberg's Ryan NY-P. The *Aotearoa* was powered by a Wright J-5 radial engine of 220 horsepower with enough fuel to last for twenty hours, quite sufficient for the Tasman flight covering 1,430 miles (2,300 km). The airplane was registered as *G-AUNZ* in recognition of its Australian and New Zealand departure and arrival points, respectively.

Guy Menzies

Kingsford-Smith made the first successful crossing of the Tasman Sea with his crew in the *Southern Cross* on 31 May 1928. Guy Lambton Menzies (1909-1940) made the first solo crossing of the Tasman Sea on 7 January 1931 in his Avro Sports Avian from Sydney, Australia to New Zealand. The Avro Avian had previously been flown from England to Australia by Kingsford-Smith, which he had named as the *Southern Cross Junior*.

Guy Menzies departed Sydney, Australia in his Avion and headed east across the Tasman Sea intending to land at Blenheim at the top of New Zealand's South Island. However, arriving in the early afternoon further south off the west coast of the South Island, he found he was off course and attempted a landing near the small town of Hari Hari, but instead, landed in a nearby swamp causing his plane to nose-over. His single-engine plane had beaten the time of Kingsford-Smith's three-engine Fokker by two and a half hours to complete the first solo Tasman Sea crossing. A memorial now marks the spot where Menzies landed.

An Avro Avian IVM, similar to the plane flown across the Tasman Sea from Australia to New Zealand's South Island by Guy Menzies. Note, the streamlined casing around the engine. The Canada Air & Space Museum in Ottawa, Canada displays this Avian.

Before Menzies departed Sydney, he claimed he was going to fly to Perth in Western Australia, to avoid any difficulties with the authorities about flying eastward across the Tasman Sea in a single-engine aircraft. Wrong Way Corrigan in 1938, used a similar excuse to cross the Atlantic after claiming he was intending to fly in the opposite direction.

In the Second World War, Guy Menzies became an RAF pilot and held the rank of Squadron Leader. But his service life was cut short along with his crew of a flying boat he was flying on 1 November 1940. They were shot down when flying from Malta to Sicily in the Mediterranean Sea. The plane and crew were never recovered.

Sir Francis Chichester

Sir Francis Chichester (1901-1971) was an adventurer, yachtsman and pioneer aviator. Born in England, he left home when he was 18 years old and immigrated to New Zealand where his entrepreneurship saw him excel at various business ventures until the Depression years. He then returned home to England in 1929 and learned to fly at Brooklands Airfield near London.

With his pilot's licence in hand, he bought a de Havilland Gipsy Moth and set out for Australia aiming to beat Bert Hinkler's record time. He arrived in Australia forty-one days later, too late to claim a record time due to engine problems en route but still a great achievement for a relatively new, inexperienced pilot. The 1,200-mile (1,930 km) Tasman Sea crossing was too far for the Gipsy Moth's range and it had to be shipped over to New Zealand. However, Chichester did claim the first solo trans-Tasman flight from New Zealand westbound to Australia, although it was not quite the easy flight he had hoped for. Swapping the Gipsy Moth's wheels for floats, which were loaned to him by the New Zealand Permanent Air Force, he set off to Norfolk Island and then Lord Howe Island, two tiny specks of land in the middle of the Tasman Sea to become the first pilot to land at these two small islands. Finding the islands was quite an incredible achievement in itself. He had to rely on celestial navigation to obtain his position from sun sights with his sextant and then do the math's long-hand, which is not an easy thing to do while flying a small plane. The Guild of Air Pilots and Air Navigators later presented him with the Johnston Memorial Trophy for his excellent navigation procedures during this flight.

When Chichester was living in Wellington, New Zealand, he was accepted as a Life Member of the Wellington Aero Club, (the aero club where this author learned to fly in 1966).

This Gipsy Moth is the same type flown by Francis Chichester on his UK to New Zealand flight and later, to Japan. This privately owned Moth is based at Hood Airfield in Masterton (named after George Hood), in New Zealand.

Landing at Lord Howe Island, his plane was damaged, which Chichester repaired himself with assistance from local islanders. He decided to continue flying around the world but a serious flying accident in Japan curtailed any more ideas of flying.

Returning to England he joined the RAF Volunteer Reserve in 1941. He used his knowledge of air navigation to instruct air force pilots to navigate when flying solo across Europe or over the Pacific Ocean, and he also wrote a book on the subject for pilots. After the war, he established his own map making business.

Aviation was not the only interest of Sir Francis; he was also a keen yachtsman. He won the first trans-Atlantic yacht race in 1960 in his yacht *Gipsy Moth III*, which was named after the plane he flew. He is also noted for achieving the first solo around-the-world circumnavigation in his yacht *Gipsy Moth* IV in 1966, for which he was knighted the following year. Truly, a pioneer aviator and yachtsman with great courage and determination to succeed.

Edgar Percival

Edgar Wikner Percival (1897-1984) from Albury in New South Wales, Australia, was a WW 1 Royal Flying Corps pilot, a charter pilot in Australia and back in England he was a test pilot for the British Air Ministry. Of interest to us here is the Percival Gull, which designed. The prototype made its maiden flight in 1932, initially built by George Parnell & Sons until Percival set up his Percival Aircraft Company in 1934 and built a total of forty-eight Gulls for air transport, record-breaking and long-distance flying. A variety of different in-line, inverted engines were available to the buyer. The Gull was developed into the Percival Proctor and used by the RAF for pilot training and general liaison duties. In 1954, the Percival Aircraft Company became the Hunting Percival Company, which built the Jet Provost until the company was absorbed into the BAC.

The Percival Gull was chosen by Kingsford-Smith, Beryl Markham and Amy Johnson for making their own long-distance record flights. Jean Batten chose the Percival Gull Six equipped with a DH Gipsy Six engine developing 200 horsepower. It was registered as *G-ADPR* and she named it *Jean*.

Jean Batten

Jean Batten's real name was Jane Gardner Batten (1909-1982), but she was more commonly known as Jean Batton. She was a New Zealand concert pianist before achieving world-wide fame as an aviatrix in the 1930s for her record making flights across the world.

With her mother, they moved from New Zealand to England where she joined the London Aero Club gaining her Commercial Pilot Licence in 1932. She obtained finance from different male friends to buy her first plane, a DH Gipsy Moth and later, the Percival Gull Six.

In 1934, she set her first long-distance record for women pilots in her Gipsy Moth when she flew from England to Australia in fourteen days and 22½ hours, four days less than Amy Johnson's record. The following year, she made the return flight to England in seventeen days to become the first woman pilot to fly from England to Australia and return.

In her Percival gull, she crossed the South Atlantic on 11 November 1935 flying via Senegal in West Africa and after a 12½ hour crossing, she arrived in Port Natal in Brazil, 61 hours and 15 minutes after departing England. This was the fastest time for any type of aircraft to reach South America from Europe. She also made the fastest South Atlantic crossing and was the first woman to fly to South America.

A year later, she departed Lympne in England on 5 October 1936 and after a six-day trip she arrived in Darwin, Australia. From there she continued to Auckland, New Zealand in a record setting eleven days and 45 minutes on the first solo flight from England to New Zealand. The following year, 1937, she

*Jean Batten's Percival Gull now hangs in the Auckland
Airport International Terminal, New Zealand.*

made the return flight to England in five days and 18 hours to achieve records out and back. This was to be her last long-distance record making flight.

She received many awards for her record flights including the Order of the Southern Cross, the CBE in 1936 plus the Harmon Trophy in 1935-36 and 1937. To these were added the French Legion of Honour and the Federation Aeronautique Internationale medal and the Britannia Trophy from the Royal Aero Club. And of course, from her New Zealand homeland, the Maori people honoured her with a *Korowai* (a Māori chief's feather cloak); they named her the '*Daughter of the Skies*'. For a young woman in her twenties, she accomplished a great deal and fame too, for her record-breaking flights. However, her fame slowly decreased until she died in obscurity on the island of Majorca in the Mediterranean Sea, in 1982 and was buried in a pauper's grave.

Sir Alan Cobham

We were introduced to Sir Alan Cobham in section 2 – Pioneers of the 20th Century, as an English pioneer aviator with many accomplishments, including long-distance pioneering flights. Two flights of interest here are his flights to Cape Town and the other to Australia. Using a de Havilland DH-50, he flew from London to Cape Town in South Africa and return, between 16 November 1925 and March 1926. The 30 June 1926, saw Cobham again

159

departing England when he became airborne from the River Medway in Kent, England, flying a de Havilland DH-50 on floats. His destination was Darwin in Australia where the floats were exchanged for a wheeled-undercarriage before he continued his trip to Melbourne; he returned via the same route to England.

Historic Flights Re-enacted

The Vickers Vimy made a name for itself when one was flown across the North Atlantic by Alcock and Brown on 14/15 June 1919. Six months later, two Australian brothers, Sir Keith Macpherson Smith (1890-1955) and Sir Ross Macpherson Smith (1892-1922) with their two mechanics James Bennett (1894-1922) and Sergeant Wallace H. Shiers departed from Hounslow Heath Airfield and flew to Darwin in Australia arriving on 10 December 1919. They received a £A10,000 prize for the first flight from England to Australia.

On 4 February 1920, a Vickers Vimy made the first flight departing from England on the 4 February 1920 and arrived in Cape Town, South Africa on 20 March 1920. This was a private venture expedition involving four aircraft departing London none of which made it all the way to Cape Town with their flights terminating in accidents flying south across Africa. Two African pilots, Lieutenant Colonel Pierre van Ryneveld (1891-1972) and his co-pilot Captain Quentin Brand (1893-1968) completed the trip in a borrowed South African Air Force aircraft.

These three pioneering flights were re-enacted nearly eighty years later by a Vickers FB-27 Vimy replica built specifically for that purpose, which made its first flight on 30 July 1994. The idea was instigated by American, Peter McMillan who flew the plane from England to Australia with Lang Kidby in remembrance of the first flight made in 1919. On this flight the plane had two, Chevrolet V-8 engines in NASCAR racing trim, or to put it simply, to run for a long period.

The Vimy made its second remembrance flight, flying from England to Cape Town, South Africa. On this flight, the pilots were Mark Rebholz and John LaNoue. The Vimy was equipped on this flight with a pair of BMW M73 V-12 engines of 321 horsepower each. At the end of its flights to Australia and South Africa it was returned to England by ship.

The American record-setting pilot, Steve Fossett (1944-2007) and Mark Rebholz made the third major flight on 2/3 July 2005, flying from Newfoundland to Clifden in Ireland. The flight lasted nearly 19 hours to complete. Again, the Vimy used a different pair of engines, this time Orenda

This Vickers Vimy replica was used by Steve Fossett and Mark Rebholze to retrace Alcock and Brown's Atlantic flight and was also flown to Australia and South Africa by other pilots. Although this plane is a replica, its recent flights are worth a mention. It is now displayed in the Brooklands Museum, Weybridge, UK.

OE600 V8's were used developing 600 horsepower each. On each flight four-bladed props of 10 feet 6 inches (3.20 m) were used.

The Vimy was donated to the International Society of Transport Aircraft Trading Foundation (ISTAT) in 2006 with maintenance provided by Brooklands Museum volunteers who kept it in an airworthy condition. It was donated to the Museum on 26 August 2006 where it is now displayed with the name *Spirit of Brooklands*.

It is interesting to remember the original flights were made over a century ago (1919-20) back in the days of the true pioneering spirit.

12 – The Circumnavigators

They Circled the Earth

Up until 1923, many pioneering flights had been made by several adventurous aviators. However, a flight circling the world was yet to be made although the French and Portuguese had made attempts, but failed. The English were about to make an attempt when the US Army Air Service took up the challenge to be the first to circumnavigate the world.

World Flight Expedition

Not having a suitable aircraft, the USAAF contacted the Douglas Aircraft Company to provide an aircraft capable of making the flight. Douglas Aircraft offered a conversion of its Douglas DT torpedo bomber which they supplied to the US Navy and suitably modified it with extra fuel tanks, six in the wings plus a fuselage tank increasing the capacity from the 115 gallons carried by the Douglas DT to 536 imperial gallons (2,437 litres) in the DWC, and other refinements for the long legs of the proposed World Flight. The wingspan was increased to 49 ft (15 m) and a tail fin of increased area plus a strengthened fuselage structure. They were built at the Douglas Aircraft plant at Santa Monica in California.

Five aircraft were built with the prototype delivered to the US Army Air Service on 17 March 1924 to train the pilots who were to fly the four aircraft on the World Flight. The aircraft were suitably named as the Douglas World Cruiser (DWC) with each of the four aircraft named after American cities, the *Boston, Chicago, New Orleans* and the *Seattle*.

The World Flight expedition departed Seattle in Washington on 2 April 1924 heading for Alaska, flying around the world westbound. The lead aircraft, *Seattle*, didn't make it any further than Alaska where it crashed on 30

The first world-circling aircraft, the Douglas World Cruiser 'Chicago'
exhibited in the National Air & Space Museum, Washington, D.C.

April 1924. The *Chicago* became the new lead aircraft with the World Flight continuing the journey across Asia and through Europe, with supplies and support provided by the US Navy and the US Coast Guard. Navigation was purely by 'dead reckoning' the most basic form of air navigation as radio navigation aids were still in the future. The next aircraft to be lost was the *Boston* which ditched off the Faroe Islands, halfway between Scotland and Iceland. The *Chicago* and the *New Orleans* continued across the North Atlantic to Pictou in Nova Scotia where the prototype, now renamed as the *Boston II*, joined the expedition for the remainder of the flight across the USA to the starting point at Seattle, arriving there on 28 September 1928 at the end of the World Flight completing the first circumnavigation by plane.

The World Flight had covered 27,558 miles (44,342 km) in just over 371 hours of flying time averaging 70 mph (113 km/h). The four pilots flying the remaining two planes that completed the circumnavigation were the pilot of the *Chicago* Lieutenant Lowell Smith (1892-1945) with his co-pilot First Lieutenant Leslie Arnold (1893-1961) and the crew of the New Orleans were pilot Lieutenant Erik Nelson (1888-1970) and his co-pilot Lieutenant John Harding (1896-1968). All six crew members including the crew of the *Boston II* received the Distinguished Service Medal for their successful World Flight.

The *Chicago* was donated to the Smithsonian Museum in Washington, D.C., on 25 September 1925 where it still remains on display. The *New Orleans* is housed in the Museum of Flying in Santa Monica, California and the wreckage of the *Seattle* is displayed in the Alaska Aviation Museum in Anchorage.

Dieudonne Costes & Joseph LeBrix

The Breguet Br 19 GR named the *Nungesser-Coli* made a world flight flown by Dieudonne Costes (1982-1973) a WWI fighter ace, a mail pilot, an airline pilot and a test pilot before he turned to making record breaking flights. His navigator and co-pilot on the world flight were Joseph LeBrix (1899-1931) a French aviator and Lieutenant Commander in the French Navy.

The world circling Breguet Super Bidon viewed in the National Air & Space Museum of France, in Paris.

They departed on 10 October 1927 from Paris, France on their world flight and returned on 14 April 1928 after covering 34,418 miles (55,390 km). As mentioned previously, they were the first to make a non-stop crossing of the South Atlantic on 14-15 October 1927 from Senegal to Brazil and then continued on via Central America to complete a tour of the USA. Their plane was shipped across the Pacific from San Francisco to Tokyo, Japan, where they continued their journey across Asia and Europe and back to Paris.

The place names of their stops across Asia and Europe on their world flight in 1927, in their previous plane the *Nungesser-Coli,* are written on the forward part of the oblique band on the *Point d'Interrogation*. On the rear oblique band around the fuselage are the names of the places they visited in the USA after crossing the South Atlantic. The *Point d'Interrogation* was the plane Dieudonne Costes and Bellonte used to cross the North Atlantic on 1-2 September 1930.

The *Point d'Interrogation,* is on display in the National Air & Space Museum of France, in Paris, as featured in section 5 – Trans-Atlantic Pioneers.

Wiley Post

Right from his early days, Wiley Post (1898-1935) was a man who accomplished many things in his relatively short life time. One of his first jobs was working on oil rigs as a roughneck where he met with an accident causing the loss of his left eye. In 1921, he spent just over a year doing jail time for armed robbery and later, he gave parachute demonstrations with a flying circus. After learning to fly, Wiley Post bought his first aircraft from the pay-out he received from his eye injury. He was later employed by oil industry businessmen, Briscoe and Hall in 1930 as their personal pilot flying the Lockheed Vega *Winnie Mae,* owned by Hall. He used the Vega to compete in the National American Race flying between Los Angeles to Chicago; he won the race to claim the prize money equal to US$112,000 in today's (2022) dollars.

In 1931, he made his first flight around the world in the Lockheed Vega accompanied by the Australian, Harold Gatty as observer to claim a new world record time. They departed from Roosevelt Field in New York on 23 June 1931 and flew via Berlin in Germany, Moscow, Omsk, Irkutsk and Khabarovsk in Siberia and on to Nome in Alaska, Edmonton in Canada and finally returning to New York on 1 July 1931 after flying 15, 474 miles (24,900 km) in eight days, 15 hours 51 minutes in their single-engine monoplane.

Another famous aircraft. This Vega was flown around the world twice by Wiley Post and the plane in which he confirmed the existence of the jet stream. Displayed here in the National Air & Space Museum in Washington, D.C.

It must be remembered, that an official world circumnavigation flight must now cover a minimum distance of 22,859 miles (36, 758 Km) equal to the length of the Tropic of Cancer at latitude 23.4° North, to qualify for an FAI record. However, Wiley Post's world flight was still a magnificent achievement for its day.

Wiley Post acquired the *Winnie Mae* from his employer, Mr. Hall and two years later he made a second circumnavigation in 7 days, 18 hours and 49 minutes from 15 July to 22 July 1933, beating his own record time. This was also the first solo flight around the world.

On 15 March 1935, while flying at high altitude he confirmed the existence of the jet stream on a flight between Los Angeles and Cleveland when he recorded a ground speed of 340 mph (547 km/h). The jet stream had first been noted by balloonist John Wise circa 1860-70s. Wiley Post was also instrumental in developing pressure suits which are now commonly used by fighter pilots and astronauts.

The Lockheed Vega was a popular plane for record–making pilots including Amelia Earhart in her red Lockheed Vega, which she used on her Atlantic crossing and other pioneering flights, covered in *section 5 – Trans-Atlantic Pioneers*. The Lockheed Vega *Winnie Mae* flown by Wiley Post, is displayed in the National Air & Space Museum in Washington, D.C. The right-hand side of the plane has a list of Wiley Post's achievements in flying around the world and record making flights.

Wiley Post and his passenger Will Rogers were killed on take-off from a lagoon near Point Barrow in Alaska on 15 August 1935. The plane had been assembled by Wiley Post from two similar Lockheed models and although Lockheed advised against the combination of parts, Wiley Post continued to build and fly the aircraft. It was purported that an engine failure on take-off resulted in the aircraft being too nose-heavy and it dived into the lagoon. The more probable cause would have been a departure stall after engine failure. Such were the hazards faced by pioneering pilots. Wiley Post's life was short but he gained fame as a pioneer aviator between the two World Wars for his many achievements.

Amelia Earhart

Amelia Earhart (1897-1937) must be the world's most famous female pioneer aviator of all time. Her pioneering flights and achievements were quite amazing.

A Lockheed Electra 10A similar to the one flown by Earhart on her ill-fated circumnavigation flight. This Electra is on show in the Museum of Transport & Technology, Auckland, New Zealand, in the colours of Union Airways.

As we saw earlier in this work, she was the first female passenger to cross the North Atlantic followed by her own solo crossing. She set many other aviation records, including seven speed-records for women between 1930 and 1937, she wrote two best-seller books and in 1929, she co-founded the female pilots' group known as *The Ninety-nines*. She became a celebrity mixing with the high society and was awarded several medals including the US Distinguished Flying Cross, the French Legion of Honour, the National Geographic Society's Gold Medal along with claiming several 'firsts' in aviation.

Amelia was an adventuristic girl from an early age and had learned to fly in the 1920s. Long-distance flying over new routes became her passion and she was the first female pilot to fly from Honolulu to Oakland in California. She also flew solo from Los Angeles to Mexico City and then on to New York.

Apart from her bright red Lockheed Vega, which is now displayed in the National Air & Space Museum in Washington, D.C., she also flew a little-known Kinner Airster and also a Pitcairn Autogyro. In 1935, after making successful pioneering flights and entering into air racing, her next ambition was to fly around the world.

Acknowledging her single-engine Lockheed Vega had served its purpose in her earlier flying, she chose a twin-engine Lockheed Electra 10A for her world flight modified with additional fuel tanks installed to increase its range. As a member of Purdue University's Department of Aeronautics, they assisted her with finance for the world trip. The famed Hollywood stunt pilot Paul Mantz (1903-1965) was her technical advisor for the flight and Captain Harry Manning was her first choice of navigator but he was replaced by Fred Noonan for his more accurate navigation calculations.

Earhart departed Oakland, California on 17 March 1937 on the first leg of her journey to Honolulu with plans to fly westbound around the world. She was accompanied on the first leg of her journey by Paul Mantz and her two navigators, Fred Noonan and Harry Manning onboard. Fred Noonan was to fly as far as Australia, while Earhart planned to complete a solo flight home. However, on 20 March 1937 during take-off from Honolulu, the plane ground-looped either from mishandling or a blown tyre causing damage, which required the plane to be shipped back to the Lockheed factory at Burbank, California for repairs.

On the second attempt at the world flight, Harry Manning declined to continue leaving Earhart and Fed Noonan to make the flight together, now re-planned to fly eastbound, departing California on 1 June 1937. Their route took them via South America, Africa, India, Southeast Asia to Lae in New

Guinea, arriving there on 29 June 1937. With just another 7,000 miles (11,300 km) to fly to reach home, they departed Lae on 2 July heading for the remote Howland Island in the Pacific Ocean on what was to be their final flight.

They never arrived at Howland Island and what happened to Earhart and Noonan has remained a mystery ever since. Several theories have been put forward as to their fate, the most common being their unconfirmed capture and execution by the Japanese military. Their disappearance has been well-covered by TV documentaries and by several authors on the subject. However, with no aircraft wreckage found and no admittance of involvement from Japan, the fate of Earhart and Noonan may remain a complete mystery forever. A sad fate for an experienced aviatrix from the pioneering days.

Howard Hughes

A year after the loss of Amelia Earhart on her ill-fated circumnavigation flight, the American, Howard Robard Hughes (1905-1976) made a speed-record flight around the world.

Hughes was a very successful business tycoon involved in several ventures including his time as a record-setting pilot, the founder of Hughes Aircraft, owner of Hughes Airlines, film director and producer, etc. However, in his later years he suffered from eccentricities and deteriorating mental health with compulsive disorders and phobias and he spent the remainder of his life as a recluse.

In his younger days, Howard Hughes circled the world in 1938 in a Lockheed Super Electra, the larger version of the Electra used by Earhart. The time taken was three days 19 hour and 14 minutes, nearly four days faster than Wiley Post's solo flight in 1933. Hughes and his four crewmen departed from Floyd Bennett Airfield in New York and circled the world via Paris, Moscow, Yakutsk in Siberia, Fairbanks, Alaska then Minneapolis, Minnesota and returned to New York on 15 July 1938.

The Electra was grossly overloaded on take-off from New York with a take-off weight of 25,600 pounds (11,611 kg) making it 10,000 lbs overweight; the plane only just managed to get airborne on the available runway after an extended take-off run. Crossing the North Atlantic saw the fuel consumption higher than expected due to the extra weight, and they only just managed to reach their first destination of Paris. Later in the flight, Hughes elected to postpone his night take-off from Yakutsk until daylight, which turned out to be a wise decision considering their maps showed the highest mountains peaks on their route were at 6,500 feet (20,000 m) when they were actually at 9,700 feet (29,500 m).

The advent of World War Two curtailed any further attempts at world-circling flights until the war was over.

First Post-World War II Circumnavigation

Not long after World War II had ended, two US Air Force Reserve Officers who were both flight instructors, were giving flying lessons to new GI recruits when they conceived the idea to fly around the world together. They were USAF officers Major George W. Truman and Major Clifford V. Evans and their aircraft of choice were two Piper PA-12 Super Cruisers, single-engine light aircraft with a conventional (tail-wheel) undercarriage. They were not designed for long-distance flying; therefore, an additional 50-gallon (227 Litre) fuel tank was installed in place of the two rear seats. Fuel was transferred to the main tanks via a pilot operated hand pump. The extra fuel boosted the planes range to about 2,600 miles (4,184 km) and an endurance of 27 hours. An extra oil tank was also placed in the cabin to feed the engine sump. Extra radio navigation equipment was also installed.

Truman and Evans had both lived on opposite sides of the USA, George Truman had lived in Los Angeles and Clifford Evans lived in Washington, D.C. From their home towns, they named their planes The City of the Angels and the City of Washington, respectively.

Departing on 9 August 1947 at Teterboro, New Jersey, USA. They flew eastbound across the North Atlantic via Greenland and Iceland to London in England. From there, they continued across Europe and the Middle East and Asia to Japan, Alaska, Canada and back across the USA to their starting point at Teterboro, New Jersey, arriving there on 10 December 1947. Making fifty-five stops in at least 19 different countries.

Major Clifford Evans was the pilot to make the first landing at Teterboro in his Super Cruiser the *City of Washington* to claim the record for the first 'modern' light aircraft to circle the world. Each pilot flew his own plane solo but they stayed together throughout their circumnavigation flight. Their flight covered 25,162 miles (40,494 km) and lasted just over four months, due to increment weather keeping both planes grounded at some stops en route.

They received a big welcome on their arrival in Washington, D.C., from the crowds and also President Harry Truman.

This Piper Cruiser (the City of Washington) was the first modern light aircraft to circle the world, after the war. It was flown by Clifford Evans, and has been on display since 2006 suspended from the ceiling of the Udvar-Hazy Center.

First Non-stop World Flight

Nearly two years after the pair of Piper Cruisers had circled the world, the USAF decided to make a non-stop circumnavigation flight.

The first aircraft to do so was a Boeing B-50A Superfortress named *Lucky Lady*. It commenced the flight departing from Carswell Air Force Base in Texas on 26 February 1949 and arrived back there five days later on 2 March 1949. Keeping the *Lucky Lady* airborne for such a long period was made possible by its air-refuelling capability, having received four in-flight refuels from Boeing KB-29 Superfortress tankers from the 43rd Refuelling Squadron while over-flying The Azores Islands, Saudi Arabia, The Philippines and Hawaii. The *Lucky Lady* covered a total route distance of 23,452 miles (37,743 km) flying at an average ground speed of 249 mph (400 km/h) for a total flight time of 94 hours and one minute. The *Lucky Lady* was flown by USAF Captain James G. Gallagher with a crew of fourteen working in shifts.

The Boeing B-50 Superfortress flown around the world was similar to this Boeing KB-50 parked in the grounds of the Pima Air & Space Museum in Tucson, Ar.

The Boeing B-50 was a post-World War II strategic bomber version of the more famous B-29 Superfortress; they had a taller tail fin and more powerful Pratt & Whitney R-4360 engines and other refinements. The B-50s were the last of the piston-engine bombers built by Boeing for the USAF, with the last B-50 retired in 1965 after spending their remaining years as air-refuelling tankers. From the total of 370 built, only five examples remain in existence as museum exhibits. The *Lucky Lady* was not so lucky at the end of its service life, as only its forward section remains and can now be seen in the Planes of Fame Museum at Chino in California. The accompanying photo shows one of the four remaining and complete Boeing B-50s; this one is displayed in the Pima Air & Space Museum in Tucson, Arizona.

Max Conrad

Max Conrad (1903-1979) was born in Winona in Minnesota and graduated from the Cotter High School in 1921. Entering a career in aviation in the 1920s, he became a fixed-base flight school operator with his Conrad Flying Services in Minnesota. He was noted for making nine record flights in light aircraft and for 25 crossings of the North Atlantic.

In 1961 he circumnavigated the world in his Piper Aztec which he named *New Frontiers*. He departed Miami, Florida on 27 February 1961 flying westbound via Honolulu, Manila, Singapore, Africa, South America and Trinidad including other stops along the way. He landed back at Miami on 8 March 1961. This was his speed- record flight averaging 123.20 mph (198.27 km/h) with his passenger Richard Jennings as official observer.

In 1952, Conrad received the Louis Bleriot medal and the Harmon Trophy in 1964. His home town airport of Winona Municipal Airport was named in his honour as Max Conrad Field.

Geraldine Mock

Geraldine Mock (1925-2004) or 'Jerrie' for short, was just your average, married woman with three children, living in Columbus, Ohio. But she had a passion – two in fact; one was her passion for flying, which she started as a young girl after a flight in a Ford Trimotor with her father. Her other passion was to fly her own plane around the world solo. She was not after any fame or glory, nor was she out to break any aviation records. However, she did fulfil both her passions and flew around the world solo, leaving Port Columbus in Ohio on 19 March 1964 and returning there on 17 April 1964.

Her husband and his friend, Al Baumeister, bought her a used Cessna 180, a single-engine light aircraft, which she named the *Spirit of Columbus;* her flight was sponsored by the local *Columbus Dispatch* newspaper and other backers. An extra fuel tank holding 183 US Gallons (695 litres) was installed in the Cessna's cabin giving a total endurance flight time of 25 hours. For navigation she used twin ADF's (Automatic Direction Finders), good for long range

The Cessna 180 that circumnavigated the world with Geraldine Mock at the controls in 1964. It is exhibited in the Udvar-Hazy Center suspended from the museum's ceiling.

reception but virtually obsolete in today's modern aircraft. Also onboard were dual VOR's for short range VHF navigation and dual radio communication receivers. An autopilot helped with keeping the plane on course.

Geraldine Mock became the first woman to fly solo around the world, completing the flight in 29½ days and covering a distance of 22,860 miles (36,790 km). Although she made the world flight just to satisfy her own desire, she was awarded a record for the fastest flight around the world for the Cessna 180s class for aircraft under 3,858 lbs (1,750 kg). In 1965 she received the FAI gold medal, which was just one of 21 awards and 15 records made during the flight.

After the world flight, her Cessna 180 was temporarily displayed at the Cessna plant in Wichita, Kansas, before being placed on permanent display suspended from the ceiling in the Udvar-Hazy Center. The Cessna Company gave Geraldine Mock a replacement aircraft in exchange for her Cessna 180.

Joan Merriam Smith

Joan Merriam Smith (1936-1965) was a young American aviatrix. She became interested in aviation at an early age and qualified for her private pilot licence at age 17 and went through the ratings to obtain her airline transport pilot licence at the age of 23. Her other aviation achievements include the following:

- The youngest woman to enter the All-Woman's International Air Race
- youngest person to fly around the world (in 1964)
- first woman to fly solo around the world following the equator
- first woman to follow the Earhart Trail
- first woman to fly a twin-engine aircraft around the world
- first woman to fly across the Pacific

She had planned to be the first woman to fly around the world solo; however, Geraldine Mock (mentioned above) departed a few days before her and also returned home first, to claim the title. For her efforts, Joan Smith received the Harmon Trophy posthumously for the *Outstanding Aviatrix of 1964*.

After logging over 8,500 hours of flight time, she was involved in two flying accidents, the second one was fatal. On 17 February 1965, she crashed in the San Gabriel Mountains near Long Beach, California. A sad end for an aspiring pilot.

The Rockwell Polar Flight

During 14-17 November 1965, the first flight was made that circled the world, not an east or westbound flight, but one overflying both the North and South Poles.

The aircraft chosen for the flight by Captain Fred Austin and Captain Harrison Finch was a Boeing 707-349 named appropriately as the *Pole Cat*. It was operated by the Flying Tigers Line, the first scheduled and charter cargo airline in the USA, which flew cargo and passengers for the US military starting in the Cold War years. Their first start-up aircraft were Budd Conestoga piston-engine planes acquired from the US Navy. The Flying Tigers flew a variety of transport aircraft ending with the Boeing 747 in 1988 when the company was bought out by Federal Express, which pioneered the overnight parcel delivery system.

The Boeing's cabin could be configured with either, or both, passenger and cargo compartments, known as a Combi version. The *Pole Cat* had seats for twenty-seven lucky passengers on the flight, including Rockwell Corporation's founder, Willard F. Rockwell who financed the flight. In the cargo section were additional fuel cells to increase the aircraft's range.

Departing Honolulu on 14 November 1965, they flew north to circle the North Pole before continuing over the pole heading south to London for their first refuel stop. The long flight to Buenos Aires in Argentina called for another fuel stop at Lisbon, due to London Heathrow's runway length restricting a maximum-weight take-off. Flying south from Buenos Aires, they circled the South Pole before heading north again to Christchurch, New Zealand for a final refuel before continuing to Honolulu to complete the first circumnavigation via both poles. The entire trip around the world was undertaken in 62 hours, 27 minutes with 57 hours and 27 minutes of flying time and the remaining five hours taken up with refuelling at their stopping points. The flight covered a total distance of 26,230 miles (42,213 km).

A continuous flight of that length required the assistance of other crew members, which included Captains Jack Martin, Robert Buck and James Gannett with three flight engineers and two navigators.

The Polar Flight was the first flight to circumnavigate the world via the Poles and was also the first flight to cross the South Pole (and Antarctica) from one side to the other without landing in the Antarctic, that is, from South America to New Zealand. The reader may recall the North Pole was first over-flown by Amundsen in the airship *Norge* in 1926.

Sheila Scott

The English aviatrix, Sheila Christine Hopkins (1922-1988) was an actress prior to becoming a pilot. She started acting in 1943 taking the stage name of Sheila Scott which she continued to use after ending her acting career. She had a brief marriage from 1945 to 1950. However, it was her aviation exploits for which she became famous.

She learned to fly in 1958 at Thruxton Airfield and she bought her first aircraft in 1959, a 1930s vintage Tiger Moth converted to a Thruxton Jackaroo. The Jackaroo had a widened fuselage to take four seats and an enclosed cockpit canopy. Eventually, flying long-distance and breaking records became her passion. Trading in her Jackaroo, she upgraded to a Piper PA-24 Comanche 260B in 1966, a single-engine, four seat aircraft with retractable undercarriage, which she named *Myth Too*. She made her first solo world flight in this aircraft departing London on 18 May 1966 and after flying 31,000 miles (50,00 km) she returned to London on 20 June 1966 having logged another 189 flying hours. Flying her *Myth Too,* she completed her second world flight in 1969-1970. Sheila Scott sold this plane the following year and in 1979 it received accident damage and its remains are held by the National Museum of Flight near Edinburgh in Scotland.

Her third solo circumnavigation was flown in 1971 in a Piper Aztec 250, a twin-engine, six seat aircraft. During this world flight, she covered 34,000 miles (55,000 km) which included crossing the North Pole, the first time for a

A Piper PA-24 Comanche similar to the Comanche flown by Sheila Scott. This privately owned example is actively flying in the UK.

176

modern light aircraft. Sheila Scott claimed over 100 aviation records, which in itself must be a record number for any one person. She received the Harmon Trophy in 1967 and in 1968 she received the OBE and the Britannia Trophy from the Royal Aero Club. The Brabazon of Tara Award was presented to her in 1965 and again in 1967 and 1968, followed by the Gold Medal in 1971 from the Royal Aero Club. This is an outstanding achievement for a female pioneering pilot.

Cliff Tait

New Zealander, Cliff Tait (1929-20??) held a private pilot's licence and an instrument rating and with 240 hours in his log book, he set-off from New Zealand on a world circumnavigation flight.

His aircraft was a Victa Airtourer, built in Hamilton, New Zealand. Power was supplied by a single Lycoming O-235 engine developing 115 horsepower to a fixed pitch propeller giving the plane a 105 mph (169 km/h) normal cruise speed. The Airtourer had two seats side-by-side with a unique short control stick mounted between the seats on the centre console for either pilot to use. Built as a training aircraft, it was a very easy and pleasant aircraft to fly; as this author found spending many hours flying Victa Airtourers. As a world circling plane, it was certainly on the small side having a wingspan of 26 feet (7.93 m) and an all-up weight of 1,993 lb (904 kg). The single, fuel tank beneath the seats held 29 imperial gallons (132 litres) of fuel, good for nearly five hours endurance but insufficient for the world flight. The quantity was boosted up to 75 imperial gallons (340 litres) increasing the endurance to about 14-15 hours of flight time. Cliff Tait took his wife's initials of JC to name his plane as *Miss Jacy*.

Cliff Tait departed Hamilton, New Zealand on 12 May 1969 and island-hopped through the South Pacific islands to Japan stopping at New Caledonia, Guam Island and Iwo Jima, to name just a few places. Unable to gain permission to land and refuel in eastern Russia, he shipped his Victa over to Vancouver in Canada to continue his world flight. Cliff flew across Canada in stages and then across the North Atlantic via Greenland and Iceland to England. His flight continued with many stops across Europe, India, Singapore and Australia. The last leg of his journey was across the Tasman Sea via Norfolk Island and home to Hamilton, New Zealand arriving on 1 September 1969. He flew for 284 hours to cover a total distance of about 30,000 miles (48,000 km) over 81 days; it was a very long flight for a small training aircraft and a great accomplishment for Cliff Tait.

The world circling Victa Airtourer from New Zealand. This must be the smallest aircraft to have circled the world. It is on display in the Museum of Transport & Technology, in Auckland, New Zealand.

Cliff went on to gain his Commercial Pilot Licence and a career as a ferry pilot delivering Victa and Fletcher aircraft from New Zealand to buyers in other countries and also collecting aircraft for import to New Zealand and of course, he broke several flight records in the process.

First Helicopter World Flight

On 6 August 1982, the Australian adventurer, helicopter pilot Dick Smith had departed from Dallas, Texas on his solo helicopter world flight. Not wanting to be outdone, two Americans, H. Ross Perot Jr (1958- ?) and his companion Jay Coburn bought a Bell 206L LongRanger II and set off three-weeks after Dick Smith from their home-town of Dallas, Texas on 1 September 1982 on their world circumnavigation flight.

They gained the FAI recognised record for the fastest helicopter speed around the world and for various place-to-place record times for helicopters.

Ross Perot donated his world-circling LongRanger to the National Air & Space Museum on 15 November 1982; it is now displayed in their Udvar-Hazy Center, in Chantilly, Va. Dick Smith was not upset for not achieving the first helicopter flight around the world, he was there to enjoy the experience, not to make records. In fact, he didn't complete his circumnavigation until the following year, arriving back in Dallas in July 1983. However, his flight was the first helicopter solo flight.

Jennifer Murray

The world's last circumnavigation flight for the 20th century must be the one flown by Jennifer Murray departing England on 8 August 1997 accompanied by helicopter instructor Quentin Smith. Flying her UK registered Robinson R-44, they flew around the world east-bound visiting twenty-eight countries during their flight, to also become the first pilots from England circle the world in a helicopter.

She commenced her flying later in life, aged 53 years and had accumulated some 600 flying hours when departing on her first world flight. The Robinson was the first helicopter to fly around the world powered by a piston engine; Dick Smith and Ross Perot flew turbine-powered Bell helicopters. Jennifer Smith repeated her flight in the year 2000, to become the first woman helicopter pilot to circle the world on her own.

Her helicopter is now displayed in the Udvar-Hazy Center, Washington close to Ross Perot's world circling, Bell Longer Ranger, pictured below.

The Spirit of Texas, the first helicopter to fly around the world, now resides in the Udvar-Hazy Center.

*The first piston-engined helicopter to circle the world was this
Robinson R-44 flown by Jennifer Murray in 1997.*

World-circling Grumman Albatross

The Grumman Albatross was an amphibian search and rescue aircraft
operated mainly by the USAF, particularly in the Korean War. It was also
flown by the US Navy and US Coast Guard from the 1940s; the Hellenic
Navy retired the last military operated Albatross in 1995. It was also used in
the civilian role as an airliner flying between the Pacific Islands. Typical of
Grumman-built aircraft, they were favoured for their ruggedness especially
during water handling.

The Albatross of interest here (N44RD) was one of the 466 built by
Grumman and it made its first flight in October 1947; it was acquired by
pilots Dennis Reid and Andy Macfie, both from the San Francisco area. They
flew the Albatross around the world in 1997 to act as a filming platform
and support plane for a film crew who were making a documentary on
Amelia Earhart's interesting and famous, but fatal attempt to make a world
circumnavigation flight. The Albatross was also available to act as a rescue

plane in the event of the plane flown by Linda Finch, representing Earhart's aircraft, having to ditch in the sea; thankfully, that eventuality didn't arise and both planes circled the world safely.

It became the first, and possibly the only Albatross to circle the world, recording a flying time of 190 hours and covering a distance of 30,338 miles (48,822 km). Dennis Reid and Macfie made thirty-eight stops in 21 countries during the two and half month trip.

The plane was donated to the Hiller Aviation Museum, near San Francisco by Dennis Reid in 2013 where it is now displayed.

Linda Finch

Linda Finch (1951- ?) was an American businesswoman and pilot. She conceived the idea to fly around the world following the Earhart Trail, the route taken be Amelia Earhart sixty years earlier. She chose the same type of plane as used by Earhart, a Lockheed Electra 10E model, which she rebuilt after finding parts of a dilapidated fuselage. Pratt & Whitney was a major sponsor of the rebuild cost and the world flight.

The world-circling Albatross now at rest in the Hiller Aviation Museum at San Carlos, California.

The Electra flown around the world by Linda Finch in 1997 accompanied by the Grumman Albatross. It is now a Museum of Flight exhibit.

Linda Finch's flight was filmed by the crew onboard the Grumman Albatross (mentioned above) which accompanied her during her flight as her safety plane and camera platform for the film crew making the documentary.

The Lockheed Electra used by Linda Finch is now displayed in the Museum of Flight in Seattle, USA.

Dick Rutan & Jeana Yeager

The reader may recall the first aircraft to fly around the world non-stop was a Boeing B-50A Superfortress in 1949. It flew non-stop, but received aerial refuelling four times during its journey. The first aircraft to fly around the world non-stop, but without refuelling, was the purpose-built Rutan Model 76 Voyager. It completed the circumnavigation flight in nine days and three minutes after departing from Edwards AFB in California on 14 December 1986 and returning there on 23 December 1986. It was flown by Richard (Dick) Glen Rutan (1938-?) who was a USAF fighter pilot, a test pilot and the Voyager's main pilot accompanied by pilot Jeana Yeager.

Dick Rutan's aviation interests began at an early age and he entered the USAF in the late 1950s where he had a long and distinguished career including his time in Vietnam. His list of trophies, medals and ribbons, etc, is extensive, too many to mention all in this work. But let it be said, he was well qualified to pilot the Voyager around the world.

Dick Rutan's co-pilot on the Voyager flight, was Jeana Lee Yeager (1952-?) who was not new to making record flights. After she met Dick Rutan, they both claimed new records in the 1980s, flying Rutan VariEze and Rutan Long-EZ planes designed by Dick's brother, Burt Rutan. Jeana Yeager set two, women's speed records, the first in 1982 and the second in 1984. She was the first woman to claim an absolute category record and received six medals in total for her record flights.

The route taken by pilots, Dick and Jeana was westbound from California covering the non-stop distance of 26,366 miles (42,432 km) and gaining a flight endurance record, while cruising at 11,000 feet (3,350 m).

Dick and his brother Burt Rutan created the idea for the world non-stop flight as early as 1981, but it took the next five years for volunteers to build the Voyager, no doubt due to other commitments, in the Rutan Aircraft Factory at the Mojave Airport in California. Typical of Burt Rutan's designs, the Voyager was of a totally unconventional design with a high aspect ratio wing spanning 110 feet (33.5 m). The fuselage pod was attached at the rear to the main wing and by the canard wing at the front which themselves were attached to the two outboard booms, which each carried a vertical fin. George Cayley would have been astonished; the Voyager was nothing like he envisioned a plane should look like back in the early 1800s! Burt Rutan's designs always go beyond the normal.

Power was supplied by two engines in the push/pull configuration; it had one Teledyne Continental O-240 tractor engine of 130 horsepower, plus one Teledyne Continental IOL-200 pusher of 110 horsepower. Both engines were used for take-off and the first part of their trip until the weight had reduced sufficiently for the flight to be continued on the one rear engine, thus saving fuel; high speed was not a priority. Built of composite structure, the airframe had a relatively light empty weight of 2,250 lb (1020 kg). The maximum take-off weight was set at 9,694 lb (4,397 kg) due to the large fuel load required for a world-circling flight and a required endurance of over 216 hours. The official cruise speed was 116 mph (187 km/h).

The Voyager's maiden flight was made on 22 June 1984. During a test flight in July 1986 off the California coast line, they broke the un-refuelled endurance record of 84 hours 32 minutes set in 1931 by Walter Lees and Frederic Bossy flying a Bellanca CH-300; they claimed a new record of 111 hours 44 minutes.

*The world-circling Voyager is preserved in the National Air
and Space Museum in Washington, D.C.*

After an aborted attempt on the world flight due to a propeller-pitch motor failure, the flight was terminated at the Vandenburg AFB. A second emergency landing was required on 29 September 1986 after one of the props threw a blade.

The Voyager was built solely to make the non-stop world flight and was then retired in 1987 and placed on display in the National Air & Space Museum in Washington, D.C.

The Voyager flight could be considered as one of the last pioneering flights to be made, a major historic aviation achievement due to the efforts and expertise of Burt and Dick Rutan and Jeana Yeager, helped by many other people in the background. With the progress in modern technology, aircraft building materials and a bit of ingenuity thrown in, it proved that the ultimate long-distance flight could be made. Dick Rutan and Jeana Yeager claimed eight world records and both received their well-earned Collier Trophy.

13 – Pioneer 'Aces' of World War One

Pioneers of Aerial Warfare

The Italian military were the first to use airplanes for bombing and reconnaissance flights during the Italian-Turkish War from September 1911 to October 1912. Their dispute was over ownership of the North African country of Libya. The Italian pilot Lieutenant Giulio Gavotti (1882-1939) dropped four small, one-pound bombs from his Etrich Taube (Dove) on a Turkish Military camp at the Ain Zara oasis in Libya on 1 November 1911; these were the first bombs in history to be dropped from a plane, although they did not cause any harm to the Turkish forces. Gavotti also flew the first military flight to be made at night time.

The Etrich Taube was designed by the Austrian, Ignaz (Igo) Etrich, based on the gliders built by Otto Lilienthal. It first flew in 1910 and was built by many different aircraft builders in Germany after the German Patents office invalidated Etrich's patent. The Taube in the attached photograph is a replica of the Rumpler-built Taube, built by Art Williams in 1984. The installed engine is an original, a rare Mercedes D.IIIa six-cylinder, water-cooled, in-line engine developing 120 horsepower giving the Taube a maximum speed of 60 mph (100 km/h). Lateral roll control is by wing warping.

During the First World War, which started on 4 August 1914, observation aircraft were used to support the ground-based military fighting in the trenches. They were flown to report on enemy progress and positions. The first observation planes were initially flown with an observer using hand-held guns for self-protection; it is recorded a rifle was first fired from an airplane on 20 August 1910. Later, machine guns were mounted on top of the wing, firing over the propeller arc become the world's first fighter planes.

Firing through the propeller arc between the rotating prop blades proved more accurate when French pilot Roland Garros and his mechanic, Jules

This example is a reproduction of the Rumpler Taube, similar to the Etrich Taube used as the world's first bomber. The single-surface wing was typical of airplane wings of that era, along with the clear, see-through doped fabric covering; painted wings and fuselages came shortly after during WWI. Lateral control is by wing warping. Now placed on display in the Museum of Flight in Seattle, Washington.

Hue, in association with aircraft designer Raymond Saulnier, devised the method of attaching deflector plates to deflect any bullets that hit the blades on his Morane-Saulnier Type L. Roland Garros became the first pilot to shoot down an enemy aircraft, on 1 April 1915, using his deflector plate system on his Morane Saulnier. He thus, became the world's first fighter pilot flying with the Escadrille 23 squadron of the Aeronautique Militaire. He was later shot down himself, leading the Dutchman, Anthony Fokker (1890-1939) to improve on the deflector system and invent the propeller synchroniser, which allowed the machine gun to fire between the propeller blades allowing greater accuracy. The German Air Services' Fokker Eindecker was the first aircraft to use a relatively reliable prop synchroniser.

Roland Garros claimed two more victories on the 15 and 18 April. However, he was himself shot down by German ground fire and captured. After eventually escaping the prison of war camp, he returned to France to re-join his squadron but was shot down once again and killed on 5 October 1918 shortly before the war ended. He has been incorrectly dubbed as the world's first fighter pilot ace but he only claimed four kills and not the five required to claim ace status.

However, the world's first one-on-one dogfight resulting in a victory, was made on 5 October 1914 when French pilot Sergeant Joseph Frantz flying a Voisin III engaged with a German pilot flying an Aviatik B.114. When Joseph Frantz's plane ran out of machine gun ammunition, his observer Captain Louis Quenalt used a rifle to kill their German opponent.

A pilot downing five enemy aircraft was dubbed an 'ace', a term introduced by French newspaper reporters. The first pilot ever to be described as an ace, was Adolphe Pegoud (1889-1915). He was a Second Lieutenant in the French Army and later, after learning to fly, he flew as a test pilot for Louis Bleriot flying the Bleriot XI monoplane. He is noted for making the first experimental parachute jump from a plane, which was sacrificed and left to crash. He was initially credited with making the first loop in a plane until it was discovered that Russian Army pilot, Peter Nesterov earned the distinction for the first loop on 9 September 1913. Adolphe Pegoud was later shot down and killed in August 1915, by one of his previous students from Germany.

The term ace is usually associated with fighter pilots, but bomber pilots, reconnaissance crews and observers also earned the ace title. Some pilot aces went on to score a high number of 'kills' or victories and became household names. Less fortunate pilots lost their lives on their first mission or soon afterwards due to inexperience, or plain bad luck. Usually, the most experienced pilot out-manoeuvred his opponent or the best-performing plane decided the winner; air superiority was in its infancy! The highest scoring 'ace of aces', was the German pilot known as the Red Baron – Manfred von Richthofen (1892-1918).

Flight training for pilots of the First World War was conducted in England, USA, Canada, New Zealand and Egypt, etc. In England, the initial military pilot training required a pilot to have an FAI licence obtained from a Flying School at his own expense and reimbursed on acceptance into the Royal Flying Corps. In the early part of the war the training was very basic and minimal, which led to excess losses in training accidents and in combat. By the end of the war, the training had improved greatly with pilots having around eighty-hours of flying time on graduation. In the USA, civilian flying schools located at various places were used by the military for initial pilot training. It is recorded 8,689 pilot cadets graduated from flight schools in the USA. In Europe, 1,674 trained as pilots and 851 as observers.

A fighter pilot's life expectancy was measured in weeks and he remained on duty until he was either killed in action, injured or relieved from duty due to a nervous breakdown, or battle fatigue as it was also known. It was not until 1942 that pilots did a 'tour of duty' before being relieved, the number of missions flown depended on the type of missions performed, bomber or fighter pilot, etc.

The few remaining aircraft used in the pilot training role and for combat in WWI are now mostly non-flying museum exhibits, some of which are pictured below. Some of these aircraft are originals and are priceless in value dating back over 100 years now, whereas others are quite often replicas built in more recent years. Originals or replicas, it is amazing how these pioneer pilots learned the art of combat flying in such fragile and relatively unstable aircraft.

The top scoring pioneer ace pilots from Germany, as well as Great Britain and its Commonwealth countries and allies, are presented below.

Manfred von Richthofen

The German fighter pilot ace, Manfred von Richthofen (1892-1918) known as the Red Baron, became the highest scoring ace in World War One with a total of eighty victories to his credit.

Richthofen came from a Prussian noble family, hence his title of Baron. He first served in the German cavalry as an officer before transferring to the

A diorama of British soldiers taking souvenirs from the Red Baron and his crashed Fokker DR.1 aircraft. Displayed in The Omaka Aviation Heritage Centre in Blenheim, New Zealand.

German Air Service and claimed his first air victory in 1916. He eventually became a Captain of his squadron, the Jagdgeschwader 1, who became known as the Flying Circus due to their frequent repositioning as the war progressed. Their Fokker DR.1 planes were easily identified by their bright-red colour scheme, which gave Von Richthofen his name of the Red Baron. He almost survived the war, but was shot down on 9 April 1918 over the River Somme area by a Canadian pilot, Captain Roy Brown, believed to have been flying a Sopwith Camel. British soldiers ransacked Richthofen and his crashed aircraft for souvenirs and clothing. An original piece of fuselage fabric from Richthofen's DR.1 plane, is now displayed close to the diorama (pictured here) of Richthofen's crash, in The Omaka Aviation Heritage Centre in Blenheim, New Zealand.

The British forces honoured him with a full military funeral as a 'Galant and Worthy Foe', which they inscribed on his coffin. He was initially buried near Amiens in France before transfer to a military cemetery at Fricourt. In 1925, his body was taken back to Germany by his brother for re-burial and was again moved in 1975 to his final resting place at Wiesbaden, Germany.

Rene Foncke

The French pilot, Colonel Rene Paul Foncke (1894-1953) was the top French fighter ace of WWI and also the top allied ace. Rene Foncke left school at the age of thirteen years and is believed to have completed a course in engineering as part of his education, although no records have surfaced to prove he attended the engineering school. His interest in aviation developed at an early age but initially, he was unable to join the air service and instead he was posted to the French Army as an engineer in 1914 experiencing trench warfare. In May 1915, he transferred to the French Air Service and learned to fly and became a pilot flying the Caudron G.3 observation planes. He was later posted to the elite Escadrille les Cigognes and became an excellent fighter pilot using his calculating and careful planning when picking targets to attack.

He claimed his first kill in July 1916 but this was not confirmed and in May 1917, he was flying a SPAD VII when he claimed his fifth victory and reached ace status. He ended the war with a total of seventy-five confirmed victories out of the 142 he had claimed. The 75 kills placed him in second ranking of the top aces after eclipsing the 53 kills claimed by Guynmeyer, France's leading ace who was killed in action in September 1917.

Foncke was a very calculating pilot improving his fighting technique and his number of kills. He was noted for his caution, avoiding dog fights but picking his targets of opportunity before going in for the kill. On one day, he claimed six aircraft downed, although Foncke himself was never shot down or injured in combat and only one bullet ever struck his plane. For all his skills as a fighter pilot and the highest scoring French ace, on the ground he was reticent and preferred his own company instead of enjoying the company of his fellow pilots and did not socialise with them very often; when he did, he tended to brag about his exploits. He never received the fame through the French newspapers that were afforded to France's leading ace, Captain Guynmeyer before he was killed in action.

Note, the SPAD aircraft were built by Armand Deperdussin's (1860-1924) company, Societe de Production des Aeroplanes Deperdussin (SPAD).

After the war, Rene Foncke entered the French Parliament and served from 1919 to 1924. He also spent time as a race and demonstration pilot. In 1926, Rene Foncke attempted to make one of the first trans-Atlantic crossings by plane with three other crew members but crashed on take-off from Long Island, New York with the loss of two of his crew. [See section 5 – Trans-Atlantic Pioneers].

A SPAD VII similar to this exhibit, was used by Rene Foncke to claim many of his victories. This one is a museum exhibit in the NMUSAF at Dayton, Ohio.

Rene Foncke received several medals for his wartime efforts, which included the Legion d'Honneur, Medaille Militaire, the British Military Cross and the Distinguished Conduct Medal plus twenty-eight Army citations; he was one of France's most decorated officers from WWI.

William (Billy) Bishop

William Avery Bishop VC, DSO and MC (1884-1956) was Canada's top ace from the First World War. He was born in Ontario, Canada and during his school days he was not very academic and gave up quickly on subjects he found too demanding to study. Although he excelled at the sport of shooting with which he benefitted from during his military career.

Billy Bishop, as he was known, went to the Royal Military College of Canada and was sent to the French frontline in 1915. Taking a dislike to the trench conditions he transferred to the Royal Flying Corps gaining his wings in November 1916. He was posted to the No 37 Squadron RFC flying BE.2c aircraft in England until his posting to France in March 1917 where he flew the Nieuport 17 fighter. Bishop gained his first air victory on his first combat mission. Within a few days he claimed four more kills to become an ace pilot, often flying on solo missions looking for targets of opportunity. His tally of kills gradually increased surpassing that of England's top ace, Albert Ball, claiming a total of seventy-two kills, more than any other pilot from the British Commonwealth. Although, historians have since questioned the validity of his total due to some of his claims lacking confirmation from reliable witnesses. His prowess in the air earned him the name of the 'Hell's Maiden' from the German pilots; he was a force to be reckoned with. He finished the war as the third top ace after Baron von Richthofen and Rene Foncke.

Between the wars, Bishop returned to civilian life with various occupations including British Air Lines chairman, and vice-president of an oil company, etc, before re-joining the Canadian Air Force and reaching the rank of Air Marshall in 1939. He was responsible for developing the British Commonwealth Air Training Plan, to provide pilots for the Second World War and later helped to establish the world-wide International Civil Aviation Organisation (ICAO) based in Montreal, Canada. Billy Bishop deserved the many medals he earned which included the VC, DSO & Bar, DFC, VC, and the MC.

A very nice example of a flying reproduction of a RAF BE.2c displayed at an air show at Masterton, New Zealand. The type was flown by Billy Bishop.

The RAF BE.2c flew with a crew of two, pilot and observer. The aircraft had a relatively large wingspan of 37 feet (11.29 m), and was armed with a .303 Lewis machine gun for the observer which were added in October 1914 to the 2c model. When flown solo, it could carry 230 lb of bombs. The RAF 1a, 90 horsepower, V-8 air cooled engine gave it a speed of 75 mph (121 km/h).

Edward Mannock

The Irishman, Edward Mannock (1887-1918) was born to Irish parents and was working in Turkey when the First World War erupted; he was interned in prison there but released due to ill health and returned to England in April 1915.

Wanting to join the military, he qualified as a Royal Flying Corps pilot in March 1917 after training on the Henry Farman and Airco DH.2 trainer aircraft. After flying training, he was sent to France to join No 40 Squadron where initially, he was a nervous pilot but eventually settled down to become quite an assertive fighter pilot with his victories starting to increase. However, because of his lower-class background, he didn't jell very well with his fellow pilots who came from a higher-class background. After becoming an ace, he was more readily accepted by the other pilots.

He flew Nieuport 17 fighters in combat before transferring onto the Royal Aircraft Factory S.E.5, which were the first of the Allied aircraft to be equipped with a Vickers machine gun, which fired through the propeller disc using interrupter gear and also a .303 Lewis gun mounted on the top wing firing over the top of the propeller. Over 5,000 S.E.5 and S.E.5a's were built during the war and found favour with many of the ace pilots who flew them.

In his leadership, Edward Mannock taught new pilots the skills of aerial combat and helped them achieve combat victories in flight. He later became the commander of Number 85 Squadron, until the 26 July 1918 when he was killed in action after claiming his last victory. He followed his victim down too low and was hit by ground fire causing him to fatally crash.

The total score for Captain Mannock was sixty-one enemy aircraft downed, an impressive score making him the fifth top ace in World War One. He received the most decorations of any pilot during WW 1 including the Victoria Cross posthumously.

An S.E.5A displayed in the Shuttleworth Collection Museum at Old Warden, UK. This was the type flown by Captain Mannock.

Andrew Beauchamp-Proctor

Andrew Beauchamp Proctor (1894-1921) DSO, VC and bar, DFC was the leading ace from South Africa flying with the RFC/RAF in the First World War.

He initially joined the South African Army serving from 1914 to 1915 before joining the Royal Flying Corps in 1917, where he served until 1921 retiring with the rank of Flight Lieutenant. His RFC training began as an air mechanic until his transfer to the Pilot Training unit at Oxford, England. He soloed after five hours of dual instruction and with ten hours logged, he transferred to RFC No 84 Squadron in July 1917, which was being reformed from a bomber to a fighter squadron flying RAF S.E.5's.

Going into combat, he made his first kill on 3 January 1918 leading to a total of fifty-four including sixteen balloons. His score on balloon kills made him the British Empire's leading balloon-killer. He survived the war but met his demise on 21 June 1921 when he was killed in a flying training accident when practicing for an air show at RAF Hendon, near London.

Robert A. Little

Captain Robert Alexander Little (1895-1918) DSO and bar, DSC and bar, was from Victoria in Australia and became the top Australian ace with forty-seven kills.

The Australian Army's Central Flying School at Point Cook near Melbourne turned down his application for pilot training. However, in 1915, he travelled to England and at his own expence he learned to fly at Hendon and joined the Royal Navy Air Service in January 1916 after graduation.

In June 1916 he was posted to Dunkirk with No 1 Naval Wing and flew Sopwith 11/2 Strutters on bombing raids. He was later sent to the Western Front flying Sopwith Pups. Despite his poor flying skills and surviving several crash-landings, he was classed as an excellent fighter pilot achieving the top score for Australain pilots with a total of forty seven kills. Just like many other fighter pilots of the war, he was shot down and killed, on 27 May 1918, a few monthe before the war's end.

The single-seat Sopwith Pup had a Le Rhone 9C 9-cylinder rotary engine developing 80 horsepower giving it a maximum speed 112 mph (180 km/h). The plane was equipped with a .303 Vickers machine gun.

Baron Willy Coppens

Willy Omer Coppens, Baron de Houthulst (1892-1986) was Belgium's leading flying ace. He survived the war and lived to the age of 94, one of the oldest surviving WW 1 flying aces.

His military career started in 1912 as a Premier Regiment Grandiers conscript. In 1914 he was transferred to the Motor Machine Gun Corps and commenced pilot training with the Compagnie des Aviateurs on 6 September 1915. Coppens arranged for two months leave from the Army and along with thirty-nine other Belgian trainees, they all went to England and paid for their own flying tuition. He qualified for his pilot licence on 9 December 1915 and went to the Farman School at Etamps in France for further training. His next move, on 8 April 1917, took him to join the Sixieme Escadrille as a Sergeant First Class flying RAF BE.2c's, two seat biplanes. Later that month he transferred to the Quatrieme Escadrille to fly Sopwith 11/2 Strutters and went into air battle for the first time.

Moving on again in mid-July, he was sent to the First Pursuit Squadron flying Nieuport 16 and 17 fighters followed by flying the Hanriott HD.1. The next month on 19 August, he was promoted to Adjutant.

A Sopwith Pup similar to the Pups flown over the Western Front by Robert Little.
This Pup is displayed in the Brooklands Museum, Weybridge, England.

A Hanriott HD.1 is one of the types flown by Willy Coppens during his war-time service. This one is displayed in the RAF Hendon Museum, London.

Just as with Andrew Beauchamp Proctor, enemy balloons soon became his target of choice and he was noted for being a champion balloon-killer. On one occasion, he attacked a German observation balloon which became detached from its moorings and rose upwards carrying Coppen's aircraft with it. After his plane slid off the top of the balloon Coppens re-started his engine and flew back to base. His last mission was flown on 14 October 1918. Attacking his last balloon, he was wounded in the leg by a bullet and crash landed his plane and taken to hospital where his leg was amputated.

His fighter pilot career ended with thirty-seven kills and possibly six more unconfirmed victories, all made while flying the Hanriott HD.1 fighter.

In 1960, he was given his knighthood and his full title of Willy Omer Coppens, Baron de Houthulst. He received many medals from Belgium, Portugal, England, France, Italy, Serbia and Poland; a well-deserved tribute to Belgium's top pilot ace and Belgium's champion balloon buster.

Francesco Baracca

Count Francesco Baracca (1888-1918) became an Italian Air Force pilot in the First World War after attending the Military Academy of Modena, in October 1907.

One of his early interests was horse riding and so it was to be expected he would attend the Piemonte Real Cavelleria Regiment as a commissioned cavalryman in 1910. He moved to Reims in France and learnt to fly there gaining his pilot licence on 9 July 1912 after which, he joined the Italian Air Force and flew with the Battaglionne Aviatori in the 5th and 6th Squadron in 1914. By May 1915, he had converted to Nieuport two-seater aircraft and soon after he joined 8A Squadron Nieuport, flying Nieuport 10s. With their low rate of climb and cruise speed being too slow, they were unsuited for the required task and in April 1916, he transferred to flying the single-seat Nieuport II. On 7 April 1916 he made history for the Italian Air Force when he shot down an Austrian Hansa-Brandenburg C.1. This was Baracca's first victory and the first for the Italian Air Force.

His luck continued as his victory record continued to climb, now flying the SPAD VII from March 1917. From October that year, he converted on to the SPAD XIII. He nearly survived to the end of the war but on 19 June 1918 he failed to return to his base after conducting a strafing raid in a SPAD XII.

The SPAD XIII was powered by a Hispano-Sulza V-8 water-cooled engine of 235 horsepower giving it a relatively high top-speed of 139 mph (223 km/h). Armament consisted of two Vickers machine guns. The wingspan of 26 feet 4 inches (8.1 m) was similar to other fighters of that era, as also was its length of 20 feet 4 inches (6.18 m).

A monument now stands at Nervesa della Batoglia, Baracca's his home town, in memory of Italy's pioneer pilot 'ace' with a record of thirty-four kills.

As a point of interest, Baracca painted his family's coat of arms on his aircraft, depicting a prancing horse. After the war, his mother presented the family's coat of arms emblem to Italy's famous race car driver and manufacturer, Enzo Ferrari (18981-1988); the emblem has been mounted on the Ferrari car bonnets ever since.

Alexander Kazakov

Alexander Kazakov (1889-1919) DSO, DFC, Military Cross, French Legion of Honour and Croix De Guerre, was a member of a Russian noble family. He entered the Russian cavalry school and graduated in 1908. In 1913, he

A Sopwith Camel suspended from the ceiling of the RAF Hendon Museum, London. This is one of the types flown by Kazakov during World War One.

commenced flying training at the Gatchina Military Aviation School before his posting to the Imperial Army Air Service, where he became a Lieutenant Colonel. In January 1918, following the Bolshevik Revolution, he transferred to the Royal Air Force where he reached the rank of Major on 1 August 1918.

As a combat pilot, he claimed twenty unofficial aircraft destroyed plus thirty-two German and Austro-Hungarian for a total of fifty-two aircraft downed, including one enemy plane that was intentionally rammed in flight. He was Russia's top pilot ace in the Russian Imperial Air Force during WWI. Note, the Russians only accepted planes destroyed over Russian territory as claimed kills.

During his fighter pilot career, he flew the Nieuport 10, 11, and 17 and then the Sopwith Camel for the RAF. On 1 August 1919, he died in a plane crash while performing at an airshow; some witnesses claimed it was suicide, not an accident.

The single-seat Sopwith Camel, had a 130 horsepower Clerget 9B 9-cylinder rotary engine giving the plane a top speed of 113 mph (182 km/h). Most WWI fighters were relatively small; the Camel was no exception having a wingspan of 28 feet (8.5 m) and a length of 18 feet 9 inches. (5.7 m). With its two .303 Vickers machine guns, the Camels were a very successful fighting machine, downing more enemy aircraft than any other type during the war. Powered by a rotary engine (the cylinders rotate around the crankshaft) engine torque assisted in making sharp right turns enabling it to out-turn its opponents.

Eddie Rickenbacker

Edward Vernon Rickenbacker (1890-1973) was born to Swiss immigrant parents in Columbus, Ohio, and as a young boy, he was a 'bit of a rascal' and prone to accidents. His early working life included engineering which led him into motor racing and entering the first Indianapolis 500 car race as a top race driver. He also claimed several racing records and was at one time the chauffeur for Major Dodd and other high-ranking US Army Air Service officers when he was based in France during the First World War. His frequent contacts with the officers enabled him to be selected as the chief mechanic in the flight school at Issoudon in France where he also qualified as a fighter pilot.

A SPAD XIII similar to the type flown by Eddie Rickenbacker in WWI. Displayed in the NMUSAF in Dayton, Ohio.

At the age of 27-years he was too old to fly as a combat pilot but managed to talk his way in and became a very competent pilot, albeit over-enthusiastic in combat. However, he managed to survive the war with twenty-six victories to his credit and received the Medal of Honour, the Distinguished Service Cross and the French Croix de Guerre.

He claimed two victories after attacking a flight of seven German aircraft on his own. Another 18-victories were claimed during the last forty-eight days of the war. No doubt he would have claimed more if the war had not come to an end. He ended the war as the USA's top scoring ace.

In 1919, he was discharged from the US Army Air Service with the rank of Captain. He was involved with several businesses and performed consultancy work for the US Government before taking on the role in 1935 as the CEO for Eastern Air Lines until his retirement in 1963. During his many business trips, he was involved in two plane crashes in which he was lucky to survive on both occasions, after receiving serious injuries in the first crash and being adrift at sea for 21-days after a war-time ditching in the Pacific Ocean.

Keith Caldwell

Born in New Zealand, Keith Logan Caldwell (1895-1980) CBE, MC, DFC and bar was a pilot in the RFC in WWI and in the RNZAF during WWII reaching the rank of Air Commodore in 1946.

Prior to WWI, Caldwell joined the Territorial Army in New Zealand and later tried to join the New Zealand Army, but was rejected. With the onset of war in Europe, he joined the first class of the Walsh Brothers Flying School at Auckland in October 1915 and paid £100 for his flight instruction and ground school, with £75 being refunded on joining the RFC. He qualified for his British Royal Aero Club Aviator's Certificate in December 1915 to become one of the first two aviators to qualify.

The Walsh brothers established the first flying school in New Zealand and their fleet consisted of several flying boats, all single-engine of course, including the first two Boeing B & W aircraft, mentioned earlier. The Walsh brothers later built their own airplanes based on the Curtiss-style flying boats

Caldwell sailed to England in January 1916, joined the RFC and was Commissioned in April 1916. With a further twenty-seven hours of training logged in England, he had a total of 35 hours flight experience before going into combat. In July, he was posted to 8 Squadron RFC flying BE.2C's and D models on observation duties near Arras in France. On 18 September 1916, he claimed his first victory, a Roland CII while flying a BE.2D. In March 1918 he moved to

74 Tiger Squadron RFC flying RAF S.E. 5A fighters. He was one of the few pilots to become an 'ace in a day' when he shot down five bombers in North Africa. He survived the war and flew his last combat mission 30 October 1918. His final victory was a Fokker D.VII, giving him a total of thirteen enemy aircraft destroyed plus eleven more sent down out of control for a total of 25 kills.

A popular story, tells of Caldwell's mid-air collision with fellow pilot Sydney Carlin from the same squadron. The story reads that Caldwell flew his damaged plane back to base by standing on the port, lower wing and reaching into the cockpit to operate the controls. During the landing flare, he jumped off the wing as the plane crash-landed. However, from Caldwell himself, he stated that he flew the damaged plane from 8,000 feet while standing on the right wing with his left foot on the right rudder pedal while he leaned out to the right as far as he could and crash-landed a short distance behind enemy lines. The enclosed photograph shows a diorama of the popular story of his flight with him standing on the left wing, presented in the Omaka Aviation Heritage Centre at Blenheim in New Zealand. Both versions are claimed as true stories from over one hundred years ago; which one is correct? We may never know.

A diorama of Keith Caldwell flying his RAF S.E. 5A by standing on the left wing after his mid-air collision. Note, the upper wing has been pushed forward out of alignment during the collision. This diorama is on display in the Omaka Aviation Heritage Centre, Blenheim, New Zealand.

After the war, he returned to New Zealand in August 1919 and entered into farming. He was also a founding member of the Auckland Aero Club. On joining the RNZAF, he was posted to England in 1943 and to India in 1945 and later still he became the station Commander at RNZAF Woodbourne in Blenheim and at RNZAF Wigram near Christchurch. He retired from the RNZAF in 1956 and returned to farming. Truly a pioneer pilot from New Zealand.

Hubert Williams

The oldest surviving pioneer WW 1 ace, was RFC pilot Hubert Williams (1896-2002); he died at the age of 106 years on 20 September 2002, eighty-four years after his last victory. He had joined the Royal Flying Corps at the age of twenty, in 1915 and at the age of 100, he took the controls of Concord on a flight to New York; what a contrast in speed and technology from his WW 1 days! He was presented with the French Legion de Honour medal when he was 102 years old for his wartime service.

14 – Age of the Airships

Airships in War & Peace

The early pioneer aeronauts (pilots of hot air balloons and airships) was covered in section 1 – The Early Pioneers. This section now covers the airships and balloons of the 20th century.

Airships were the first type of aircraft to be controllable in flight starting with the dirigible *La Caroline* in 1784. Several airships were built and flown in those early days and all could be classified as experimental airships until the advent of the Zeppelins in 1900, which ushered in the era of civilian and military airship use.

Airships can be classified into three groups of non-rigid, semi-rigid and rigid types:

- The non-rigid types uses their internal gas pressure to maintain their shape. They are known as pressure airships, or Blimps and were common in the war years as barrage balloons and those operated by the Goodyear Tire & Rubber Company for their public relations and tourist flights, advertising and as camera platforms.

- The semi-rigid airship became popular in later years of airship operations. They were noted for having a keel to support the structure to prevent the envelope from kinking (bending) in the middle. Up until the end of the 19th century, all airships were of the non-rigid or semi-rigid type and were making some progress towards being successful in their own right.

- The rigid type of airship has an internal metal framework to hold the envelope's shape with individual gas bags located within the main envelope to provide the required lift. The rigid type was designed and developed by the German, Count von Zeppelin and built by his company Luftschiffbau Zeppelin. The first Zeppelin, LZ 1 made its first flight from the shores of Lake Constance in south Germany on 2 July 1900. They were classed as dirigibles and were more successful than other earlier airships. They were commonly known as Zeppelins.

It is commonly believed the early Zeppelins from 1914 onwards were built of duralumin, a metal much stronger and lighter in weight compared to other metals. In fact, it was not until the 1920s to 1930s when duralumin was introduced for building airships from the Zeppelin LZ-127 onwards and the US Navy's *Los Angeles, Akron* and *Macon*.

Germany was at the forefront of airship engineering with the founding in 1909 of the German airline, Deutsche Luftschiffahrts Aktiengesell (DELAG). The airline operation ended in 1914 with the advent of WWI, when the airships switched to carrying bombs to Paris, London and other cities. Liege in Belgium, was the first city to be bombed by the Zeppelins in August 1914. From 1915, the Zeppelins carried out bomb raids over south-east England and the 6 September 1916, will be remembered as the night when sixteen Zeppelins raided London killing 557 civilians and injuring many others.

Although the Zeppelins had a low flying speed, initially they proved difficult to shoot down, due to the Zeppelins being able to fly higher than the British fighters. Later fighters that could reach the Zeppelin's altitude still had difficulty in shooting them down. Although the airships used highly flammable hydrogen for their lift, the bullets entering the balloon failed to ignite the gas due to there being no oxygen, which is of course, required to make fire. It was discovered the use of incendiary bullets mixed in with ordinary bullets could ignite the hydrogen and bring down the airships.

The first German airship to be shot down during WWI was the LZ 37 from the German Imperial Navy on the night of 6/7 June 1915. While returning to its base at Gontrode in Belgium from a raid on Calais with two other airships, it was attacked by Sub-Lieutenant Reginald Warneford (1891-1915) in his Moraine-Saulnier Type L Parasol scout plane. Warneford dropped six 20-pound bombs on the LZ 37 airship setting it on fire and bringing it down to crash near Ghent in Belgium. Eight crew members were killed including the captain and one other crew member survived with minor injuries. This event marked to first time an airplane had attacked and destroyed a lighter-than-air aircraft, earning Reginald Warneford the Victoria Cross and a place in aviation history.

The first pilot to destroy a German airship over England, was Lieutenant William Leefe Robinson (1895-1918) on the night of 2/3 September 1916 over the village of Cuffly in what is now known as Hertfordshire. Flying his converted night fighter B.E.2c, he attacked and shot down the German airship Schutte-Lanze SL 11 flying at 11,500 feet (3,500 m).

The last German airship to be shot down in WWI was the Zeppelin L.53, claimed by Lieutenant S.D. Cully (1895-1975) flying a Sopwith Camel 2F1 on 11 August 1918. For his achievement, he was awarded the Military Cross. Cully and his Sopwith Camel were launched from a platform towed by the *HMS Redoubt*, which was a common way to launch fighters to attack the airships. The Camels were armed with twin Lewis .303 machine guns mounted on the upper surface of the top wing where they could fire above the propeller arc. The attached photograph of the Sopwith 2F1 is the actual plane used by Lt. Cully and was photographed in 2015 by this author in the Imperial War Museum, London.

The Sopwith 2F1 Camel featured here, was the last British fighter to shoot down a Zeppelin airship. It was flown by Flight Sub Lieutenant Stuart D. Cully operating from the HMS redoubt in 11 August 1918.

The use of German airships for bombing raids on England gradually ended with the introduction into service of the Gotha heavy bombers in August 1917. The improved Gotha IV and V versions enabled the Imperial German Air Service to conduct the first strategic bombing raids on England, inflicting many deaths and injuries. As a result, the British formed the Home Defence Network with Sopwith Camels and anti-aircraft guns, forcing the Germans to switch to night raids.

Von Zeppelin

The 18th and 19th centuries saw many experimental balloons and airships flown in the USA and Europe on a trial-and-error basis with the *Le France* in 1884 being the most successful and controllable airship of those early pioneering years.

In July 1861, the US Navy used observation balloons for the first time in the American Civil War (1861-1865) at the Battle of Bull Run. In 1863, the German, Count Ferdinand von Zeppelin (1838-1917) at the age of 25 years received the chance to fly as a passenger in one of the balloons operated by the Union Army of the Potomac.

Zeppelin's first airship, was the LZ-1 (LZ for Luftschiff Zeppelin) built by the company he founded, Luftschiffbau Zeppelin, located at Friedrichshafen on Lake Constance in Germany. It made its maiden flight on 2 July 1900 flown by von Zeppelin and Theodore Kober (1865-1930).

The prototype LZ-1, was 420 feet (128 m) in length and 38 feet 6 inches (11.7 m) in diameter and carried seventeen cells filled with 399,000 cubic feet of hydrogen gas. Mounted in tandem below the airship were two gondolas each carrying two 14-horsepower Daimler engines, each driving a propeller mounted on out-riggers on each side of the airship. Longitudinal pitch control was achieved via a sliding weight below the airship. It was devoid of stabilising elevators and fins, which made control difficult on its maiden flight on 2 July 1900. Count Zeppelin's airship failed to impress or make any sales to the military and the airship was dismantled.

The DELAG company's first airship was the *LZ-10 Schwaber*, capable of carrying twenty passengers. Over a five-year period until 1914, the airship company carried 34,000 passengers on 1,500 German internal route and sight-seeing flights. The *LZ-120 Bodensee* was Germany's first post-WW1 airship to be built and it initiated a return to scheduled flights between Berlin and Friedrichshafen in Southern Germany. A fleet of twelve airships were used to carry passengers between ten of Germany's largest cities. It introduced thousands of passengers to air travel, especially the rich and famous, entertainers, businessmen and politicians, etc. Several airships were destroyed due to fire or bad weather, usually by wind too strong for the airships to handle.

Count von Zeppelin is considered to be the 'Father of the dirigible airship'.

Hugo Eckener

Airship pioneer, Hugo Eckener (1868-1954) was born in Flensburg, Germany and as a young child, he was not very academic. However, he later attended the University of Leipzig and gained a Doctorate in psychology but never pursued that as a career. Instead, he went into journalism and while working for the Frankfurt Zeitung newspaper, he reported on the new *Zeppelin LZ-1* and *LZ-2* airships, later working part-time for the Zeppelin Company as their publicist from 1908. His interest in airships grew and in 1911 he gained his airship pilots license. During his Military service in the First World War, he was not allowed to go into combat, instead his service of instructing new pilots to fly airships was considered to be of greater importance. He eventually became the company's chief airship commander replacing von Zeppelin when he died in 1917.

Hugo Eckener became the commander of the rigid airship *Graf Zeppelin* in 1928, Germany's most famous and successful airship. Eckener set many airship records flying the *Graf Zeppelin* with one of his most notable flights occurring on 1 October 1928 when he flew the first flight to carry passengers by airship from Friedrichshafen, Germany to the Naval Air Station in Lakehurst, New Jersey, USA, arriving there on 15 October. In August 1929, he made the second flight to circle the world in the *Graf Zeppelin*; the Douglas World Cruisers were the first to circle the world in April 1924.

Hugo Eckener had become a well-known hero in Germany for his airship flights, which he promoted as successful German engineering. Eckener was instrumental in the development of the German airships and their trans-Atlantic passenger-carrying flights with the *Graf Zeppelin*.

At the end of WWII, Eckener returned to newspaper journalism and with a partner they founded their newspaper *Sudkurier*. Hugo Eckener died in 1954 at Friedrichshaven, close to the home of the Luftschiffbau Zeppelin Airship factory and base.

The Giants of the Skies

From the start of the 20th century, airships were used in great numbers by the military and for carrying passengers across the North and South Atlantic routes in competition with the ocean liners, before they were replaced by the flying boat era and later still by landplanes. The 1930s saw the demise of the airship's reign; airplanes were becoming faster, more manoeuvrable and could carry greater loads.

Regular airship flights across the North Atlantic became routine affairs for Eckener and the *Graf Zeppelin*, from Frankfurt-am-Main to Lakehurst, New Jersey. From 1931 to 1937, the South Atlantic was flown by the *Graf Zeppelin* a total of 136 times to Recife and Rio de Janeiro. In all, the *Graf Zeppelin* flew over a million miles and made a total of 590 flights including a world-circumnavigation in 21 days.

The *Graf Zeppelin* was joined by the *LZ-129 Hindenburg* in 1936, which became the flagship of the Zeppelin fleet, measuring a colossal 803 feet (245 m) in length and 134 feet (41 m) in diameter to become the world's largest airship. It too, made several flights including seventeen return trips across the North Atlantic and later was used by the German Nazi Government to perform several propaganda flights prior to the war. Its last flight ended in disaster when attempting to moor to its mast on arrival in Lakehurst on 6 May 1937. It has never been confirmed, but it was concluded leaking hydrogen gas was ignited by a static spark with the resulting fire totally engulfing the *Hindenburg*. Of the ninety-seven crew and passengers on board, thirteen passengers and 22 crew members were killed plus one person on the ground. The *Hindenburg* commander was Captain Max Pruss (1891-1960) on its fatal flight.

Up until then, the Hindenburg Company had flown accident-free operations thanks to the safety procedures put in place by Eckener. Over time, the Company management had over-ridden some of Eckener's procedures leading to lax safety performance by new and less experienced airship commanders.

After the Great War, the Zeppelin Company built the rigid airship *LZ-126* named by the US Navy as the *USS Los Angeles* which became their longest serving airship from November 1924 until June 1932. It was returned to service in 1933 for a few more years to replace the lost *USS Akron*. Eckener was the commander on the delivery flight to Lakehurst for the US Navy.

The first rigid airship operated by the US Navy was the *USS Shenandoah* which made its first powered flight on 24 September 1923. It was the first US airship to use helium for its lift, which at the time was in short supply and the *Shenandoah* held most of the helium then available in North America. The *Shenandoah's* claim to fame was for being the first airship to cross North America. However, as with other airships, its service life was short lived; it was lost in a storm in September 1925 over Ohio on its 57th flight.

The British airship, the *R101,* was the world's largest aircraft when it was introduced into service with its first flight in 1929. However, it too, had a short service life before it crashed in France during 1930. The *USS Macon* and *USS Akron* were the world's largest airships when they were launched. The parasite biplane concept was trialled on both of these airships, which carried four Curtiss F9-C Sparrowhawk fighters, stored in their on-board hangers. The planes were launched and recovered using the plane's trapeze gear attached to supports on the airship. The *USS Macon* also had a short life span after receiving storm damage and being forced down and wrecked on 12 February 1935. Most of the crew were saved. The *USS Akron* operated from 1931 through to its last flight on 4 April 1933 when it too crashed during a severe thunderstorm, off the New Jersey coast. Its crash involved the greatest loss of life in airship disasters; seventy three of the 76 persons onboard were lost. Despite the large proportions of airships, they cannot handle severe weather.

Although quite numerous in their heyday, the operation of airships has waned considerably except for a small number, which continue to operate mainly for promotional purposes to this day. The end of serious airship operations has come to a close; however, the sport of hot air balloon flying is now the domain of sport pilots who use them solely for pleasure flying and tourist flights in many countries around the world. The more serious balloonists use them for record breaking flights, as we will see shortly.

Army Balloon Factory

The Gondola featured here, was first used on the *Beta-I* airship built by the Army Balloon Factory at Farnborough, England, making its first flight in April 1910 with a single, 35 horsepower engine. It was a successor to the *Nulli Secundas* and the *Baby*, earlier airships built at Farnborough.

In 1912, the engine was removed to check in-flight handling without it in place. The Gondola was damaged during these tests and after repair work was completed it was paired up with the non-rigid *Beta-II* airship, a rebuild of the *Beta I* with a lengthened balloon envelope. The single engine was later replaced by a pair of Clerget 50 horsepower engines driving four-blade props.

Hydrogen was its main source of buoyancy-lift with an engine driven pump used to inflate the envelope's ballonet with air as required due to any loss of hydrogen. The airship was operated by a crew of three in a boat-shaped Gondola, as shown in the photograph below.

The Beta-II was built as an experimental airship and was used to pioneer the method of mooring airships to masts and to experiment with aerial photography, etc. Because of the successful outcome of its experimental work, the Beta became the forerunner of other small airships used for anti-submarine duties during the war.

Looking very much like a canoe, this is the gondola car from the Beta-II/ HMA 17 balloon, in the Science Museum, London.

All British military airships were initially flown by the Army; however, that changed in 1914 when their control was transferred to the Royal Navy Air Service (RNAS) and the *Beta-II* was renamed as the *HMA (His Majesty's Airship) No 17*. In the early days of WWI, it was used as an escort airship for military cargo ships crossing the English Channel to deliver supplies to the Continent. In 1916 the *Beta-17* was retired from use and the Gondola was donated to the London Science Museum where it remains on display with its two engines attached.

Goodyear Airship – Pilgrim

The *Pilgrim* was the prototype of several small, non-rigid, Blimp airships built by Goodyear in 1925 as airship pilot trainers and sporting airships. The *Pilgrim* pioneered the use of helium gas in airships which is far safer than extremely flammable hydrogen.

The *Pilgrim* was flown on its maiden flight by Jack Yolton on 3 June 1925 from Akron, Ohio with hydrogen for its lifting power within its original envelope of 47,700 cubic feet. This envelope was replaced in April 1929 with a larger capacity envelope of 55,000 cubic feet with which it made its first flight with helium.

This was Goodyear's first airship intended for civilian use as a private airship in line with private yachts and launches, but it was not to be, the public showed little interest. However, the *Pilgrim* became the first of Goodyear's promotional airships which are still used to today, 97 years after the *Pilgrim* first flew.

The *Pilgrim's* overall length was 105.5 feet (32.2 m) with a maximum diameter of 31 feet (9.45 m). To put that into perspective, the *Graf Zeppelin II* and the *Hindenburg* were both 804 feet (245 m) in length with a diameter of 135 feet (41 m).

The gondola had seating for the pilot and two passengers in a quite luxurious cabin with upholstered seats and mahogany veneer fittings; a mechanic in the rear attended to the engine. The gondola's cabin measured 14.5 feet (4.42 m) in length with a width of 3 feet 9 inches (1.14 m). The single, Lawrence radial, air-cooled engine of 60 horsepower drove a pusher prop that was attached to the rear of the gondola giving the *Pilgrim* a cruise speed of 40 mph (65 km/h).

Another unique feature of the gondola was its attachment directly to the envelope, a first for any airship, as opposed to all previous airships where

*The Pilgrim represents the pioneering days of airships dating back nearly 100-years.
It is displayed siting on its ground support frame in the Udvar-Hazy Center.*

*This airship gondola is one of the most-used airships built by
Goodyear. It is now displayed in the Udvar-Hazy Center.*

the gondola was suspended underneath. Having the gondola attached was possible due to the non-flammable nature of its helium lift gas; previous airship gondolas were suspended to keep them (and their engines) away from the flammable hydrogen in their envelopes. An attached gondola is now a feature of all airships since 1925. The *Pilgrim* had its own portable mooring mast allowing it to moor on any piece of ground that was large enough. A single wheel below the gondola helped for ground-handling manoeuvres.

During its six-years of operation, the *Pilgrim* clocked up 2,880 hours in the air, carried 5,355 passengers and made a total of 4,765 flights until its retirement on 30 December 1931. Goodyear gifted the *Pilgrim* to the Smithsonian Museum where it is now displayed along with *Airship C-49* in the Udvar-Hazy Center.

Goodyear Airship C-49 Control Car

The Goodyear Company built the airship *C-49* which was used by the US Navy from 1942 until its return to Goodyear on 24 January 1946. It was given the designation of *L-5* by the US Navy who used it to train new airship pilots at Moffett Field in California and also for the occasional patrol flight.

On its return to Goodyear after the war, the control car was rebuilt and mated with the Goodyear non-rigid (Blimp) in 1969 for use as their promotional aircraft named the *Goodyear Blimp*. In 1975, it was renamed as the *Columbia IV* and it logged several thousand hours of flight time in corporate work, as a night time advertising board and for carrying many passengers. It was seen at sports events such as the 1984 Summer Olympics in Los Angeles and Super Bowls events, etc. It has also appeared in several movies.

The *C-49* had a varied working life including military service and commercial utility work spanning forty-four years from 1942 through November 1986, making it one of the longest serving airships to remain in use. The *C-49* was donated to the Smithsonian Museum in November 2011 and placed on display in the Udvar-Hazy Center, Chantilly, Va.

Goodyear L-8 Control Car

The day started with a routine Navy airship patrol over the sea and ended as a complete mystery. On the morning of 16 August 1942, the Goodyear-built airship *L-8* was prepared for flight and launched from Treasure Island near San Francisco in California into a light breeze and an overcast sky with a cloud base at around 1,000 feet. It headed west to patrol the coast looking for Japanese submarines, which had previously sunk some allied shipping in the area.

The US Navy had bought the *L-8* from the Goodyear Tyre & Rubber Company in 1942. It was lifted by 123,000 cubic feet of helium and had a length of 150 feet (46 m) with a diameter of 47 feet (14.3 m). Its two Warner Super Scareb engines of 145 horsepower each powered the pusher props and gave the airship a cruise speed of 50 mph (80 km/h).

The *L-8* was crewed by two experienced airship crewmen, Lieutenant Ernest Cody and Ensign Charles Adams. Ernest Cody at the age of 27 years old, was the senior airship pilot at the US Navy's Airship Patrol Squadron 32, although relatively new to airships with 756-hours flying experience. He was a very capable pilot and Navy officer and well-liked with his quiet and calm attitude. On this patrol he was the pilot-in-command although with far less experience than Adams, who was 38 years old with 2,281 hours of flying time in over twenty years' service, but who had only received his commission on the previous day. Therefore, Cody was his superior officer on this first patrol together. Both men were married.

Cody and Adams made a routine departure from their base just after 6 a.m. and went on station in their patrol area near the Farallon Islands off the Californian coast from San Francisco. Spotting an oil patch on the sea surface they went to investigate; it could be a sign of a submarine in the area. They dropped two smoke flares to mark the area and reported this action by radio to their base at around 7.40 a.m. However, after over an hour of searching there were no signs of any submarines. The *L-8* had covered the area from a height of 200-300 feet and as low as 30 feet at one stage. Their actions had been noticed by the crews of a fishing boat and the cargo-carrying Liberty ship the SS *Albert Gallatin*. Cody and Adams were also seen within the airship's gondola by the crew of both vessels. It was to be the last time anyone would see the *L-8* crew.

The 7.40 a.m. radio contact was the last one received from the airship crew and they failed to respond to calls from their base. Eventually, two Vought Kingfisher floatplanes were sent out to investigate and the *L-8* was seen by the crew of one of the Kingfishers at 11 a.m., apparently flying under control. The crew of a Pan Am Clipper flying boat had spotted the *L-8* flying over the Golden Gate Bridge a few minutes earlier at 10.49 a.m., as if returning to its base. The *L-8* was also observed by crowds of people on the land as it drifted in across the coastline to eventually crash-land in a San Francisco suburban street at 11.30 a.m. When locals went to investigate, it was discovered the two crew members were not onboard and have never been found.

A full investigation was launched and apart from the gondola door being latched open, there was no sign of any trouble between Cody and Adams in the gondola, no radio calls for help and the airship was in perfect working order when it departed on its patrol mission. Several theories were put forward to explain the crew's disappearance, but nothing was conclusive. From a routine patrol, their disappearance remains a mystery to this day.

The L-8 spent the remainder of the war as a training airship for the US Navy before its return to the Goodyear Company where it was renamed as the America; It was used as a camera ship at sports events around the USA until its retirement in 1982. The L-8/America was donated in 2003 to the National Naval Aviation Museum in Pensacola, Florida where it was restored to its L-8 Navy livery and placed on display.

The control car from the Goodyear L-8 airship with a mysterious past. Now on show in the National Naval Air Museum, NAS Pensacola, Florida.

British Airships R-33, R-34, R-101 & R-100

Across the Atlantic in England, the *R-33* was built by Armstrong Whitworth as a class *R-31* rigid airship. The *R-33* made its first flight on 6 March 1919 for the Royal Navy Air Service, but was too late to serve in World War One. The RNAS later merged with the Royal Air Force and the *R-33* gave ten years of service, based at RAF Pulham Airship Station in Norfolk.

Most British military airships at the time were taken out of service and scrapped due to the British government putting an end to airship development and their use due to financial reasons. However, as a civilian airship from 1920, the *R-33* was registered as G-FAAG with a nickname of *The Pulham Pig*. It was instead, placed in storage at the Royal Airship Works at Cardington, Bedfordshire until 1925 when it was reconditioned and once again took to the air. It was used for testing parasite fighter aircraft attached to her underside and also for research work in preparation for building the airship *R-101*, amongst other airship duties. The discovery of metal fatigue in 1928 finally brought her useful life to an end. She was dismantled with only the front half of her control car remaining, which was placed on display in the RAF Hendon Museum, in outer London.

Her sister airship the *R-34* (section 5 – Trans-Atlantic Pioneers) made the first double crossing of the North Atlantic from RAF East Fortune near Edinburgh to Mineola, New York, with a return to RNAS Pulham in July 1919. On arrival in New York, Major E. M. Pritchard descended by parachute from the airship to organise the ground handlers in the mooring procedure. He made history by becoming the first person to arrive on the North American continent by air from Europe. The reader may recall the first airplane to cross the Atlantic from America to Europe was a US Navy Curtiss NC-4 two months earlier in May 1919.

The rigid airship *R-101* was the world's largest airship at the time it was built measuring a length of 777 feet (236.8 m) with a diameter of 131 feet (40 m). The German-built *Hindenburg* was larger still, arriving on the scene in 1936. The *R-101* was an experimental airship funded as a government project by the Air Ministry, as opposed to the earlier *R-100*, which was privately funded. She was built by the Royal Airship Works at Cardington and made her maiden flight on the 14 October 1929. However, her service life was also short-lived. It crashed on 5 October 1930 at Beauvais in northern France while en route to India on her first overseas trip. Of the fifty-four people onboard, 48 died in the crash including the captain Major George Herbert Scott (1888-1930) an experienced airship commander. George Scott was previously the captain of the *R-34*, the first airship to make a double crossing of the Atlantic in July 1919. Also lost were several government officials responsible for the British rigid airship programme and various workers from the Royal Airship Works. The loss of the *R-101* was the worst civilian airship disaster and brought about the demise of the British airship industry.

The airship *Vickers R-100* was designed by Barnes Wallace of Dam Buster fame for the Airship Guarantee Company in England . It made its maiden flight on 16 December 1929 after the *R-101* had entered service. She flew a trip to Montreal departing on 29 July 1930 and returned to Cardington arriving on 16 August 1930 to prove regular trans-Atlantic passenger services were feasible. However, the loss of the *R-101* put an end to those plans leading to the *R-100* being scrapped. The German airship company DELAG remained the World's sole airship operator across the Atlantic for a few more years. The use of airships waned after these unfortunate accidents to be replaced by conventional aircraft, which were becoming more and more common and far more efficient and safer.

Double Eagle II & V

Ben Abruzzo (1930-1985) was an American balloonist and businessman. He was part of the crew that flew the balloon *Double Eagle II* across the Atlantic with Max Anderson and Larry Newman.

They departed from Presque Island, Maine, USA on 11 August 1978 and landed six days later in Miserey, France on 17 August. They covered a distance 3,120 miles (5,000 km) in a total of 137 hours and 5 minutes of flight time. Their gondola was a small 6 feet by 8.5 feet (1.84 by 2.59 m) housing the three crew members and their food, ballast and equipment. All three men received a Gold Medal each, for their successful first crossing of the Atlantic in the helium-filled balloon. The gondola is now displayed in the Udvar-Hazy Center. Sixteen previous attempts had been made to cross the Atlantic but all had failed; five people died during their attempts.

The *Double Eagle V* was the first manned balloon to fly across the Pacific Ocean with a crew of four including Ben Abruzzo, Larry Newman, Ron Clark and Japanese Rocky Aoki, who partly financed the trip.

Departing from Nagashima, Japan on 12 Nov 1981, they covered 5,768 miles (9,283 km) in 84 hours 31 minutes of flying time before they landed near Covello in California. They gained the record for the longest distance flown by a balloon at that time.

The *Double Eagle V* balloon contained 400,000 cubic feet of helium and was approximately 130 feet (40 m) high. Its gondola had a boat-shaped hull for flotation in the event of a water ditching. Their planned cruising altitude was 26,000 (8,000 m) feet to catch the high-speed westerly winds of up to 150 mph (240 km/h). However, their altitude varied considerably reaching a maximum of only 22,000 feet where the wind speeds were lower giving them an average ground speed 68.3 mph (110 km/h).

At the end of the first day when 200 miles (320 km) from Japan, they flew through a storm picking up a heavy load of ice on top of their balloon forcing them down from 19,000 feet to 4,200 feet. A ditching in the sea and ending their Pacific crossing looked quite possible until the ice melted in the warmer temperatures at lower altitudes allowing the balloon to ascend back to higher levels. Changes in day and night air temperature also caused changes in cruise altitude due to the heating and cooling and hence, buoyancy of the balloon's helium.

Ben Abruzzo (1930-1985) was an American businessman and balloonist. He received the Congressional Gold Medal and also the FAI Diplome Montgolfier, the highest award given for ballooning achievements. He promoted Albuquerque as a centre for the sport of ballooning. He died in 1985 when his Cessna 421 crashed after take-off along with five other people onboard including his wife. Max Anderson with Don Ide, lost their lives in the 1983 Gordon Bennet balloon race while trying to land before a storm in Bavaria.

However, the first manned balloon to cross the USA on a non-stop flight was flown by Max and Kris Anderson on 12 May 1980. Again, they used a helium-filled balloon, which they named *Kitty Hawk,* a nod towards the place where the Wright brothers made their famous first flight in 1903.

Breitling Orbiter 3

The *Breitling Orbiter 3* was built by the British company of Cameron Balloons at Bristol as a Roziere-type balloon with the sole purpose of flying around the world non-stop, which it achieved in March 1999.

The balloon's envelope reached 180 feet (55 m) high and was part hot air balloon and part helium gas balloon. A chamber held the helium within the balloon's envelope and was surrounded by the hot air heated by six propane burners from a collection of titanium cylinders some of which were stored either side of the gondola. At lift-off, the helium bag was part-filled allowing expansion of the gas by heat from the sun to support the purpose-built gondola,

The capsule for the Breitling Orbiter 3 balloon, which circled the world non-stop in 1999 is now an Udvar-Hazy Center museum exhibit.

which was pressurised giving a cabin altitude of 10,000 feet (3,000 m) when the balloon was flying at 33,000 feet (10,000 m).

The pilots were Swiss Bertrand Piccard (1958- ?) a psychiatrist and balloonist and Englishman Brian Jones (1947-20?) and were the last of the pioneer balloonists and the first to circumnavigate the world by balloon, non-stop in March 1999. They departed from Chateau-d'Oex in Switzerland and headed south-west to Mauritania in North Africa for their official start line for the world flight. After circling the world, they landed in Egypt after covering a total distance of 25,361 miles (40,814 km) in 19 days 21 hours and 55 minutes of flight time.

The *Breitling Orbiter 3* gondola is now a museum exhibit in the Udvar-Hazy Center, Chantilly, Va.

Other balloon records include a climb to 51,761 feet (15,800 m) on 27 May 1931 by Dr. Auguste Antoine Piccard (1884-1962) a Swiss physicist and inventor, with Paul Kipfer. Dr. Piccard was the grand-father of Bertrand Piccard, mentioned above. They were the first pilots to enter the stratosphere using a pressurised balloon gondola designed by Piccard and they were the first humans to see the earth's curvature from a high altitude. The purpose of their high altitude flight, was to study the upper air atmosphere. In 1932, Piccard exceeded his own FAI record when he reached nearly 55,000 feet.

This altitude was later exceeded by Steven and Anderson who climbed to over 70,000 feet (21,200 m) on 11 November 1935. This record was eclipsed by two officers from the US Navy, Commander Malcolm Ross and Lieutenant Commander Victor Prather when they reached 113,740 feet (34,667 m) in their balloon, in 1961.

In 1960, USAF Captain Joe Kittenger claimed the longest free-fall sky-dive record during his jump from 103,000 feet (31,400 m) while wearing a special version of a NASA type space suit. This record was later eclipsed in the year 2012.

15 – The Air Racing Era

The Challenge for Speed

Air racing first started in France in 1906 with the Gordon Bennett Cup race for hot air balloon pilots. Other air races for airplanes have been flown over the years mainly in Europe and North America and still continue to this day. Some races are flown point-to-point, as we shall see shortly, other races are flown on closed-circuit courses such as those held at Reno, Nevada since 1964. The races are held in different categories and commonly flown with souped-up WWII fighter aircraft, special home-built racer planes and also jets. The Americans are far more competitive in their air racing compared to the British who are more relaxed about their sport.

Gordon Bennett Cup

The Gordon Bennett Cup (also known as the Coupe Aeronautique) was the first race ever to be held for balloon pilots and was initially sponsored by the American *New York Herald* owner and millionaire sportsman, James Gordon Bennett, Jr., (1841-1918). The aim of the race was simply to fly as far as possible from the launch site. The first race departed from Paris, France on 30 September 1906, which was won by Frank Purdy Lahm (1877-1963). Frank Lahm was dubbed as the (American) 'nation's first military aviator', serving as an officer in the USAAC and the Army Air Force.

The prestigious Gordon Bennet Cup race was hosted by the winning country's team in the following year's contest. The race was held annually from 1906 to 1938 apart from 1931 when it was cancelled, followed by a temporary cessation during WWII due to the hosting nation of Poland being invaded. It was not until 1979 before the race was reinstated by the American, Tom Heinsheimer and it continues to be held annually to this day. It is now the world's oldest race for balloon pilots.

The record for the longest time aloft of 92 hours went to the German pilots, Wilhelm Eimers and his co-pilot Bernd Landsmann. Distance records were continually being broken over the years by various competitors and tragically, some pilots lost their lives due to thunderstorms and other accidents during the races.

In 1909, Gordon Bennett opened a race for powered aircraft held in conjunction with the Grande Semaine d'Aviation de la Champagne at Reims, France that was sponsored by local makers of champagne; it was the world's first aviation meeting held for heavier-than-air aircraft. The first race covered a twelve-mile (20 km) distance and was won by the American, Glen Curtiss at 46.77 mph (75.27 km/h). The last race held in 1913, extended to a total distance of 124 miles (200 km) which was won at a speed of 124.8 mph (200.8 km/h), demonstrating how the speeds of those pioneering aircraft quickly increased, even more so in the years that followed. The last Gordon Bennett race for powered aircraft was held in 1920.

From the first balloon flight in 1783 flown by the Montgolfier brothers, the sport of ballooning is still enjoyed by many privileged individuals who fly their balloons for enjoyment or attempt to make further records in long-distance flying. And what a spectacular site it is to see a flock of balloons becoming airborne in the still, early morning or evening air.

London to Manchester Air Race

The British newspaper, the *Daily Mail*, offered a £10,000 prize in November 1906 to the pilot of the first powered aircraft to fly from London to Manchester within a twenty-four-hour period. The rules cited that no more than two en route landings were permitted on the 185-mile (298 km) route and the departure and arrival points were to be within five miles of the *Daily Mail* offices in London and Manchester.

It was not until 1910 before the challenge was taken up by just two aviators, British pioneer aviator Claude Graham-White (1879-1959) and French aviator, Isadore S.M. Louis Paulhan (1883-1963) who was commonly known as Louis Paulhan. He was an early French pioneer aviator who started his aviation career when he joined the French military balloon school. He later won a Voison biplane in which he taught himself to fly and gained his pilot licence from the Aero Club of France. He flew frequently in England and America as an air show exhibition pilot and also competed at various flying meetings, which included competing and winning Britain's London to

Manchester air race, as mentioned above. And like similar pioneer aviators at the time, he also claimed altitude and endurance record flights.

Graham-White was the first to depart from Park Royal in London early on 23 April 1910 to become the first pilot to make a night-time take-off; his first stop was made at Rugby. His next landing was caused by an engine malfunction on his Farman III biplane at Lichfield, where his plane suffered wind damage while on the ground and had to be returned to London for repairs.

In the meantime, Paulhan made his departure from London on 27 April with Graham-White departing soon after with the hope of passing Paulhan. But it was not to be. Paulhan won the race and the *Daily Mail* prize of £10,000. Graham-White had further mechanical problems with his plane and accepted defeat. The two competing aviators had lunch together at the Savoy Hotel in London on 30 April 1910 to celebrate Paulhan's win of the first long-distance air race to be held in England. Forty years later in 1950, Louis Paulhan then 67 years old retraced his route as a passenger in a Gloster Meteor T7, a two-seat jet trainer aircraft, taking about thirty minutes from London to Manchester. He then had a reunion with his rival Graham-White arranged by the *Daily Mail* newspaper.

The Coupe de la Meurthe

The Potez 53 racing aircraft was built by *Aeroplanes Henry Potez* at Aubervilliers in France, a company established in 1919. Three Potez 53 planes were built to compete in the *Coupe de la Meurthe*, an aeronautical speed competition, which was open to all international competitors. The speed competition was instigated by French oil businessman, Henry de la Meurthe in 1909, but it was to be another three years before the first competitors took up the challenge, on 12 April 1912. Several races were held over the years, with the race distance varying with each race. The last race was flown in 1936.

The Potez company fulfilled the requirement with their Potez 53 winning the 1933 race on 23 May. The winning pilot was Georges Detre in the aircraft pictured here. During the winning race, he clocked-up a speed of 200.58 mph (322.81 km/h), while competing against company test pilot Lemoine in another Potez 53, but he failed to complete the race. His other opponents were Captain Ludovic Arrachart flying a Caudron C.360; however, he fatally crashed following an engine failure during a training run. The two other

The 1933 Coupe de la Meurthe winning aircraft, was this purpose-built Potez 53 race plane, now displayed in the Air & Space Museum in Paris.

The winner in the 1925 Schneider Trophy Race at Hampton Roads in the USA. It now hangs in the Pioneers of Flight gallery at the National Air and Space Museum in Washington, D.C.

pilots were Raymond Delmotte, the chief pilot for Caudron who was flying a Caudron C.362 and from England, Nick Comper was flying one of his designs, a Comper Swift.

The Potez 53 displayed in the Air & Space Museum in Paris and pictured here, was the outright winner in 1933. It was powered by a Potez 9B nine-cylinder radial engine giving 310 hp. The Potez 53 design has similarities with the Bee Gee Racers from America, having a radial engine, circular cross-section fuselage, low wing monoplane with its single-seat cockpit set towards the rear of the fuselage.

The winner of each race was awarded 20,000 francs. The de la Meurthe cup itself valued at 10,000 francs, was presented by the Aero-Club de France.

The Schneider Trophy

The Schneider Trophy, or in French, the Coupe d'Aviation Maritime Jacques Schneider, was introduced to be awarded to the winner of a race for seaplanes held each year until the winning team had won three consecutive races. The idea for the races was instigated by the Frenchman, Jacques Schneider (1879-1928) in 1910. He was a financier, aircraft enthusiast, a balloonist and a racer of floatplanes. His interest in aircraft was stemmed from a meeting with Wilbur Wright in 1908. However, a boating accident left him disabled and unable to continue his love of racing and flying. He had noted that the progress of floatplanes and flying boat's performance was less than that of their land-based counterparts. At a banquet on 5 December 1910, Schneider presented his idea of a race for floatplanes to promote and encourage the progress in aviation technology especially in engine design and aerodynamic streamlining for drag reduction and hence, greater speed.

The course was to be over a triangular circuit initially of 170 miles (280 km) extending to 220 miles (350 km) in later years with the race planes departing at 15-minute intervals. Three consecutive wins within five years were required to win the Schneider Trophy, with the pilot of each of the three winning races to receive 75,000 francs each. The winning country hosted the next race, which was held twelve times between 1913 and 1931. It turned into a speed contest which saw the speed of aircraft increase from 45 mph (73 km/h) in 1913 to 328 mph (528 km/h) in 1929. This was a good example showing the increase in performance of aero engines and aircraft over a few short years. The French, Federation Aéronautique Internationale (FAI) were the contest's official judges. It also became a very popular spectator sport with over 250,000 people watching the final race.

The twelve races are covered briefly as follows:

- 1913 the first race was flown at Monaco and won by French pilot Maurice Prevost (1887-1952) in his Deperdussin Monocoque at a speed of 45.71 mph (73.57 km/h).

- 1914 again at Monaco, won by British pilot Howard Pixton in a Sopwith Tabloid at 86.83 mph (139.74 km/h).

- 1919 held at Bournemouth, UK, won by Italian, Guido Janello flying a Savoia S.13, speed unknown.

- 1920 held at Venice in Italy and won by a Savoia S.12 flown by Luigi Bologna at a speed of 107.2 mph (172.6 km/h).

- 1921 held at Venice again and won by Italian Giovanni de Briganti in a Macchi M.7-bis with a speed of 117.85 mph h (189.66 km/h).

- 1922 flown at Naples and won by Britain, flown by Henry Biard in his Supermarine Sea Lion II with a speed of 145.72 mph (234.51 km/h).

- 1923 at Cowes UK and won by USA pilot David Rittenhaus in a Curtiss CR-3 reaching 177.27 mph (285.29 km/h).

- 1924 races were cancelled.

- 1925 the first race held in the USA at Baltimore, flown by US Army pilot James Doolittle in a Curtiss R3C-2 at a speed of 232.57 mph (374.28 km/h).

- 1926 at Hampton Roads in the USA and won by Italian Mario de Bernadi flying a Macchi M.39 to 246.49 mph (396.69 km/h).

- 1927 saw a return to Venice in Italy with British pilot Sidney Webster flying a Supermarine S.5 to a speed of 281.66 mph (453.28 km/h).

- 1929 at Calshot, Hampshire, British pilot Richard Waghorn flew his Supermarine S.6 to 328.64 mph (528.89 km/h).

- 1931 on the Solent, UK, the race was won outright by Britain after winning three consecutive racers; flown by RAF pilot Flt Lt John Boothman flying a Supermarine S.6B to a record speed of 340.08 mph (547.31 km/h).

The Curtiss R3C-2 won the 1925 Schneider Cup race in Baltimore on 25 October flown by James (Jimmy) Doolittle with an average course speed of 232. 57 mph (373.4 km/h). He achieved a world speed record of 245.7 mph (395.4 km/h) on the following day. In the 1926 race, the same plane was flown by US Marine Corps pilot, Lieutenant Christian Schlit to an average speed of 231.4 mph (371.7 km/h) gaining second place. That race was won by the Italian team who hosted the 1927 race in Italy.

The winning Curtiss R3C-2 is now displayed in the National Air & Space Museum in Washington, D.C.

With the British gaining a win in each of the last three races, they became the final winners of the Schneider Trophy. A few days later, the race-winning Supermarine S.6B (S1596) was flown by RAF pilot Flight Lieutenant George Stainforth to become the first pilot to exceed 400 mph and to claim a new, world-speed record of 407.5 mph (655.80 km/h). This record still remains for piston-engine powered floatplanes.

The Schneider Trophy Cup has been on long-term display in the London Science Museum in South Kensington, London close to the race-winning Supermarine S.6B. The second Supermarine S.6 (N248) used in the race is

The Supermarine S.6A entered the same race as the S.6B but was disqualified due to cutting the corner inside of a marker. Note, the large propeller with a very course pitch for high-speed flight, in the days before constant-speed propellers. It is now in the Solent Sky Museum, Southampton, UK.

The Supermarine S.6B was the outright winner of the Schneider Cup race. The plane and cup has been on display for many years in the Science Museum in London.

on display in the Solent Sky Museum in Southampton near to where the last Schneider Trophy winning races were held. It had competed but received a disqualification.

The designer of the Supermarine S.6 racing planes, Reginald J. Mitchell CBE, FRAeS, (1895-1937) also designed the famous Spitfire which was a progression of the S.6 racers design.

The Thomson Trophy Races

The Thomson Trophy race was a closed-course pylon race held annually from 1929 to 1939 and again after WWII when it was run from 1946 through 1961. The races were major events on the aviation calendar during the Golden Age years of the 1930s. The race covered 10 miles (16 km) around the pylons which marked out the closed-circuit course.

Most races were run at Cleveland, Ohio before the war and post-war the races were held at Detroit, Los Angeles, Dayton in Ohio, NAWS China Lake in California; however, the majority of the races held at Edwards AFB in California.

The well-known Roscoe Turner, won the highest prize of all races at US$22,000 when he won the 1938 race at Cleveland flying a Laird-Turner Meteor LTR-14 to speeds reaching 283.42 mph (456 km/h). The following year Turner again flew the same plane and reached 282.54 mph (455 km/h) to win another US$16,000.

Racing continued post-war with surplus WWII fighters converted for racing, a separate jet-powered division was established post-war to enable military jet aircraft to compete in the races. The Mach 2 Convair B-58 Hustler jet bomber won the final race in 1961 at the impressive speed of 1,302 mph (2,095 km/h)! It was flown by USAF Major Harold E. Confer at Edwards Air Force Base in California.

Comparing the aircraft speeds in the 1930s at less than 300 mph (475 km/h) to the B-58 Hustler's Mach two speed, emphasizes the progress in aircraft performance attained in just over twenty years of development from the 1930s to the 1950s.

The Gee Bee Racers

The Gee Bee Model R Super Sportster racing planes were designed and built by the Granville brothers, hence the name Gee Bee, at Springfield, Massachusetts, with the sole purpose to win the Thomson Trophy air race in 1931.

The prototype made its maiden flight on 13 August 1932. They were designed to have the smallest fuselage with the largest possible engine, a single Pratt & Whitney R-985 Wasp Junior of 535 horsepower. This was later up-graded to the P&W R-1340 Wasp developing 800 horsepower for a speed record attempt. The Gee Bee's airframe had a wingspan of 25 feet (7.62 m) and a length of 17 feet 8 inches (5.38 m). The maximum take-off weight was 3,075 lb (1,394 kg) quite heavy for such a small airframe, which gave a rather high stall speed of 90 mph (145 km/h); however, this was reduced later reduced to 65 mph (105 km/h). The cockpit was placed far aft to improve visibility during turns when racing.

The purpose-built Gee Bee racers were popular race planes for their high-speeds (at that time). In 1931, Lowell Bayles flew his Gee Bee Model Z at Cleveland to win first place and US$7,500. In 1932, again at Cleveland, Jimmy Doolittle (1896-1993) flew a Gee Bee GBR-1 reaching 252.7 mph (407 km/h) to win the race and gain the prize of US$4,500. He favoured the Gee Bee for its high speed and in the same year he raised the FAI speed record for landplanes when he reached 296 mph (476 km/h); the seaplane record

A Gee Bee racing plane of the 1930s. They were unstable and hard to fly, but Jimmy Doolittle favoured them for their high-speed. Note the cockpit just forward of the tail fin. A Thomson Trophy stands beside this Gee Bee R-1, a non-flying replica displayed in the San Diego Air & Space Museum, San Diego, Calif.

The MacRobertson Race winning aircraft, the DH-88 Comet 'Grosvenor House', is now owned and displayed by the Shuttleworth Collection Museum, Old Warden, UK.

at that time stood at 407.5 mph (655.8 km/h) gained by the British in the Supermarine S.6B floatplane in September 1931.

The Gee Bee's with their high power/weight ratio were quite a handful for some pilots to fly. They also suffered from instability and aerodynamic aileron flutter causing the first four planes to fatally crash. Lowell Richard Bayles (1900-1931) who won the 1931 Thomson Trophy race, was killed on 5 December 1931 in a crash at Detroit, Michigan while attempting to gain a new landplane speed record.

MacRobertson Trophy Air Race

The MacRobertson Trophy Air Race was the brainchild of Sir Harold G. Smith (1890-1983) the Mayor of Melbourne in Victoria, Australia, as part of the 1934 Melbourne Centenary celebrations. The race was planned not only for the Melbourne Centenary but also to promote an extension of the air route through the British Empire countries in the Middle East and on to Australia to provide a continuous air route. It would then ensure an established service for air mail, civilian passengers and military personal with their equipment, if required.

The air race, also known as the 'World's Greatest Air Race', was flown from RAF Mildenhall in England to a landing on the Flemington Racecourse in Melbourne covering a total distance of about 11,300 miles (18,200 km). Compulsory stops were required at Baghdad in Iraq, Allahabad in India, Singapore, Darwin and Charleville in Australia and finally Melbourne with another twenty-two optional fuel-stops available en route, all organised the Royal Aero Club in England.

The total prize of £15,000 was funded by Sir Macpherson Robertson. He was an Australian confectionary manufacturer, hence the name of the race. Aircraft of any size were eligible to enter with no restriction on the number of crew and the aircraft were to be equipped with sufficient rations and emergency supplies. The winning categories included aircraft performance based on handicap, completing the race within sixteen days and for the aircraft with the fastest speed.

Initially, over sixty aircraft applied to enter the race, with twenty aircraft actually participating and departing from England on 20 October 1934. A variety of aircraft types were entered including transports, old bombers and three DH-88 Comets built by de Havilland to special order. Jim and Amy Mollison flew the DH-88 Comet *Black Magic,* but failed to complete the race.

*Roscoe Turner and Clyde Pangborn's Boeing 247 in which they claimed
second place in The MacRobertson Trophy Air Race. Displayed in
the National Air & Space Museum, Washington, D.C.*

The British entry, the DH-88 Comet *Grosvenor House* (G-ACSS) was the outright winner completing the race in less than three days (seventy-one hours to be exact); it was flown by Flight Lieutenant C.W. Scott and Captain Tom Campbell Black, who also won the first prize of £10,000. The DH Comet is noted for being one of the first aircraft with a stressed skin construction, a retractable undercarriage, variable-pitch Ratier propellers (not constant speed) and an enclosed cockpit, setting the standard for future aircraft to come. The outright winning DH-88 Comet is on display in the Shuttleworth Collection Museum at Old Warden in Bedfordshire, UK.

Coming in second was the Dutch crew in a Douglas DC-2 named *Uiver* (PH-AJU) which was flown by K. D. Parmentier, C. van Btugge Holland, J. J. Mol and B. Prins. They won the handicap section in 90 hours and 13 minutes.

An interesting side story is attached to the Dutch DC-2 *Uiver (Stork)*. During the race, it was crossing New South Wales in Australia at night and the crew became lost in a thunderstorm. Getting low on fuel, they elected to make a forced-landing near Albury. Hearing the plane overhead, local residents used their car headlights to mark a landing path on the racecourse for the DC-2. It landed safely apart from local residents having to pull the plane out of the mud on the following morning. The *Uiver* went on to finish the race coming in second. With thanks to the Albury community, the Dutch

Airline KLM, owners of the *Uiver,* made a donation to the Albury Hospital and gave the town's Mayor, Dutch nobility. A Douglas DC-2 is now being restored at Albury Airfield in NSW by the Uiver Memorial Community Trust, in memory of the *Uiver.*

The original DC-2 *Uiver* was lost in a fatal accident in Iraq on 20 December 1934, while en route to the Dutch East Indies. It was the first DC-2 to have a fatal crash with the loss of its seven crew and passengers.

The American pilots, Roscoe Turner, Clyde Pangbourne and Reeder Nichols flying their Boeing 247D (NR257Y) were placed third in the transport aircraft section after the Dutch DC-2 and the third overall position with a time of 92 hours 55 minutes, in their plane that was leased from United Airlines specifically for the race. It was retired circa 1953 and donated to the National Air & Space Museum in Washington, D.C., wearing the colours of United Air Lines. This Boeing 247 was the first production aircraft off the assembly line.

As for the fate of the MacRobertson Air Race trophy itself, it is believed to have been melted down for its metal as part of the WWII war effort.

Captain Tom Campbell Black

Captain Tom Campbell Black (1899-1936) was an English pioneer aviator and equestrian. He became a household name along with Charles Scott after winning the MacRobertson Trophy Air Race in 1934.

As a youngster, he was schooled at Brighton College before going to the Royal Navy College in Greenwich near London. He became a pilot with the Royal Naval Air Service before transferring to the RAF where he saw active service in WWI and gained the rank of Captain.

He moved to Africa in 1922 and with his brother they worked on a coffee plantation as its managers in Kenya. Tom Black's interest also included horse show jumping, horse racing and horse breeding. He became the chief pilot and managing director of Wilson Airways in Kenya when it was formed in 1930. He also formed a friendship with aviatrix Beryl Markham in Kenya when he became her instructor. In 1932, he resigned from the airline and returned to England to become the personal pilot to horse breeder Lord M. Furness. Two years later in 1934, he won the MacRobertson Air Race with Charles Scott, as mentioned above.

He was severely injured at Liverpool Airport in a ground taxiing collision with a RAF bomber when he was struck by the bomber's propellers; he died from his injuries soon after.

Charles W. Scott

Flight Lieutenant Charles W. Scott (1903-1946) was educated at the historic public Westminster School attached to Westminster Abbey in London, England; it dates back to the 14th century.

Charles Scott went to British Guiana to work on a sugar plantation in 1920 as his first employment but returned to England after eighteen months and joined the RAF in 1922. He received a short service commission as a pilot officer and went through the ranks to become a Flight Lieutenant. In 1926 he left the RAF and returned to civilian life where he turned to making record flights as a pilot flying on various trips around Australia with the Queensland & Northern Territory Aerial Services, later shortened to QANTAS, now Australia's international airline.

Scott claimed three record flights between England and Australia; the first was in April 1931 when he delivered a de Havilland DH.60 Moth, arriving in Darwin in nine days 4 hours and 11 minutes. His second record flight was made in the opposite direction, back to England flying another DH Moth bought by his backer Lord Wakefield, in which he returned to Australia to claim his third record. For these three record-breaking flights he was awarded the Air Force Cross. Along with Captain Tom Black, he crewed the DH.88 Comet in the MacRobertson Air Race, which they won, as mentioned previously.

Charles Scott managed Cobham's Flying Circus for a while before competing in other air races. He also spent time ferrying aircraft across the North Atlantic and was a factory test pilot for de Havilland Canada flight testing newly built Mosquitos and giving type-conversion instruction to new Mosquito pilots. After the war, in a depressed state he chose suicide; a sad end for such an adventurous pioneer pilot.

The Bendix Air Races

The American, Paul Mantz (1903-1965) was a movie stunt pilot and race pilot who bought the North American P-51 Mustang named *Excalibur III* as surplus government property, with which he used to enter several air races including the Bendix Air Races in 1946 and 1947. The cross-country Bendix races had been postponed due to WWII and resumed in 1946. The Mustang came in second in 1948 flown by Linton Carney and in 1949 it came in third flown by Herman Richard 'Fish' Salmon (1913-1980) a barn-stormer, race pilot and later a test pilot for Lockheed.

Famed stunt pilot Paul Mantz, owned and flew this Mustang in the Bendix Air Races before selling it onto Captain Charles Blair who flew it across the North pole.

Paul Mantz had the Mustang's wings converted to 'wet wings' to enable a larger fuel load to be carried allowing him to fly non-stop from the USA's West Coast to Cleveland, Ohio for the start of the Bendix Race. He claimed a coast-to-coast speed record both ways in his Mustang in 1947.

Paul Mantz sold Excalibur III to airline pilot Captain Charles Blair who also made record flights in the plane including the transpolar flight across the Arctic in 1951 (see section 9 – Arctic Aviators). The Merlin engine-powered P-51 Mustangs were the planes of choice for several air racing pilots and P-51 Mustangs won the four post-WWII Bendix races.

Reno Air Races

Most aviation enthusiast today will be familiar with the Reno Air Races but less familiar with its full title of STIHL National Championship Air Races. It is an annual event organised by the Reno Air Race Association (RARO) since 1964 and dubbed 'the fastest motor sport on Earth'. It was initially held at the Sky Ranch airfield with its 2,000 feet airstrip. However, with the closure of Stead Air Force Base at Reno, Nevada in 1966, it was opened as a public airfield and renamed Reno Stead Airport.

The racing program consists of 2½ days of pilot qualifying races followed by 4½ days of pylon racing around the closed, ovoid circuit of three miles

(4.8 km) for the Formula One and biplane contestants and eight miles (13 km) for the faster jet pilots and the unlimited class aircraft. Pilots enter one of the six classes depending on their aircraft's performance and reach speeds up to about 500 mph (800 km/h). It is truly a spectator sport with the thrill of fast airplanes roaring past the public stands at 500 feet viewed by the 250,000 people who attend the races. And of course, it would be a far more exhilarating experience for the pilots too!

Many famous race pilots have flown the Reno Air Races including one of the top race pilots, Darryl Greenamyer.

Darryl Greenamyer

The American, Darryl Greenamyer (1936-2018) was a well-known pilot on the American Air Race circuit. He flew with the USAF Reserve before becoming a Lockheed test pilot flying their SR-71 aircraft. He entered the Reno Air Races in the unlimited class and had his first win in 1965 and went on to become the third most successful Reno Air Race pilot. He acquired an ex-WWII Grumman Bearcat which he had converted with the help of his engineering friends back at Lockheed. Better streamlining was achieved by using a smaller cockpit canopy, wings of shorter span, a larger four-blade propeller and a special mix of high-octane fuel, etc, which all helped to increase the Bearcat's top speed. With his converted Bearcat, Greenamyer increased the speed record for piston-engine aircraft to 483 mph (777 km/h) breaking the FAI Class C-1 record set thirty-years previously by the German Messerschmitt Me 209 in 1939, flown by the German pilot, Fritz Wendel. Greenamyer's record has since been eclipsed by Lyle Shelton also in a Bearcat in 1989 and later in 2017, by Steve Hinton in his highly modified P-51 Mustang. The National Air Race was won six times by Greenamyer in his brightly-painted, yellow Bearcat, which is now a museum exhibit in the Udvar-Hazy Center.

The Last Great Air Race

The Last Great Air Race as it was known, was flown in 1953 from London Heathrow Airport to Christchurch International Airport in New Zealand. It was also known as the London to New Zealand Air Race.

The race was held in two sections, the speed and the handicap sections. The speed section was flown by five English Electric Canberra jet-powered bombers, three from the RAF and two from the Royal Australian Air Force. The winning plane was an RAF Canberra PR.3 WE139 flown by Flight

The 1969 record-breaking Bearcat flown by Darryl Greenamyer in which he won several races and claimed a world speed record. The brightly-coloured Bearcat is now on display in the Udvar-Hazy Center.

This RAF Canberra won the speed section of the race covering over 12,000 miles. Note the map on the fuselage side depicted the route flown by this aircraft. The RAF Hendon Museum, London UK, displays this Canberra.

Lieutenant Roland (Monty) Burton AFC (1918-1999) and his navigator, Lieutenant Don H. Gannon DFC (1923-2006) both from 540 Squadron RAF. They flew a total distance of 12,270 miles (19,750 km) at an average speed of 495 mph (797 km/h) to win the Harewood Gold Cup and the prize of £10,000, which they donated to the RAF Benevolent Fund. Their time en route was twenty-three hours and 51 minutes, a record time which still stands today as of 2022. This winning RAF Canberra is on display in the RAF Museum Hendon, in London.

The handicap section was won by a Douglas DC-6B operated by the Dutch airline KLM in a flying time of forty-four hours and 29 minutes. A Vickers Viscount from BEA came in second in the handicap section flown by Captain Baillie and his crew. A New Zealand Air Force Handley-Page Hastings was withdrawn from the race at Ceylon, now known as Sri Lanka.

The Harewood Gold Cup was named for the Christchurch suburb of Harewood, which was the original name for the city's International Airport, where the race ended.

Several other races were held in Europe and America during the early year of pioneering aviation, all to encourage the growth of aviation and improve aircraft performance.

16 – The Record Makers & Breakers

Faster, Further and Higher

Since the beginning of flight, pioneer aviators have aimed to fly faster, further and higher. With the advancement of aircraft performance over the years, records for speed, distance, endurance and altitude have continually been made and broken. As record-making pilot Cliff Tait aptly stated, "records are made to be broken". A few of these pioneering record-making pilots are listed below.

Ferdinand Delagrange

The French pioneer aviator, Ferdinand Leon Delagrange (1872-1910) was one of the first pioneer aviators. He was born in Orleans, France and was schooled at the Ecole des Beaux-Arts studying sculpturing; some of his work was presented in several exhibitions in Paris.

The Voisin brothers built their first airplane, a Voisin 1907 biplane which was bought by Delagrange after it made its first flight at Bagatel on 30 March 1907, flown by Gabriel Voisin. It was their first aircraft sale which established their aircraft manufacturing business, one of the world's first. The Voisin 1907 became a very successful early French aircraft, which Delagrange used to gain many records gradually raising the speed and distance travelled by those early pioneering aircraft. He entered several air race meetings in France, and also attended the *First Flying Meeting* in England held at Doncaster from 18-23 October 1909.

On 8 July 1908, Therese Juliette Peltier (1873-1926) became the first woman in the world to make a flight in a fixed-wing aircraft when she flew with Delagrange as his passenger, when Peltier visited Turin in Italy to make demonstration flights.

Ferdinand Delagrange was killed when his plane crashed at Bordeaux, France on 4 January 1910. Such were the hazards faced by the early pioneer pilots in their frail machines.

Maurice Prevost

The first aircraft to exceed 100 mph (160 km/h) was a Deperdussin Monocoupe flown by the French pioneer pilot, Maurice Prevost (1887-1952) when he entered the Gordon Bennett Trophy race on 28 September 1913. At the time, he would have been the fastest man on earth! The plane was the first type to be built with a monocoque fuselage covered with plywood, appearing in 1911. A monocoque fuselage has a load-bearing surface skin-covering, which supports the internal structure of the fuselage.

It was mentioned earlier, Maurice Prevost was the winner of the first Schneider Trophy air race held on 16 April 1913 in his Deperdussin at a mere 45.71 mph (73.56 km/h).

The Key Brothers

The two brothers, Algene Key (1905-1976) and Fred Key (1909-71) became interested in aviation at the end of the First World War. In the 1920s they joined the new breed of barnstorming pilots calling themselves the Flying Key Brothers. During the Depression years, their local airfield at Meridian in Mississippi was about to be closed and the Key brothers decided to make an endurance record flight to help publicise the airfield and keep it open.

They had previously gained a long-endurance record which was soon eclipsed by another pilot, which stood at 533 hours. To gain back their record, they organised a second flight using a borrowed Curtiss Robin J-1 Deluxe from its owner William H. Ward Jr., which was named Ole Miss.

Two previous attempts at reclaiming the record were thwarted by problems shortly into the flights. However, on the 4 June 1935, they departing from Meridian Airfield in Mississippi and remained airborne for a record breaking 653 hours and 34 minutes, returning to Meridian Airfield 27 days later on 1 July. They flew a distance of 52,320 miles (84,200 km) all in the vicinity of Meridian, equal to more than two circuits around the world. They were able to stay airborne with food supplies dropped down from the support plane (another Robin) through a hatch in the cabin roof of the Ole Miss.

Air refuelling was accomplished in a similar manner via a hose from the support plane using a valve designed to cut the fuel flow when it became detached. A modified version of this valve is now used on all military air refuelling aircraft.

During the flight, the Robin's Wright J-6-5 Whirlwind 165 horsepower engine consumed at total of 5,500 imperial gallons (25,003 litres) of fuel at 8.4 gallons per hour and 250 imperial gallons (1,136 litres) of oil. Engine maintenance and lubrication was possible by using the walkways attached to each side of the engine. The job of looking after the engine went to Fred due to his smaller body size creating less drag, while the aircraft's speed was reduced to 80 mph (130 km/h). The two brothers shared the flying and the single bunk atop the ferry fuel tank in the cabin and had to contend with day and night flying through all weather conditions including thunderstorms.

Their flight gained the publicity the brothers had hoped for and to honour their achievements, the airfield was renamed, during their flight, as Key Field. It is still in operation and is known today as the Meridian Regional Airport.

The Key brothers were the first to use VHF radio in a plane in place of the HF radio, which caused too much static. Having the radio enabled them

This Curtiss Robin J-1 Deluxe was used by Algene and Fred Key to reclaim the endurance record in 1935. A Curtiss Robin was also used by Wrong-Way Corrigan on his trans-Atlantic trip in July 1938. The Key Brother's Curtiss Robin is shown here in the National Air & Space Museum, Washington, D.C.

to request food and supplies to be delivered to them in flight. Ending their record-breaking flight, they were welcomed back by an enthusiastic crowd of 35,000 local people.

Both Algene Key and Fred Key became bomber pilots in WWII and both completed their tours of duty without coming to any harm and they were both rewarded with medals for their war service. Algene Key rose to the rank of Colonel before retiring from the USAF in 1960. Returning home to Meridian, he became the local Mayer in 1965 for a short time, and also the Manager of the Meridian Municipal Airport from where their endurance record breaking flight was held.

In 1955, Fred Key flew into what is now Washington's Dulles Airport to donate their fully restored Curtiss Robin *Ole Miss* to the Smithsonian's National Air & Space Museum in Washington, D.C.

Rolland Garros

The Frenchman, Eugene A.R.G. Garros (1889-1918) commonly known as Roland Garros, was a pioneer air race pilot and flight record maker. In 1909, Rolland Garros learned to fly in a Demoiselle monoplane and gained his pilot licence in July 1910. He competed in several air races from 1911 in his Bleriot XI and came in second on the Paris to London and return air race. Garros claimed an altitude record of 12,960 feet (3,590 m) on the 4 September 1911, but this record was eclipsed a year later by Phillip von Blanche from Austria on 6 September 1912. Garros then reclaimed the record by climbing to 18,410 feet (5,610 m).

He made the first non-stop flight across the Mediterranean Sea from Saint-Raphael in the south of France to Bizerte in Tunisia on 23 September 1913. During the flight, he had engine problems twice in his Morane-Saulnier G monoplane but was able to keep the engine running to a safe landing in Tunisia with only a few minutes' worth of fuel remaining. The flight had taken seven hours and 53 minutes with a fuel endurance of eight hours.

Apart from his record-making flights, he also joined the French Army in 1914 as one of the first World War One pilots flying reconnaissance flights before becoming a fighter pilot, as we saw earlier in section 13.

Howard Hughes

The eccentric, American millionaire businessman, Howard Hughes (1905-1976) was introduced in section 12 – The Circumnavigators, for his world record flight. The Hughes Aircraft Company built two aircraft of interest here.

The first one was his Hughes H-1 Racer, which he designed in conjunction with Richard Palmer and Glen Odekirk; it first flew in September 1935.

It was a single-engine airplane of advanced design for its time with retractable undercarriage, aerodynamic streamlining including flush riveting, and a low wing of 25 feet (7.6 m) span with wing fillets. The H-1 was powered by a Pratt & Whitney R-1535 radial engine of 700 horsepower, fine-tuned to produce 1,000 hp for air racing. On the 13 September 1935, Howard Hughes made the maiden flight of his H-1 Racer and also claimed a world speed record (for land planes) on the same flight at 352 mph (566 km/h) over a course of 3 km at Santa Ana in California. At the end of his record flight, his plane was out of fuel and he made an off-airport, dead-stick landing causing minor damage to his aircraft. His plane was repaired with wings of greater wingspan attached at 31 feet 9 inches (9.68 m) making it more suitable for long-distance flights. He gained a transcontinental time-record when he flew the 2,490 miles (4,000 km) between Los Angeles and Newark, New York in 7 hours, 28 minutes and 25 seconds on 19 January 1937. The record flight was the last flight made by Howard Hughes, although other pilots flew the Hughes Racer.

Howard Hughes tried to sell the type to the USAAC but they were not interested in the design claiming it was unsuitable for their requirements. However, WWII fighters had a strong resemblance to the H-1 with their radial engines, retractable undercarriage and aerodynamic refinements.

It should be mentioned, a Macchi M.C.72 gained the speed record for seaplanes at 440.7 mph (709.2 km/h) in October 1934, a speed greater than Hughes' landplane record. The Hughes Racer was presented to the Smithsonian Museum in 1975 and now resides in the National Air & Space Museum in Washington, D.C.

The Hughes Aircraft Company also built the world's largest flying boat, the Hughes H-4 Hercules, also known as the Hughes Flying Boat or more commonly as the *Spruce Goose* due to it being built mostly of spruce wood. It still remains the world's largest wooden aircraft and also the largest flying boat, intended as a trans-Atlantic US military transport during the Second World War. However, it was too late to be placed in service and it only ever made one flight, flown by Hughes and his crew, just a few feet off the water at Long Beach, California on 2 November 1947. The *Spruce Goose* was stored in a special climate-controlled hanger until after the death of Howard Hughes when it was then acquired by the Aero Club of Southern California who leased it to the Wrather Corporation for public display near the passenger liner *S.S Queen Mary* at Long Beach. In 1993, the

Spruce Goose made the long trip to its new owners, the Evergreen Aviation & Space Museum at McMinnville in Oregon. In 2001, the museum opened its doors allowing the public to again see this very iconic, one-of-its-kind aircraft.

Jacqueline 'Jackie' Cochrane

'Jackie' Cochrane (1906-1980) must rank as the most outstanding female aviatrix of all time with her many accomplishments, service to the aviation industry and the aviation records and medals she has achieved.

A true pioneer woman pilot and business executive, she was elected to be the director of the Women's Flying Training Detachment, which soon merged with the Women's Auxiliary Ferrying Squadron led by Nancy Love to form the Women Airforce Service Pilots of WWII (known as the WASPS). They flight-tested service aircraft (from trainers to bombers) and ferried them from the factories to their bases within the US during WWII.

Jackie Cochrane is also noted for the following:

- She claimed several flight records including the first female pilot to exceed the speed of sound (supersonic flight) in a Royal Canadian Air Force, North American Sabre 3 jet on 18 May 1953.

- She was the first woman pilot to fly above 20,000 feet and set an altitude record of 56,072 feet in a Northrop T-38 Talon in October 1961.

- Flying a Lockheed F-104C Starfighter, she claimed three world speed records; 1,429 mph over a 25-km course, a speed of 1,302 mph over a 100-km course and a speed of 1,135 mph over a 500-km course.

- She was the first female to take-off and land on an aircraft carrier

- The first female pilot to fly a bomber across the North Atlantic in 1941 and the first woman to pilot a jet aircraft across the North Atlantic.

- In the early 1960s, she flew the Goodyear Blimp accompanied by its captain, R. W. Crosier.

In addition to her numerous record flights and achievements, Jackie Cochrane was awarded numerous medals and honours including the DSM, DFC (three times), the Legion of Merit and the Gold Medal from the FAI.

A side view of the Hughes H-1 Racer flown by Howard Hughes. A long-term resident on display in the National Air & Space Museum, Washington, D.C.

A nicely preserved Northrop Talon, similar to the plane in which Cochrane set two FAI records. This one is displayed in the Pima Air & Space Museum, Tucson, Ar.

A North American Sabre similar to the one in which Cochran became the first female pilot to exceed the speed of sound on 18 May 1953 at Rogers Dry Lake in California. This aircraft is parked outside in the Pima Air & Space Museum, Tucson, Ar.

She was also inducted into various 'Halls of Fame' and became the director of Northwest Airlines in the USA, to name a few of her achievements. Cochrane was truly a pioneer aviatrix with many accomplishments and awards for her contributions to the growth and progress of aviation.

Flights over 5,000 Miles

The first non-stop flight to exceed 5,000 miles was flown by Russel N. Boardman (1898-1933) and John Polands (1901-1985) on 28-30 July 1931. The flight from New York's Floyd Bennett airfield to Istanbul in Turkey was made in a Bellanca Special J-300, a high wing monoplane named *Cape Cod*. The flight lasted for 49 hours and 20 minutes to cover the great circle distance of 5,011 miles (8,065 km).

A single-engine Vickers Wellesley bomber claimed a new world long-distance record in 1938, when it flew from Egypt to Australia, a distance of 7,162 miles (11,526 km).

In recent years, long-range passenger jets routinely remain airborne on their 14-15-hour flights, much to the boredom of their passengers. However, over half a century ago on 1-2 October 1957, a TWA Lockheed Constellation flew from London to San Francisco, covering a distance of around 5,350 miles (8,610 km) taking 23 hours and 19 minutes. This record still stands for the longest duration of a piston-engine powered airliner on a non-stop passenger flight.

Captain William Odom

The Beech V-35 Bonanza was one of the first civilian light aircraft to be built after the end of World War II and the Bonanza has proved to be very popular ever since. The prototype V-35 made its first flight on 22 December 1945 and was superseded by the straight-tail Bonanza A36 version, which is still in production.

In 1949, the fourth Bonanza prototype off the production line, pictured here, made a non-stop record run from Honolulu, Hawaii to Teterboro in New Jersey on 7-8 March 1949, with former US Army Air Corps Captain William 'Bill' Odom (1919-1949) at the controls. Flying non-stop for 36 hours and 2 minutes he covered a total distance of 4,957 miles (7,977 km) at an average ground speed of 146.3 mph (235 km/h). He not only covered the distance from Hawaii to the US West Coast but he continued flying to cross the whole USA as well! A long-range fuel tank was installed in the rear of the cabin to extend the Bonanza's range. A total of 225 imperial gallons (1,030 litres) of fuel was consumed on the trip to Teterboro with about 10 imperial gallons (45 litres) of fuel remaining, good for a further twenty minutes flying time or about 72 miles before the tanks ran dry. The total cost of the fuel for the flight was US$75.00; that sounds very cheap compared to today's prices!

Apart from other long-distance flights, William Odom also flew around the world twice in a Douglas A-26 Invader in 1947, however these flights were not recognised as FAI records. He also entered a few air races. While flying a North American P-51 Mustang in the Thomson Trophy Air Race he lost control of his plane and it fatally crashed on 5 September 1949.

The record-breaking Beech V-35 Bonanza was donated to the Smithsonian plane museum, however, it was borrowed by Peter F. Mack, which he renamed as the *Friendship Flame* and flew it around the world visiting thirty countries. The Bonanza was restored in 1975 with a polished metal finish and red trim. It is on display again in the Udvar-Hazy Center, Chantilly, Va.

This record-making V-tail Bonanza flew non-stop from Hawaii to Teterboro in New Jersey in 1949. It is seen here in the Udvar-Hazy Center, near Washington D.C.

The Truculent Turtle

The US Navy claimed a distance record flight in excess of 5,000 miles in September 1946. They chose the third Lockheed P2V-1 Neptune off the production line for the record flight. The Neptune was a maritime long-range aircraft used by the US Navy and other navies of the world after entering service in the early 1960s.

The reason for the flight was to publicize the US Navy's new, long rang, anti-submarine aircraft. It was also used to study the physiological effects of the crew on lang-range patrol flights and the use of pressure pattern navigation, a method developed in the 1920s for airship navigation and for use by WWII long-range bombers and the piston-engine transports used by the airlines before the advent of jet transport aircraft.

The Neptune used for the flight was named by the Navy as the *Truculent Turtle*. On 9 September 1946, it departed from Perth, Western Australia bound for Washington D.C., but had to land short at Columbus, Ohio due to getting low on fuel. Flown by a crew of four, the 11,235 miles (18,080 km) flight lasted for 55 hours 17 minutes equivalent to two and a half days of non-stop flying, travelling across the Pacific Ocean and the USA. The Neptune was equipped with extra long-range fuel tanks to extend its normal range of 4,110 miles (6614 km) and was devoid of its normal military armament. A more streamlined nose cone replaced the normal cone to reduce the front-area drag. At the time of its flight, it claimed the record for the longest point-to-point distance flown for a non-refuelled flight by a piston-engine aircraft.

The US Navy's Neptune record was held for forty years before it was eclipsed in 1986 by the Rutan Voyager which remained airborne for a total of nine days during its non-stop circumnavigation flight (mentioned in section 12 – The Circumnavigators).

The *Truculent Turtle* used for the record flight has been placed on display in the National Museum of Naval Aviation in Pensacola, Florida.

Max Conrad

Maxwell Arthur Conrad Jr., (1903-1979) was an American pilot who was noted for making long-distance record flights. Known as the *'Flying Grandfather'* he claimed nine FAI records in the light aircraft category during the 1950-60s. Not only did he gain nine aviation records, he also gained ten children with his wife!

During his early flying days, he operated his own Fixed-Base Operator (FBO) business from 1929 before getting into long-distance record flying. He made several trans-Atlantic flights in his single-engine Piper PA-24 Comanche 250, notably from Casablanca in Morocco to Los Angeles and also from Casablanca to El Paso in Texas, a distance of 7,668 miles (12,340 km) from 2-4 June 1959. In March 1961, Conrad made a west-bound flight around the world in his twin-engine Piper PA-23 Aztec covering a total distance greater than the length of the Equator, which he crossed twice during the flight.

The US Navy's Truculent Turtle is now presented in the National Museum of Naval Aviation. It is displayed suspended from the ceiling with several US Navy fighter aircraft displayed below. This photo was supplied courtesy of the National Museum of Naval Aviation in Pensacola, Florida.

Other long-distance flights include a record flight from Cape Town to St. Petersburg in Florida in his Piper PA-30 Twin Comanche on 26 December 1964 covering a non-stop distance of 7,878 miles (12,678 km). Conrad won the Harmon International Aviation Trophy for his flight from Casablanca in 1964.

Fastest Trans-USA Flight

The fastest trans-continental flight was achieved by a Lockheed SR-71A Blackbird flown by Lieutenant Colonel Ed Yielding as pilot and his RSO Lieutenant Colonel J.T. Vida on 6 March 1990. Departing from their Air Force base at Palmdale, California they headed off-shore to gain altitude and refuel from a Boeing Stratotanker at the start of their record-breaking run from overhead Oxnard on the south California coast to Dulles International Airport near Washington, D.C. The aircraft achieved four National Aeronautics Association speed records en route and three FAI records. Colonel Yielding and Colonel Vida covered the trans-continental distance of 2,405 miles (3,869 km) in one hour, 7 minutes and 53 seconds. To put this into perspective, Yielding and Vida returned to California on a United Airlines Boeing 767, a flight that lasted for five hours. Their average speed on the record flight was Mach 3.3 or 2,124 mph (3,419 km/h). At the end of this record-setting flight, the Blackbird (61-7972) was retired from service and donated to the Smithsonian's Udvar-Hazy Center plane museum near Dulles Airport where it is now displayed. This same Lockheed Blackbird had previously achieved the fastest time between New York and London in one hour, 54 minutes.

This same Blackbird also claimed a speed record between London and Los Angeles covering the distance of 5,446 miles (8,764 km) in three hours, 47 minutes.

Colonel Yielding was a pilot of exceptional experience. He earned an engineering degree and joined the USAF as a combat pilot flying McDonnell Phantoms for eight years and then spent time as a Lockheed Blackbird instructor/pilot and test pilot. He also spent time over the Soviet Union observing Russian submarine movements at their bases on the Barents Sea coast and he also flew special air missions in the Grumman C-20 Gulfstream III aircraft. After 23 years of active service, Colonel Yielding retired from the USAF and flew for Northwest Airlines logging over 13,000 hours of flight time. In 2007, he was inducted into the Alabama Aviation Hall of Fame.

This Lockheed Blackbird is the fastest plane to cross the USA covering the distance in one hour and seven minutes. At the end of its record-breaking trip to Washington Dulles Airport, it was placed on display in the Udvar-Hazy Center.

Cliff Tait

From high-speed flight, we now turn to low-speed flight. New Zealander, Cliff Tait had earlier flown his Victa 115 single-engine light aircraft around the world solo. Returning home, he gained his Commercial Pilot Licence and ferried aircraft to and from New Zealand breaking several records in the process. His records include:

- A double crossing of the Tasman Sea from Christchurch to Sydney, Australia and return in a Fletcher top-dressing aircraft, in one day.

- Regaining the London to Auckland record first set by Jean Batten in her Percival Gull in 1936 at just over eleven days and then claimed by Judith Chisholm in her Cessna 210 in 6½ days. Cliff gained the record in 4 days 7½ hours.

- 28 speed records mostly between London and Auckland. Nineteen of these records remain unbroken.

Dick Smith

Australian pilot, Dick Smith (1944-20?) is another pilot with time on his hands. He is noted for several long-distance and circumnavigation flights around the world. His list of flights includes the:

- First solo helicopter flight across the North Atlantic in his Bell JetRanger III, in August 1982.

- First solo helicopter flight around the world, in 1983.

- First helicopter to land at the North pole, in 1987.

- First world circumnavigation landing at both poles in a de Havilland Twin Otter, in 1989.

- First non-stop balloon flight across Australia, 1993.

- First east to west circumnavigation by helicopter, in 1995.

Flight Over Mount Everest

Douglas Douglas-Hamilton, the 14th Duke of Hamilton (1903-1973), an RAF Squadron Leader with RAF Lieutenant David McIntyre, both from RAF 602 Squadron, made the first flight over the world's highest mountain, the

29,029 feet (8,848 m) Mount Everest on 3 April 1933 during their Houston–Mount Everest flight expedition. They were accompanied by an observer and cinematographer, Lathem Blacker and Sydney Bonnett respectively. They were flying in two separate planes, a Westland Wasp PV-6, the prototype of the Westland Wallace bomber and a modified Westland PV-3. Both planes were flown by the RAF between the two wars as general-purpose biplanes.

The Australian adventurer/balloon pilot, Chris Dewhurst and three crew were the next people to fly over Mount Everest in October 1991, after being granted permission by the Nepalese Government.

It is interesting to note, commercial airliners avoid flying over Mount Everest and the surrounding Himalayan mountains due to the height of the mountain peaks. A pressurization failure on the plane would prevent the plane descending to a low enough altitude of 14,000 feet where oxygen masks would no longer be required.

Nesterov and Lincoln Beachey

The Societe Anonyme des Etablissements Nieuport was started in 1909 by Edouard Nieuport as one of the world's pioneering aircraft manufacturing companies. The Nieuport IV was a monoplane initially powered by a Gnome Omega rotary engine of 50 horsepower and later with a 100-horsepower engine. It was built for pilot training and sport pilots and used by various military forces as an observation plane, particularly by the Russians who also built them locally under licence at the Dux factory near Moscow. It was in a Nieuport IV.G that a Russian military pilot, Lieutenant Peter Nikolayevich Nesterov (1887-1914) performed the world's first aerobatic loop on 27 August 1913. He was promptly arrested and held for ten days on the charge of risking government property; however, the charge was soon rescinded and replaced with a promotion.

The Russian test pilot Valery Pavlovich Chkalov (1904-1938) later performed 250 loops within 45 minutes.

The American pioneer aviator and barnstormer, Lincoln Beachey (1887-1915), was the first pilot in North America to perform a loop, doing so in November 1913. He flew a Curtiss Pusher biplane built with a re-enforced structure to take the stresses of aerobatic flight and powered by a Gnome rotary engine which continued to run when the plane was inverted. His plane received the name of 'Little Looper'.

Lincoln Beachey was born in San Francisco, California, and by the age of eighteen he was flying powered airships and received his airplane pilot license

This Curtiss Model D Headless Pusher was the first US aircraft to perform a loop, flown by Lincoln Beachey. This is the original plane, now housed in the Hiller Aviation Museum, San Carlos, Calif.

in 1910. He was recognized by Orville Wright and other fellow aviators as *'the world's greatest aviator of that era'*. He was employed by Glen Curtiss as his demonstration pilot and he gave many public exhibitions including aerobatic flights; he also claimed an altitude record, all of which brought him world-wide fame.

Lincoln Beachey died on 14 March 1915 while flying his routine at San Francisco in his latest aircraft. Pulling out from a loop, the plane's wings were overstressed and folded upwards and Beachey crashed into the water. A sad end to a very skilled pilot of the pioneering days of aviation. He is largely forgotten these days but his plane, the *'Little Looper'* lives on for the memory of Lincoln Beachey, in the Hiller Aviation Museum at San Carlos, south of San Francisco.

17 – Mail Planes

The Pioneer Mail Pilots

The aeronaut, John Wise (1808-1879) made the world's first air mail delivery for the US Postal Service in his hot air balloon, the *Jupiter* on 17 August 1859, when he delivered 123 letters from Lafayette to Crawfordsville in Indiana. He was the pioneer of what was to become a major, world-wide industry in air mail and parcel delivery services, which started many years later in 1918 in the USA.

The US Air Mail Service

From 23 September 1911, the first of several experimental postal delivery flights were made in the USA sponsored by the government. Recognised as the world's first official air mail pilot, Earle L. Ovington (1879-1936) flew the first air mail from Long Island, New York a short distance of six miles to Mineola using his own aircraft, a Bleriot XI monoplane built in America. This was the start of experimental air mail flights in the USA, which were initially operated by the US Army Air Service (USAAS) until 12 August 1918 when the US government officially established an air mail service operated by the US Postal Service. The air mail was first delivered by surplus WWI de Havilland DH.4 aircraft, until they were eventually replaced by special purpose-built single-engine aircraft, as we will see below.

The first official flight was made on 15 May 1918 by Lieutenant George Leroy Boyle, a newly qualified pilot from the US Army Air Service, flying one of their six Curtiss JN-4 Jenny biplanes. However, his first flights were not very successful when he flew south from Washington, D.C., instead of flying north to New York via Philadelphia; his flight ended in a crash-landing in a field about twenty-miles from Washington. On his second attempt he again went far off-course, resulting in his termination of service as an air mail pilot.

Nearly 7,000 Curtiss Jenny's were built during WWI for training pilots of the US Army Air Corps and Britain's Royal Flying Corps. Post war, they became very popular civilian training aircraft and owner/pilot aircraft. A Curtiss Jenny was the type used for the first official American air mail flight. The Jenny featured here, was part of the first batch of twenty-five Jenny JN-4D's sent to the Army Air Corps and was bought by the Smithsonian in November 1918, just after WWI ended.

Unlike Boyle who failed right from the start, Lieutenant James Edgerton (1896-1973), also fresh out of flight school, successfully flew the first air mail from New York to Washington, D.C., the reverse route attempted by Boyle, on the same day. Edgerton made fifty-two flights as an air mail pilot covering over 7,000 miles, the most miles flown by any of the Army postal pilots and logging over 100 accident-free flight hours. The following year he was promoted to be the Post Office's Chief of Flying Operations.

The first air mail flights between New York and Chicago began on 17 December 1918 and was extended through to San Francisco on 8 September 1920 to complete the Transcontinental Air Mail Route, the longest route crossing North America from New York to San Francisco via Chicago. The route was pioneered by well-known pilots, Eddie Rickenbacker and Bert Acosta.

When the Post Office handed over the routes to private companies, the western portion of the Transcontinental route became known as Contract Air Mail route 18 (CAM 18) starting on 8 September 1920. The western portion between San Francisco and Chicago was operated by the Boeing Air

Transport Company and at the same time, the eastern half of the route from Chicago to New York was allotted to National Air Transport. From 1 July 1924, the full trans-continental route was flown both day and night. By the end of 1930, a total of thirty-four CAM routes had been established covering the USA. However, due to the Air Mail Scandal of 1934, all CAM route contracts were cancelled with the air mail routes taken over by the USAAC until private companies filled the contracts leading to the start of the new airline industry.

Airports were relatively scarce in those early years of flight. However, from the 1920s onwards, airports began to flourish across North America, allowing the air mail routes and later, the airlines to expand. Newark Airport close to New York was at one time the world's busiest airport until LaGuardia Airport opened on 2 December 1939, which was situated much closer to New York City.

The early aircraft had minimum flight instrumentation, which at times made it a very risky occupation having to fly in all weather conditions and then later, also at night, typically flying at low altitude. Despite the dangers of their profession, there was no shortage of civilian barnstormer pilots and pilots returning from World War I who were willing to take on the risk, although many died as a result of pushing themselves and their planes beyond their limits. For example, in 1918 the first year of operation, the US Postal Service employed forty pilots but by the end of the first year of operation, half of the pilots had been lost in accidents, mostly weather related and some by engine failures. In 1928, three-engine planes were introduced capable of carrying greater loads and new air routes were gradually added to the list virtually covering all of North America.

Many company air mail pilots became household names; one pilot of special interest was James (Jack) Knight (1892-1945). He was the first airmail pilot to fly the night mail, flying from North Platte in Nebraska to Chicago on the night of 22 February 1921. He continued flying the route after his relief pilot failed to arrive at their meeting point to swap planes. By continuing on further, Jack Knight helped to prove the Air Mail Service could survive without having to transfer mail to trains at night-time, thus saving the Postal Service money. Congress approved money for the service to continue, and Jack Night became the USA's most famous pilot before Charles Lindbergh appeared on the scene.

Charles Lindberg was also an air mail pilot starting on 15 April 1926 flying the CAM 2 route between Chicago and St. Louis and return for the Robertson Air Service, where he served as their chief pilot assisted by three other pilots,

Thomas P. Nelson, Harlan 'Bud' Gurney and Philip R. Love. He survived several crashes without serious injury and made four parachute jumps, twice as an airmail pilot, earning him his nick-name of Lucky Lindy. His time as an air mail pilot was relatively short. A year later in May 1927 he shot to world fame after making his famous trans-Atlantic flight to Paris.

One of the more notable air mail pilots whose name is still around was Elrey Borge Jeppesen (1907-1996). He is best remembered for his Jeppesen navigation charts, known as Jepp Charts to present-day pilots. They originated from his notes of useful information on en route landmarks, which he gave out to fellow-pilots to help them navigate cross-country.

Most people will associate Bill Boeing with his plane-building Boeing Company, but he did do a very short stint as an airmail pilot. Flying with Eddie Hubbard in one of his own aircraft, a Boeing Model C-700, they flew the world's first international airmail flight on 1 March 1919 when they flew the airmail route from Seattle, Washington State over the boarder to Vancouver in Canada.

Most air mail pilots were men, but there was at least one exception. Katherine Stinson (1891-1977) was the fourth woman in the USA to gain a pilot licence. She was a true pioneering, record making, exhibition pilot and was the first woman pilot to fly the air mail for the US Postal Service, from Chicago to New York. She inspired her brothers to form the Stinson Aircraft Company; although now long out of business, Stinson airplanes are still favoured by pilots of vintage aircraft today and many Stinsons are found in aviation museums.

The first jet airliner to carry air mail was the Canadian built Avro Canada C-102 Jetliner prototype, which flew the first airmail by jet aircraft in North America from Toronto, Canada to New York. The Jetliner was the sole flying prototype which made its maiden flight on 10 August 1949. It could have been the world's first jet airliner but was beaten into the air by the de Havelland Comet a couple of weeks earlier. The jetliner was scrapped in 1956 with no production models built.

Pan American Airways were awarded the Foreign Air Mail route 5 (FAM 5) flying between Miami, Florida and the Panama Canal Zone. The South American Grace Shipping Company merged with Pan Am to form the new company of Pan American-Grace Airline, or Panagra as it was known, who flew the FAM Route 9 from Panama down the west coast of South America commencing their service on 12 July 1929. The services from the USA were later expanded to cover all over South America. The attached photograph shows a Fairchild FC-2 built in 1927. This was one of the first Fairchild's to be used by Panagra in South America on the FAM 9 route. It was displayed in the Smithsonian Museum in Washington D.C.

Across the Atlantic in Europe, the pioneer pilot Claude Graham-White was the first pilot to carry mail in an airplane in England, in 1910.

The French Aeropostale

The Frenchman, Pierre-Georges Latecoere (1883-1943) was a pioneer aviator and industrialist. He was the founder and pioneer of aircraft manufacturing during WWI with his company based in Toulouse in southern France, now home to one of the world's major aircraft builders, Airbus Industrie. After the war, he established the air mail company, Compagnie General Aeropostale, more commonly known as Aeropostale. On 25 December 1918, the company's pioneering flight from Toulouse to Barcelona in Spain, was flown by Rene Cornemont (1891-1978) and accompanied by Latecoere in a Salmson biplane, one of the many Salmsons built by his company for the French Army.

Latecoere used a fleet of Breguet 14 planes for his air mail and passenger service to Morocco in North Africa from September 1919. This was extended to Dakar in Senegal on the west coast of Africa by 1925, stopping at several cities en route. From Senegal, the mail was shipped across to Brazil, where it was transferred back onto the South American division of Aeropostale aircraft and flown to the main base in Buenos Aires for onward delivery to various destinations in South America.

By 1927, the company had been sold to Marcel Bouilloux-Lafont who lived in South America. In 1932, Aeropostale merged with other companies and was eventually named as Air France, now the international airline for France.

Saint Exupery

Antoine Marie Jean-Baptiste Roger comte de Saint Exupery (1900-1944) known simply as Saint Exupery for short, was a French aristocrat, writer, poet, journalist and pioneer mail pilot. He was as well-known for his flying as he was for his writing. As a writer, one of his most famous works was the book, *The Little Prince,* which was translated in over 300 different languages. Another book of his was the *Wind, Sand and Stars,* based on his experience when his plane was forced down in the Sahara Desert; another book was called, *Night Flight.* As a pioneer aviator he flew as an air mail pilot between France and North Africa for the French, Lignes Aeriennes Latecoere which later became Aeropostale. He was appointed as manager of the Cape Juby office in Southern Morocco in 1927. Any air mail pilots forced down in the desert were frequently kidnapped by Nomadic tribesman and held for ransom; Saint Exupery became adept at negotiating with the tribesmen for their release, for which he received the French Legion of Honour medal.

In World War Two, he managed to join the Free French Air Force despite being too old to be accepted, plus he had some mobility issues caused by more than one plane crash. He flew reconnaissance patrols in P-51 Mustangs based on the island of Corsica, south of France. On 31 July 1944, he was shot down and fatally crashed into the Mediterranean Sea. Parts of the undercarriage off his Mustang were found on the sea-bed off the coast of Marseilles in the year 2000 and recovered in 2003; the parts are now displayed in the National Air and Space Museum of France.

Jean Mermoz

Jean Mermoz (1901-1936) took three attempts to gain his pilot licence before succeeding in 1921. Like many pioneer pilot of his time, he became a military pilot in 1922, after joining the French Air Force where he was sent on operations to Syria in Western Asia. In 1924, back in France, he met Saint Exupery in Toulouse, and became a pilot for the Lignes Aeriennes Latécoère (Aeropostale) flying the Casablanca to Dakar route in 1926. During one of his many trips across the western end of the Sahara Desert, an engine failure resulted in a forced landing where he was held hostage by rebel Tuaregs (semi-nomadic people from the north-west Sahara region) until freed due to the efforts of Saint Exupery. Five other pilots were less fortunate and killed.

The first commercial airmail flight was flown across the South Atlantic from Saint-Louis in Senegal to Natal in Brazil on 12-13 May 1930, by pilots Jean Mermoz, Jean Dabry and Leopold Gimie. The 1,900 miles (3,058 km) flight taking 19-hours and 35-minutes flown by two Latecoere 28 seaplanes, carrying 270 lb (122 kg) of mail on each flight. One plane acted as a backup in the event of a forced landing on the sea by Jean Mermoz, who received the credit for the flight. His Latecoere 28 was named the *Comte de La Vaulx*, for Henry de La Vaulx (1870-1930), a balloonist with other interests in the early days of aviation including being a cofounder of the Aero Club of France and also a cofounder of the FAI.

Jean Mermoz was posted to South America and became the chief pilot for Aeropostale and pioneered the route to Santiago in Chile becoming their first pilot to cross the Andes Mountains. Mermoz also pioneered night flying in

South America flying the unmarked route between Natal in Brazil and Buenos Aires in Argentina.

Mermoz and Saint Exupery both became prominent Aeropostale pilots flying for the new airline of Aeropostale Argentina, a subsidiary company of Aeropostale formed in the late 1920s with Saint Exupery as the company director and Jean Mermoz as the chief pilot. Saint Exupery flew the companies first commercial flight on 1 November 1929 and he recorded his South American experiences in his book *Night Flight*, mentioned above, which was also made into a movie.

Mermoz was a true pioneering pilot having crossed the Sahara Desert, the South Atlantic and the Andes and also introduced night flying in the Aeropostale operations. Unfortunately, he met his demise during his 28th South Atlantic crossing in December 1936. Mermoz and his four crew members were flying a four-engine Latecoere 300, named the *Southern Cross* on their weekly, westbound trip from Dakar. He returned to Dakar shortly after take-off with a mechanical problem and departed soon after when minor maintenance was performed. Four hours into the flight, the last radio contact was made with Mermoz. The loss of the plane was believed to be caused by poor aircraft maintenance and possibly losing a propeller, which damaged the aircraft leading to a fatal ditching in the ocean, although sabotage has also been mooted as a possible cause.

He was dubbed, 'France's Lindbergh'. His memoirs from letters to his family was published many years later, titled *Pioneer of the Sky*.

Henri Guillaumet

Henri Guillaumet (1902-1940) was a French aviator well-known as a pioneer of new route-finding and as an Aeropostale pilot flying across the South Atlantic Ocean. A regular service was established in July 1929 from Buenos Aires to Santiago in Chile. Henri Guillaumet (1902-1940) was a regular pilot flying the dangerous route across the 20,000-feet high Andes Mountains.

It was on his 92nd flight on 13 June 1930 when he made a forced landing on a glacier due to bad weather near Laguna el Diamante, in Mendoza. He abandoned his Potez 25 mail plane and walked for a week through snow-covered terrain back to civilisation where on the 19 June he was found by a 14-year-old boy, who took him back to his village where he was given shelter, suffering from the effects of hunger and exposure.

At one stage, Henri Guillaumet was appointed as managing director of Air France. However, at the start of WWII on 27 November 1940, Guillaumet was flying a four-engine Farman F.220 airliner across the Mediterranean Sea with Jean B.P.E. Chiappe (1878-1940) who had been appointed as the High Commissioner for France to Lebanon. However, they were shot down by mistake by an Italian fighter involved in a battle near Sardinia; Guillaumet and Chiappe with three other passengers were all killed.

Henri Guillaumet, Saint Exupery and Jean Mermoz all died while doing what they loved, flying planes.

Walter Varney & Leon Cuddeback

Walter Thomas Varney (1888-1967) was an early US pioneer aviator, WWI pilot and an airline executive. He joined the US Signal Corps in WWI as a pilot in the Aviation Section. Post-war, he set up his own aviation school and air taxi service in northern California and in October 1925, when the Air Mail Act awarded contracts to private companies, Varney Air Services became one of the first companies to receive an airmail contract route. He was the founder of Varney Airlines on 28 March 1926 and he based his company in Boise, Idaho. His company flew the air mail route C.A.M. 5 from Pasco, Washington to Elke, Nevada via Boise, Idaho using a fleet of six Laird Swallow mail planes.

His company's first mail flight was inaugurated on 6 April 1926, flown by Leon Cuddeback from Pasco to Elke in Nevada, a distance covering 445 miles (715 km) with 207 lbs (94 kg) of mail over some of the USA's most rugged, back-country terrain. The return flight was flown by pilot Franklin Rose, who flew off-course in bad weather and crashed-landed out in the wilds. Rose spent the next two days walking out to civilisation carrying his 95 lb (43 kg) sack of mail.

It was soon discovered their Laird Swallows were underpowered with their Curtiss OX-5, 90 horsepower engines; these were replaced with the more powerful Wright J-4 engines of 200 hp. The Swallows were eventually replaced by Stearmans, Boeing Model 40s and the Boeing 247, etc, as time went by with company expansions and mergers. Varney Airlines merged with Boeing Airlines in 1931 and in turn, Boeing Airlines and other companies merged to form United Airlines. Continental Airlines was also founded by Walter Varney after he established Varney Speed Lines in 1932, which also merged years later with United.

Leon Dewy 'Lee' Cuddeback (1898-1984) learned to fly in 1921 at the Varney School of Flying at San Mateo, California and then became an instructor for the school and then chief pilot for Varney Air Lines while

Walter Varney concentrated on the business side of his airline. Cuddeback flew the first scheduled civilian air mail flight on CAM 32 on 6 April 1926. In 1924, Leon Cuddeback was made a Lieutenant Colonel and in 1942 he was promoted to Major in the US Army as an air transport specialist.

A Laird Swallow OX-5 restored in the colours of Varney Airlines, one of the first Air Mail airplanes in 1926. Now displayed in the Museum of Flight, Seattle.

The Laird Swallow mail plane was designed by Buck Weaver and built by the Swallow Airplane Manufacturing Company in Wichita, Kansas. The Swallow made its maiden flight in 1920 and was followed by a production run of fifty Swallow OX-5 version and many more variants of the type. It had a wingspan of 32 feet 6 inches (10 m), an all-up weight of 2,200 lbs (1,000 kg) and a cruise speed of 85 mph (137 km/h) over a maximum range of 450 miles (725 km).

The Swallow pictured here was built in 1928 as a Swallow Commercial (or OX-5 Swallow) and later restored with a Continental W-670 radial engine of

Some authorities claim the start of the Postal Service CAM routes as being the start of the airline industry, with Leon Cuddeback as the first American airline pilot who flew the first US airline flight. However, the first airline to operate was the St. Petersburg-Tampa Airboat Line in Florida, which operated briefly in 1914, several years before Varney Airlines commenced operating in 1926.

220 hp. It is finished in the colours of Varney Airlines, although this aircraft was not used by them. After its restoration, it was flown by Buck Hilbert in 1976 for United Airlines 50th Anniversary. It is now displayed in the Museum of Flight in Seattle, Washington.

Boeing Model 40

The Boeing Model 40 came about due to a competition from the US Postal Service for a new aircraft type with a Liberty engine to replace the aging de Havilland DH.4's. Boeing designed and built the Model 40 prototype powered by a Liberty engine, which made its first flight on 7 July 1925. It was bought by the Postal Service; however, the contract for new aircraft went to the Douglas Aircraft Company for their Douglas M-2 design.

The Boeing Model 40 design languished until late 1926, when it was revived at the instigation of air mail pilot Eddie Hubbard (mentioned above) powered by a Pratt & Whitney R-1690 Hornet engine and redesignated as the Model 40B. It became Boeing's first commercial aircraft to go into full production, with a total of seventy-five built between 1925 and 1932 as a mail plane with seats for two passengers (later with four passengers) plus 1,200 lb (549 kg)

A full-size replica of a Boeing Model 40B mail plane is on display in the Museum of Flight in Seattle.

264

This Douglas M-2 mail plane was built in 1926 and flown by Western Air Express. It is seen here in the Udvar-Hazy Center.

of mail. The Pratt & Whitney Hornet engine of 525 hp gave the Model 40B a cruise speed of 125 mph (200 km/h) and a range of 535 miles (860 km).

As can be seen in the photo overleaf of the Model 40B replica, the hatch for the mail bin is located between the engine and the passenger cabin which has two seats in tandem with a door for each seat; the forward door is slightly ajar. Typical of its day, the pilot sat in an open cockpit, placed further to the rear. This example is presented in the colours of the American Railway Express with the C.A.M. 18 logo on the rear fuselage. It is shown here displayed in the Museum of Flight in Seattle.

Incidentally, a Boeing Model 40 was the first aircraft to fly with a rubber de-ice boot, now common on many aircraft. The test aircraft was flown by Wesley L. Smith in March 1930, to test a rubber boot designed by William Geer, which was mounted on a wing strut. Smith and Geer were both WWI Army Air Service pilots and Smith later became an air mail pilot.

Douglas M-2

In 1918, one of the first type of mail planes was the de Havilland DH.4 biplane, mentioned earlier. The Douglas Aircraft Company designed the Douglas Air Mail One, based on the Douglas O-2, but it never went into production. A few refinements to the design, evolved into the Douglas M-2, which allowed for a single passenger to occupy the front cockpit during mail delivery flights. Western Air Express was the forerunner of Western Airlines and they used Douglas M-2's on their Contract Air Mail routes between Los Angeles, Las Vegas and Salt Lake City starting in April 1926. The Douglas mail planes proved to be reliable and popular with the pilots who flew them.

The Douglas M-2 pictured here, was built as an M-4 but was later reverted to an M-2 version. It was flown by Western Air Express from June 1927 until 1930 when it was involved in an accident. It changed hands several times over the years before being used again by Western Airlines for display in 1940.

Pitcairn Mailwing

Aircraft designer, Agnew Larson designed the Pitcairn Mailwing as a development from the Pitcairn PA-4 Fleetwing II, which was followed by several other mail planes and sport plane designs. Of the 106 Pitcairn Mailwings built, most were used by the US Postal Service and flown by Eastern Air Transport, later Eastern Air Lines, flying the routes of C.A.M. 19 through the USA's eastern states.

The Mailwing was a single-engine and single-seat biplane with a fabric covered steel-tube fuselage and wooden wings with a span of 33 feet (10.06 m). Power was provided by a Wright J-5 engine developing 220 horsepower giving the plane a maximum speed of 131 mph (211 km/h).

The Mailwing prototype (NC-2895 pictured here) made its maiden flight in 1927 and was taken on by Eastern Air Transport who used it extensively until 1934, when it was converted to carry passengers in private ownership; it also spent some of its life in the crop-dusting role. After suffering an accident, it was bought by Eastern Air Lines' employees led by John Halliburton who had it restored and presented to Eastern Air Lines president, Captain Eddy Rickenbacker, who donated it to the National Air & Space Museum in 1957 after its restoration where it is now on display.

Stearman Senior Speedmail

This Stearman 4EM Senior Speedmail was designed by Lloyd Stearman and built by his company, Stearman Aircraft. The Speedmail featured here is one of forty-one built. The prototype first flew in 1930 as a development from the Stearman C3, having a larger fuselage and a choice of engines with increased

The prototype for the Pitcairn PA-5 Mailwing is now on show in the National Air and Space Museum, Washington, D.C.

A Stearman 4EM Senior Speedmail exhibited in the Canada Aviation & Space Museum at Ottawa, Canada

power to carry heavier loads. The Stearman 4's were built as single-seat mail planes and personal transports in various versions.

Retired from flying the Air Mail routes, some were used in the crop-dusting roles and others as private planes. This Speedmail, pictured here, was operated by Canadian Airways Ltd., and is now owned by the Canada Aviation & Space Museum in Ottawa.

Northrop Alpha

The Northrop Alpha made its maiden flight in 1930 as a mail plane with seating for six passengers in the enclosed cabin forward of the open cockpit. Progress in building more reliable engines and an increase of knowledge in aerodynamics produced improved aircraft design and resulted in the USA's first production aircraft with all-metal, semi-monocoque construction and wings built with multiple cells, stressed skin and with wing-root fillets. It was also the first commercial aircraft to have rubber de-icing boots on the wing's leading edges and tailplane as standard equipment. The wingspan was 41 feet 10 inches (12.8 m) on the Alpha and the same wing design was later used on the Douglas DC-2 and DC-3 airplanes. Power was provided by a Pratt & Whitney R-1340 Wasp radial engine of 420 horsepower propelling the Alpha along at a cruise speed of 145 mph (233 km/h). It had quite an excellent range of 1,650 miles (2,650 km).

The Northrop Alpha of interest here was registered as NC11Y and was first flown by Transcontinental & Western Air (TWA) on 20 April 1931, from San Francisco to New York making thirteen stops along the way. Transcontinental & Western Air (TWA) officially changed its name, but kept the initials, to Trans World Airlines in 1950. In 1975, TWA re-acquired their original Northrop Alpha, which is now on display in the National Air Space Museum in Washington, D.C.

Dassault Falcon 20

Air mail was the domain of the Postal Service of each country using the established airlines for its delivery. However, in 1973 a new player came onboard. A private company was founded by Frederick W. Smith, now well-known as Federal Express (or FedEx) which pioneered the overnight parcel delivery service in the USA using a fleet of thirty-three Dassault Falcon 20 business-type jet aircraft. The aircraft were converted to carry cargo with loading through an enlarged side door and with a strengthened floor. The

*A Northrop Alpha with TWA markings hangs suspended in the
National Air & Space Museum in Washington, D.C.*

*This Dassault Falcon pioneered the overnight express parcel delivery service
for the FedEx Company. It was donated to the Smithsonian in 1983 on
its retirement and is now displayed in the Udvar-Hazy Center.*

Dassaults allowed FedEx to deliver parcels overnight to anywhere in the USA through its cargo hub in Memphis, Tennesse. The company has grown over the years to become world-wide with bases in several countries and their aircraft fleet now consists of a variety of full-size jet transport cargo aircraft. FedEx acquired the Flying Tiger Line in 1988 to become the largest airline devoted solely to carrying cargo.

The days of open-cockpit biplanes flown by the pioneer pilots at a height of 200 to 500 feet above ground level are now long gone; these days, air mail pilots can enjoy the comfort of a warm and pressurised flightdeck, flying in the flight levels with modern radio navigation equipment to guide them along their route.

18 – Aircraft of the Fledgling Airlines

The Pioneer Airlines

The modern airline industry that we are all familiar with today, originally started with the pioneer airlines that developed out of the Air Mail industry, using 'first-generation' single-engine light aircraft followed by aircraft built specifically for the fledgling airlines, such as the Fokker Trimotor, Ford Trimotor, Junkers J-52, etc. The next generation of airline aircraft started with the 'world's first modern aircraft' the Boeing 247, quickly followed by the Lockheed Electra, Douglas DC-2 and the famous DC-3 that helped many airlines to get off the ground, or should I say, become established?

Initially, the first airline was flown by airships not airplanes. The German company DELAG (German Airship Travel Corporation) was the world's very first passenger airline which used a fleet of twelve airships to carry passengers between ten of Germany's largest cities, starting in 1909. The company's first airship was the LZ-6, previously operated by the German Army after its maiden flight on 25 August 1909. It was destroyed in a hanger fire the following year. Over a five-year period until 1914, DELAG carried 34,000 passengers, attended to by male flight attendants; the world's first flight attendant was Heinrich Kubis, employed from March 1912.

The international airline industry started with the British airship, the *HM Airship R*-34 which was the first aircraft of any type to carry passengers across the North Atlantic from England to New York and return when the service started on 2 July 1919. As an aside, it is purported the New York's Empire State Building, built in 1930, was built specifically as a base for airships, with the intention the visiting airships would moor onto the mast at the top of the building. However, it was never used by airships.

To continue with the modern airline industry… One of the greatest advances in airline aircraft, was the introduction to service of the Boeing

Model 307 Stratoliner in July 1940 with the American company, Pan Am. The Boeing 307 was significant for being the first passenger plane with pressurisation, which would have been greatly appreciated by the early airline passengers, but is now taken for granted on modern airliners as a necessity for flying in the upper flight levels, or at any altitude above 14,000 feet. And of course, we must not forget the important role played by the flying boats which made the first long-range international flights possible by fixed-wing aircraft, particularly across the North Atlantic Ocean.

After the Second World War ended, we saw the age of modern passenger aircraft crossing the North Atlantic on a regular basis. The 23 October 1945, saw the restart of passenger flights by the American Overseas Airline using Douglas DC-4 piston-engine airliners, which cruised across the Atlantic at a low altitude of around 8,000 feet or so; the aircraft were not pressurised. Unlike today's modern non-stop flights across the Atlantic by the jet transports, the piston-engine types required fuel stops en route at places such as Gander in Newfoundland and Shannon in Ireland before the final stage to Hurn Airfield at Bournemouth; London Airport, now known as London Heathrow, opened later on 25 March 1946. The Douglas DC-4 was replaced by the DC-6 and DC-7 airliners. The Lockheed Constellation was the last of the big piston-engine airliners, powered by four Wright R-3350 twin-row radial engines, before being replaced by the aforementioned jet transport aircraft.

The first of the jet transports to appear on the scene was the British-built de Havilland Comet airliner. It made its first passenger flight on 2 May 1952 flying from London to Johannesburg, flown by Captain A.M. Majendie; it was the pioneer plane of jet transport. The Comet was followed by the first of the Boeing jet transports, the Boeing 707 which was introduced into service by Pan American World Airways on 26 October 1958. Twelve years later in January 1970, saw the introduction of the first Jumbo Jet, the Boeing 747, which pioneered the mass transportation of passengers, making airline flights affordable to most of the travelling public. The Russian Tupolev 144 supersonic airliner entered service on 31 December 1968 for a short career, just before the Aerospatiale/BAC Concorde was introduced for the more discerning passenger, cutting the trans-Atlantic crossing times in half.

In 1914, the world's first scheduled domestic airline (using airplanes, not airships) was launched as the St. Petersburg-Tampa Airboat Line, in Florida. It flew the short 18-mile route between these two cities in 23 minutes using a Benoist XVI flying boat; the journey by rail took about five hours or more. However, it was the first of the pioneering airlines to operate a scheduled fixed-wing air service, which started on 1 January 1914 running two return flights each day. The public were allowed to bid for the first airline ticket and travel on the inaugural flight. Abraham C. Pheil, the former Mayor of St. Petersburg won the bid at US$400 to become the first passenger on a scheduled airline.

The three Benoist biplane flying boats were each powered by a single pusher engine of 75 horsepower. The first scheduled flight was flown by the airline's chief pilot, Antony (Tony) Habbersack Jannus (1889-1916) to become the world's first (fixed-wing) airline pilot. He had previously flown a Benoist biplane in 1 March 1912 at St. Louis Airport, Missouri, from which Captain Albert Berry had made the first 'attached type' of parachute jump from a fixed-wing airplane, in the USA, one of the first men to make a jump.

Tony Jannus was born in Washington, D.C. At the age of 21 years, he watched an air show in Baltimore, Maryland, which aroused his interest in aviation and with his brother Thomas, they both took flying lessons and qualified to become test pilots for the pioneer aircraft builder, Thomas W. Benoist, in St. Louis, Missouri in 1911. With the St. Petersburg-Tampa Airboat Line using Benoist aircraft, Jannus was appointed as the airline's chief pilot.

After the airline ceased operations, Jannus went to work for the Curtiss Aeroplane Company as a test pilot in July 1915. He flew the Curtiss JN-3 prototype which was developed into the famous Curtiss JN-4 Jenny. He was posted to Russia to train Russian pilots in combat flying, using Curtiss airplanes and while flying with two Russian crewmen, near Sevastopol in present day Crimea, the engine developed a malfunction and they crashed into the Black Sea. All three crewmen were killed and the body of Tony Jannus was never found. A sad end to the life of the world's first airline pilot.

The St. Petersburg-Tampa Airboat Line in Florida, was the pioneer of airlines and the start of the globalised airline industry, but it only survived for four months until the 5 May 1914 and failing to turn a profit, it was closed down.

In contrast, KLM Royal Dutch Airline was founded in October 1919 in Amsterdam, which has been the airline's base ever since. KLM's first flight was made on 17 May 1920 with a de Havilland DH.16 flown by Jerry Shaw on the airline's first route when he flew from Croydon Airport, London to Amsterdam. Its long-range international flights commenced in 1924 with flights serving Jakarta in the Dutch East Indies and in 1930, the island of Curacao in the Dutch West Indies was included. Its fleet of aircraft have included the Fokker F.VII, DC-2, -3, -4, -5 and -6 before moving into the jet-age with the Douglas DC-8. It was the world's first airline to use the Douglas DC-2, which was slightly smaller than its more famous DC-3 replacement.

The airline is still in business today serving destinations in seventy countries and is the world's oldest airline and one of the few airlines to have survived such a long life-span. The airline's name of 'KLM' are the initials for its name in Dutch, the Koninlijke Luchvaart Maatschappij, (very hard to pronounce unless you speak Dutch) which translated to English gives its name of Royal Aviation Company. The Dutch Queen Wilhelmina bestowed the title of Koninlijke (Royal) when the company was founded.

Back in North America, on 23 May 1926, Western Air Express made claims to be the world's first airline to fly the 'first scheduled airline passenger service' and it also became the first profitable airline. However, it must remembered, the St. Petersburg-Tampa Airboat Line in Florida had claimed the first scheduled airline flight in 1914, albeit for only a few months. Western's first route was a regular air mail run, CAM 4, covering a distance of 650 miles (1,050 km) from Salt Lake City to Los Angeles. The first airline passenger on a Western Air Express scheduled service was Salt Lake businessman, Ben Redman, who had made the first airline reservation, therefore he was credited as the company's first passenger. He was accompanied by J.A. Tomlinson, another Salt Lake City resident. These first two passengers sat on the mail bags with a box-lunch for their meal; no cabin service in those early days. Their pilot was C.N. 'Jimmy' James, the regular pilot on the air mail run.

Charles Lindberg was the chief pilot for the Robertson Aircraft Corporation, previously known as the Robertson Air Service, which merged with the Colonial Air Transport and Southern Air Transport to become American Airways, later renamed as American Airlines.

The Transcontinental Air Transport (TAT) was initially known as The Lindbergh Line. It was formed by Charles Lindbergh and his financiers to become a major player in the USA's pioneering airlines. The company's Ford Trimotors carried 8-10 passengers per flight. The first flight departed the US east coast on 7 July 1929 bound for the west coast alternating with trains at night time, cutting the travel time to less than 48-hours, much quicker than the 72-hour train-only journey. Lindbergh was the Captain on the first flight with his wife Anne acting as cabin crew (hostess). The airline was short-lived, on 25 October 1930 the company merged with Western Air Express (which had an Air Mail contract) to form Transcontinental & Western Air (TWA). The name was later changed to Trans World Airlines, which survived as a major American airline until 2001.

National and Varney would later become important parts of United Air Lines (originally a joint venture of Boeing and Pratt & Whitney). Eastern Air Transport, later Eastern Air Lines grew out of Pitcairn Aviation.

Juan Terry Trippe (1899-1981) was also an early air mail company owner and went on to establish Pan American Airways (PAA) founded on 14 March 1927, flying mail from Key West in Florida across to Havana in Cuba. It eventually grew into the international airline as Pan American World Airways until its demise in 1991.

Western Air Express, Varney Air Lines, American and United all used the Stearman 4-EM Senior Speedmail at some stage in their operations, stemming from its popularity as a mail plane. A photo of a Stearman 4-EM appears in the previous section on mail planes.

Most of the early American airlines emerged from air mail companies. However, Delta Airlines emerged not from flying the mail, but from the crop-dusting company of Huff-Daland Dusters Inc, which was founded on 2 March 1925 to become the world's first crop dusting company. The Duster was the first aircraft designed specifically to spray the cotton crops to eradicate the boll weevil infestation of the 1920s. The Huff-Daland Duster was developed from the Huff-Daland Petrel 5, which were built for the US Navy. A fleet of eighteen Dusters were built with two examples now remaining of which one is now displayed in the Udvar-Hazy Center. It is of a unique design, being devoid of flying or landing wires as normally found on biplanes; instead, it has truss-bracing between its cantilever wings. Its vertical fin and rudder is

A Huff-Daland Duster, in the Udvar-Hazy Center. Delta Airlines originated from the Huff-Daland crop-dusting company, not from an air mail company.

also unusual being combined as one unit and having a vertical leading edge, Mooney aircraft style.

With new airlines becoming established, Huff-Daland expanded its business interests and turned to flying passengers and mail between Dallas, Texas and Jackson, Mississippi using Travel Air 6000 aircraft. From Huff-Daland's crop-dusting and passenger service, Delta Air Services was formed on 3 December 1928 and named after the nearby delta of the Mississippi River. Passenger-carrying operations began on 17 June 1929 and in 1945, the Company was renamed to Delta Air Lines.

Many small airline operators throughout America sprang up over the years, some merging with the larger established airlines as mentioned above; however, many of the small and also large airlines have succumbed to failure for various reasons.

On the other side of the world, Australia's international airline, QANTAS was established a year after KLM, on 16 November 1920 by Sir Hudson Fysh, Sir Fergus McMaster and Paul McGuinness at Winton, Queensland. Their first aircraft was a surplus Avro 504K followed by other aircraft such as the RAF BE.2e, de Havilland DH.9's, DH.50s and DH.86's. It became an international airline in 1934 using Short S.23 Empire flying boats on the Darwin to Singapore route. It is the world's third oldest operating airline by date but the second oldest airline to have remained in continuous operation after KLM. The airline's name QANTAS is taken from its original name of Queensland and Northern Territory Aerial Services.

Pioneer Aircraft Manufacturers

Several aircraft manufacturing companies became established between the wars, building planes for the fledgling airlines. New types were coming on-line such as the Fokker F.13 and F.VII/3m Trimotor, Curtiss Condor and Ford Trimotor in America, Focke Wolfe 200 Kondor from Germany and various types from de Havilland in England. The British-built Handley-Page 42 was one of the largest biplanes ever to be built having four 550 horsepower Bristol Jupiter 9-cylinder radial engines (four engines were rare in the 1930s). It had a wingspan of 130 feet (39.6 m) and was flown by a crew of three and carried 38 passengers. However, only eight examples were built.

Anthony Fokker had a very successful aircraft company in Germany building many famous aircraft for the Imperial German Air Service. At the end of the war, he transferred his company to Holland in secrecy and manufactured aircraft mostly for civilian aircraft companies. During the 1920s and 30s, Fokker was the world's largest and most successful aircraft company.

Junkers F.13

The Junkers F.13 was a very early passenger transport aircraft, designed by Otto Reuter for the Junkers Aircraft and Motor Works company in Germany. The Junkers F.13, had an outer covering of corrugated aluminium alloy skin, common to many Junkers Aircraft of that era. The two pilots sat in an open cockpit with the four passengers enjoying the relatively better comfort of a closed cabin; they were also the first to have the use of seatbelts in an aircraft.

The F.13 entered service in 1921 flown by Junker's own airline, the Junkers Luftverkehr RG, which merged into Germany's national airline, Luft Hansa in 1926, (a previous company to Germany's present-day national airline, Lufthansa, which was established as a new company in 1953). The type was used by several other airlines, as well as being put to use as a bomber in WWII; the US Postal Service also found a use for it, however, it was retired before the start of WWII.

In later years, 2016 to be precise, the F.13 was reintroduced to production powered by a single Pratt & Whitney R-985 Wasp Junior engine. The new version of the F.13 was certificated and built with each having a $2.5 million price tag. But, I am digressing here.

Farman Goliath

The Farman F.60 Goliath was built by the Farman Aviation Works in France who built sixty Goliaths. It was initially designed as a bomber, but being too late for war service it was redesigned as a 12-seat passenger transport. The prototype was the first of about sixty Goliaths to be built making its maiden flight in January 1919. It was placed into scheduled service on 29 March 1922, first flying the Paris to Croydon, London route flown by the Campagnie des Grands Express Aeriens. It was the world's first long-distance international airline, pioneering passenger flights to several destinations throughout Europe.

The Goliaths were powered by two Salmson CM.9 radial engines of 260 horsepower each giving the Goliath a maximum speed of 110 mph (177 km/h). Looking very much like a railway carriage, it was of the usual biplane

An original Junkers F.13 is displayed in the Air & Space Museum in Paris, France.

configuration of that era with a wingspan of 86 feet 9 inches (26.4 m) and a maximum take-off weight of 11,905 lb (5,400 kg). The pilot sat in an open cockpit just visible in the photo between the two forward upper-wing support struts. Four of the twelve passengers were carried in an enclosed cabin forward of the cockpit and the remaining eight were seated in the rear cabin, although in 1919, a maximum load of twenty-five passengers were carried on a weight-to-altitude record flight reaching 16,732 feet (5100 m).

All that remains of the Goliath fleet is the fuselage of the third one built, named the *Isle de France*, registered as F-HMFU. This sole example is a museum exhibit in the Air & Space Museum in Paris, France.

Boeing Model 80A-1

The Boeing Model 80 biplane was one of the first airliners to be built by the Boeing Airplane Company for operation by its own airline, Boeing Air Transport, which was established on 17 February 1927; it was also used by other operators. They flew as twelve-eighteen passenger/mail planes on scheduled routes.

The prototype Model 80A made its maiden flight on 27 July 1927 and was soon upgraded to the Model 80A-1, powered by three Pratt & Whitney R-1690 Hornet radial engines developing 525 horsepower each. This version first flew on 18 July 1929 with seats for 18 passengers with the two-flight crew having the comfort of an enclosed flight deck. The wingspan was 80 feet (24.39 m) and the length of 56 feet 6 inches (17.22 m). Their maximum take-off weight was 17,500 lb (7,940 kg) with a cruise speed of 125 mph (201 km/h). Boeing chose a biplane layout to better cope with the smaller airfields

The Farman Goliath was built as a French bomber/passenger transport aircraft flying many routes around Europe. The photo shows the remains of the last Goliath, now displayed in the National Air & Space Museum in Paris.

A Boeing 80A-1, one of Boeing's first airliners, is now on display in the Museum of Flight at Seattle, USA.

and those at higher altitude on its routes. The Ford Trimotors and Fokker aircraft had already been replaced by high-wing monoplane layouts. In May 1930, Boeing Air Transport introduced the use of flight stewardesses on their aircraft, with the requirement they were all single ladies and registered nurses.

The Boeing featured here is the sole remaining, original Boeing Model 80. It was found in a dump at Anchorage Airport in Alaska in 1960 and returned to Seattle where it was restored for display in the Museum of Flight. In the top-left of the photograph is a DC-3, the next generation of airliners to arrive on the scene.

Fokker VII/3m Trimotor

Anthony Fokker's aircraft manufacturing company became well-established when he built fighter planes during WWI. After the war, he turned to building aircraft for the civilian market as the world's largest aircraft manufacturer during the late 1920s. His three-engine Fokker VIIa/3m airliners carrying from eight to twelve passenger were very popular with the fledgling European and North American airlines after it entered service during 1925. It also found favour with private individuals who used them on long-distance pioneering flights as we saw earlier in this work. However, a Fokker F.10, variant of the

F.VII was involved in a fatal accident in the USA and the Fokker fleet were soon replaced by the American-built Boeing and Douglas types with their stronger metal construction.

Fairchild FC-2

Pan American Airways were awarded the Foreign Air Mail Route 5 (FAM 5) flying between Miami, Florida and the Panama Canal Zone. The merger of Pan Am and the South American Grace Shipping Company resulted in the new company of Pan American-Grace Airline, or Panagra as it was known. The services from the USA were later expanded to cover all over South America.

Panagra expanded its fleet from the first Fairchild P-1 single-engine high-wing monoplane to include Ford Tri-Motors, Sikorsky S-43 flying boats and Douglas transports from the DC-2 through the DC-8 jet transports when the company merged with Braniff International Airlines on 1 February 1967.

Panagra used several Fairchild FC-2 aircraft and one of special interest to us here, although unconfirmed, is believed to be the first aircraft flown by Peruvian Airways on 13 September 1928 from Lima to Talara in Peru. It could also have flown one of the first international air mail flights between Lima and Guataquil in Ecuador.

This Fairchild FC-2 was presented by Panagra to the National Air & Space Museum, Washington, D.C., in 1949. The logo of Grace and PAA can be seen on the fuselage side.

Ford Trimotors

The Ford Trimotor was the first transport aircraft to be built in relatively great numbers, a total of 199 were built by the time production ended on 7 June 1933. It first appeared on the scene after its maiden flight on 11 June 1926, as the USA's largest aircraft flying for the fledgling airlines in the 1920s and was instrumental in establishing the USA's trans-Continental Airways System. The type was chosen by Pan American to establish its first international air route between Florida and Cuba. It was also used by many other airlines around the world and by private companies for executive transportation, from 1927 onwards. The Ford Trimotor was nick-named the *'Tin Goose'* due to its metal construction, a method first introduced to aircraft manufacturing by the German, Hugo Junkers.

The Ford Trimotors were flown in airline service with a flight crew of two plus a stewardess with eleven passengers. It had a length of 49 feet 10 inches (15.19 m) and a wingspan of 74 feet (22.56 m). Power was provided by three Wright J-6-9 Whirlwind engines of 300 horsepower each, giving a cruise speed of 107 mph (172km/h).

This 1929 Ford Trimotor 5-AT-B was once owned by Pan American Airways System. Note, its relatively small fin area with a larger rudder attached. It is on show in the San Diego Air & Space Museum in California.

Commander Richard Byrd chose a Ford Trimotor for the first flight over the South Pole on 27-28 November 1929. A Trimotor was used by Scenic Airways for Grand Canyon tourist flights and was still flying in 2011 and the Experimental Aircraft Association at Oshkosh have been operating two Trimotors for several years on site-seeing flights.

As a front-line airliner, the Ford Trimotors career was rather brief being replaced by the more modern twin-engine Boeing 247 and the Lockheed Electras and later still, by the Douglas DC-3 and other larger aircraft. However, it was not the end of the line for the Trimotor; it remained in service with smaller, third-level airlines carrying passengers and freight and it even saw service in WWII moving military supplies.

At least eighteen survive in private ownership or as museum exhibits; a Trimotor 5-AT-B, built in 1929 was restored by American Airlines and donated to the National Air & Space Museum in Washington, D.C. [See photo in section 10 – Antarctic Pioneers, Byrd's Antarctic Expedition]. The second Trimotor, displayed in the San Diego Air & Space Museum in California, is also a 5-AT-B model built in 1929.

Junkers J-52/3m Trimotor

The Junkers Ju 52/3m was derived from the single-engine Ju 52. The 52/3m made its first flight on 13 October 1930 and entered airline service with several European and South American airlines. They could carry up to seventeen passengers or three tons of cargo. During WWII, the German Luftwaffe used them, as did other air forces for transporting military troops, cargo and also as bombers.

One of its most obvious and unusual features was its outer skin covering made from corrugated duralumin metal. Junkers had pioneered this type of construction when they built their Junkers J.1, in 1916-17, the world's first all-metal aircraft. The Ju 52/3m was initially powered by Pratt & Whitney R-1690 Hornet radial engines and later by P&W R-1340 Wasp engines. Also, the German BMW and the British, Bristol Pegasus VI engines were used on some models. The Ju 52 had a relatively long service life, being in production from 1931 through 1952 when a total of 4,835 were built, making it one of Europe's most successful airliners at the time.

The Ju 52/3m pictured here was built in Spain by CASA as a 352-1 model. Germany's Lufthansa Airline used it for a while for promotional flights before it was passed on in 1987 to the RAF Cosford Museum

The RAF Cosford Museum displays this well-preserved Ju52/3m-CASA 352-1.

The Boeing Model 80, Fokker Trimotor, Ford Trimotor and Junkers Ju 52 mentioned above, represent the progression from the biplane configuration of the Boeing Model 80 to the high-wing layout of the Fokker and Ford Trimotors to the low-wing Junkers Ju 52. Also similar was the three-engine layout of these aircraft; three engines were required due to the relatively low power of aero engines of that era.

Boeing Model 247

The Boeing 247 is considered to be the world's first modern airliner, which made its maiden flight on 8 February 1933 and entered service soon after on 22 May, with the Boeing Air Transport Company.

The Model 247 introduced the concept of the standard layout for most modern aircraft that were introduced over the years that followed. It has an all-metal construction with retractable undercarriage, trim tabs, an autopilot, de-ice boots on the main wings and tailplane, a cantilevered low wing and twin engines. This basic airframe layout has been improved upon by advances in aerodynamic refinements and improved engine technology, which have been introduced over the years.

The Boeing 247 was the first twin engine aircraft capable of continued flight after an engine failure, now a requirement for all multi-engine aircraft in order to achieve certification. The Boeing 247 could maintain an altitude of 11,500 feet (3,500 m) on one engine at maximum all up weight. It was powered by Pratt & Whitney R-1340 Wasp radial engines of 500 horsepower each, driving variable pitch propellers. The Pratt & Whitney engines gave the 247 a higher speed than the Boeing P-12 fighters of the day and it had a very low landing speed for a twin-engine aircraft, down to 62 mph (100 km/h), therefore flaps were not installed.

Although the Boeing 247 was perfect in many ways, its carrying capacity of only ten passengers and a stewardess, soon made it too small as a potential plane for the growing airlines. Boeing built seventy-five, which were operated mostly by their own Boeing Air Transport company.

A Boeing 247D was flown by Roscoe Turner and Clyde Pangborn in the MacRobertson Air Race from England to Australia. This aircraft is now displayed in the National Air & Space Museum, Washington, D.C. Two other examples of the Boeing can be found in museums; one has been on display in the Canada Aviation and Space Museum on Ottawa, Canada since 1967. The second one is displayed in the Museum of Flight in Seattle, Washington State, arriving there in April 2016, all pictured within this work.

A well-preserved example of the first 'modern airliner', this Boeing 247 has returned home to Seattle where it was built, and placed on display in the Museum of Flight.

Lockheed Model 10 Electra

The Lockheed Electra was introduced after the Boeing 247, when it made its maiden flight on 23 February 1934. It was of the same layout as the 247 having twin-engines, low-wing, retractable gear and built of metal construction.

The Electra was designed by Hal Hibard (1903-1996) and Lloyd Stearman (1898-1975) who later established his own manufacturing company where he designed and built the well-known Stearman biplane trainer, a type still favoured by many owner/pilots today. The Electra was one of the first designs to be influenced by 'Kelly' Johnson (1910-1990) when he was a student at the University of Michigan. He later became the Chief Designer at Lockheed where he produced many, now-famous designs.

A Model 10E Electra was flown by Amelia Earhart on her attempted around-the-world flight in 1937. An Electra also flew the first North Atlantic commercial return crossing flown by Dick Merrill (1894-1982) and J. Lambie in 1937, for which they received the Harmon Trophy. It was favoured by several major airline operators in Latin America, Europe and of course, in the USA too. It was used by secondary airlines, charter operators and by other private companies for personal transport.

This Lockheed Model 10A Electra was one of three operated by Trans-Canada Airlines and later by the RCAF during WWII. In June/July 1967, it made a world circumnavigation flight in remembrance of Amelia Earhart, flown by Ann Pellegreno. It is now on show in the Canada Aviation & Space Museum, Ottawa, Canada.

The Electra 10 was powered by Pratt & Whitney R-985 Wasp Junior SB engines of 450 horsepower each driving Hamilton Standard constant-speed propellers. The introduction of constant-speed propellers greatly improved aircraft performance allowing the Electra 10 a cruise speed of 190 mph (306 km/h) and a range of 810 miles (1,300 km).

The Lockheed Electra 10A featured here was registered as CF-TCA (for Trans Canada Airways, its original owner); it was one of three Electras they operated. It was later owned by Lee Koepke from Detroit, Michigan and was used by Ann Pellegreno to circle the world in June/July 1967 following the Earhart Trail from Oakland, California and return, (see section 12 – The Circumnavigators). It is now housed in the Canada Aviation & Space Museum in Ottawa.

The Model 10 Electra was developed into the Model 12 and Model 14 as the Super Electra, which were used by the USAAF designated as the Lockheed C-36. Lockheed named its different models including the Electra, from the stars, planets and constellations, etc.

The Flying Boat Era

Flying boats have been mentioned briefly within this work in different sections. This section is devoted to the role played by the long-distance flying boats in establishing the early airline services, particularly across the Atlantic and Pacific Oceans in the 1930s. Their time in airline service was relatively brief and interrupted by WWII, although the military also used them to their advantage during the war. After the war, landplanes had progressed to flying longer distances and eventually replaced the old, lumbering flying boats.

Pan American Airways (PAA, later Pan Am) was founded in 1927 to become one of the largest international airlines based in the USA. Flying boats became an integral part of Pan Am's fleet in those early days of the airline. The Sikorsky S-38 and S-40 were introduced by the airline in 1931 opening up the South American services from their base in Florida. In 1937, their flying boats were operating across the North Atlantic to Europe from their Norfolk, Virginia base, typically stopping for fuel in Bermuda and the Azores Islands. From 22 November 1935, Pan Am commenced its proving flights westward across the Pacific Ocean from San Francisco, stopping at place such as Honolulu, Wake Island, Guam and Manila in the Philippines. The first passenger flight to Manila was inaugurated on 21 October 1936. Other destinations followed including flying mail-only flights to Canton in China and Hong Kong with Martin M-130 flying boats. Hong Kong and

Auckland in New Zealand were eventually added to their passenger routes.

The future Empire air routes to Cape Town in South Africa, were surveyed by Alan Cobham while flying a de Havilland DH.50F on floats. In June 1926, he also surveyed the route to Melbourne, Australia for which he received the Air Force Cross and a knighthood from HM King George V. Alan Cobham also surveyed other Empire routes to India and Cairo in Egypt using a de Havilland DH.66 aircraft owned by Imperial Airways.

Imperial Airways Ltd., commenced operations on 26 April 1924 on the London-Paris route using de Havilland DH.34 and later, Handley Page FH.W8f aircraft from 3 November that year. The company used a variety of aircraft on its international routes including Armstrong Whitworths, Vickers, Boulton & Paul, Supermarine and Bristols, etc. Imperial Airways also operated the Short Empire flying boats throughout Asia and Africa along their routes connecting the British Empire colonies. Having a shorter range than the American Clipper flying boats, they were unsuitable for the North Atlantic routes.

To overcome their short-range problem, Imperial Airway's Technical General Manager, Robert Hobart Mayo (1891-1957) put forward the idea of using a Short S.21 Maia flying boat with a pylon attached on top of the fuselage to carry the smaller Short S.20 Mercury, four-engine float plane, (yes, it had twin floats). Both aircraft used their power for the take-off and climb to cruise altitude and then separated with the Short S.20 Mercury crossing the Atlantic Ocean and the Short S.21 Maia returning to its base. Several experimental test flights were made to prove the concept would work. On 21 July 1938, with Captain Donald Bennett at the controls, the first Atlantic non-stop commercial flight was made carrying newspapers and mail flying from Foynes on the south-west coast of Ireland to Boucherville in Montreal, Quebec.

The Short S.21 Maia was a slightly enlarged version of the Short Empire flying boat. Imperial Airways were supplied with two aircraft for training their crews in preparation for passenger carrying flights, but before any progress was made the planes and their crews were acquired by the RAF when WWII started.

After Pan Am was established on its South American routes, it turned its attention to the lucrative North Atlantic route, dominated by the German airships and the luxury ocean-going passenger liners. After some trial flights starting on 5 July 1937 by Imperial Airways with their Short Empire flying boats and Pan Am's Sikorsky S-42, it was to be another two years before passenger services commenced. The 8 July 1939 saw the introduction of Pan Am's

Boeing 314 Clippers on their first scheduled North Atlantic run from the USA's east coast to Southampton via Newfoundland and Foynes on the west coast of Ireland.

At the time, the flying boats had a longer range than the landplanes but fuelling stops were still required on the long North Atlantic crossing. The Clippers offered a very luxurious first-class service and accommodation, for those who could afford it. However, WWII intervened two months later and the service was curtailed. In later years, an airport was built at Shannon, just across the Shannon River from Foynes, which became an important port-of-call for trans-Atlantic fixed-wing land planes. However, throughout the war years, Pan Am continued flying world-wide in support of military operations using their flying boats.

As an interesting side-note; a museum is located at Foynes dedicated to the history of the flying boat operations out on the harbour. The museum is inside the original terminal building and a mock-up of part of a Boeing B314 flying boat can also be entered to get an idea of the large size of the flight deck and passenger accommodation.

Captain Edwin Musick

Captain Edwin Charles Musick (1894-1938) became well-known as a captain with Pan American World Airways flying the Martin M-130 Clipper flying boats across the Pacific in the 1930s.

The young Edwin Music and his parents moved to California from Missouri in 1903. While attending college, he worked as a car mechanic before switching to aircraft mechanics with the Glen Martin Company. His interest in aviation started when he was a 16-year-old after attending an air show. Two years later he built his first aircraft with friends which didn't fair very well, crashing after rising a few feet off the ground. That experience induced him to take some flying lessons at a Los Angeles flight school in 1913, launching him into his future airline career. To build up flying experience, he began flying as an exhibition pilot in 1915 before joining what was to become the US Army Air Service, where he instructed new pilots during World War I at San Diego, Texas and Florida, rising to the rank of Second Lieutenant in the Marine Flying Corps. With the war ended, he started his own flying school in Florida and by then he had over 10,000 flying hours in his log book at the age of 24 years; quite an achievement for such a young pilot!

Two years later in 1920, his airline career began when he started flying for small airlines until Pan American Airways was established in 1927 where

This photograph shows an original S-43 Baby Clipper painted in the colours of a US Marine Corps JRS-1 from VMJ-2 Squadron. It is displayed in the grounds of the Pima Air & Space Museum, Tucson, Arizona.

he became their chief pilot on their Caribbean routes in 1930. With the introduction of the Sikorsky S-42 flying boats, Musick was called upon to perform the flight-testing for the company, with which he claimed ten world records for the flying boat class of aircraft.

Captain Musick pioneered many of the company's new routes across the Pacific flying Martin M-130 Clippers including the first airmail flight across the Pacific in the *China Clipper* with his First Officer R. Sullivan on 22 November 1935. He also flew the first scheduled trans-Pacific passenger flight on 21 October 1936 in the *China Clipper* flying from San Francisco to Manila in the Philippines; his crew included First Officer Harold Gray, who later became Pan Am's president after Juan Trippe retired in 1978, and navigator Fred Noonan who was lost along with Amelia Earhart on her attempted world flight. Musick continued to pioneer other routes across the Pacific for Pan Am including flights to Auckland, New Zealand arriving there on 29 March 1937. Captain Musick became well-known for his pioneering flights across the Pacific in the 1930s for which he held the most flying records of any pilot during that time. He received the Harmon Trophy in 1936 for making the first commercial flight in the *China Clipper*.

While on a cargo and proving flight through Pago Pago in American Samoa, Captain Musick and his crew of six died when their plane exploded in flight (possibly due to fuel being dumped and igniting) and crashed into the sea after reporting an engine problem. None of the bodies were ever recovered.

The Martin M-130 made its first flight on 30 December 1934 and was introduced into service on 22 November 1935. They were built by the Glen L. Martin Company in Baltimore, Maryland, and were officially named as the Martin Ocean Transport but were more commonly known as the M-130. However, all of Pan Am's flying boats, the *Hawaii Clipper* and the *Philippine Clipper* and including the Sikorsky S-42 and Boeing B314 flying boats were always referred to as *China Clippers*. All three Martin M-130s that were built, were lost in accidents. The *Hawaii Clipper* was lost on 28 July 1938 en route from Guam to Manila, the *Philippine Clipper* was lost in California in January 1943 when on a return flight from Hawaii. The *China Clipper* was the last one to be lost on 8 January 1945, when it broke up and sank with no survivors when landing at Port of Spain, Trinidad in the West Indies.

The M-130 carried a crew of six and up to 36 passengers. It had a wingspan of 130 feet (39.7 m) and a maximum take-off weight of 52,252 lbs (23,702 kg). The four Pratt & Whitney R-1830 Twin Wasp radial engines gave the plane a cruise speed of 130 mph (209 km/h) and a range of 3,200 miles (5,150 km). Its service ceiling was a low 10,000 feet (3,048 M). [The service ceiling is reached when the rate of climb has reduced to 100 feet per minute].

A follow on from the Sikorsky S-42 flying boats mentioned above, was the smaller S-43 Baby Clipper, introduced to service in 1935. It was very similar in appearance to the earlier and larger model, the S-42. The most noticeable difference between the S-42 and S-43 was the number of engines, four P&W Hornet radials of 700 hp each on the bigger S-42 versus two P&W Hornet radial engines of 750 hp on the S-43. Also, the S-42 had twin vertical fins as opposed to most of the S-43 having single fins. Less noticeable was the larger wingspan and total length of the two aircraft and of course, the S-42 was heavier at 38,000 lbs (17,237 kg) with a maximum weight of 19,500 lb. (8,845 kg) for the S-43. Internally, the S-42 carried 25 passenger and the S-43 carried eighteen passengers.

The first airline customer to use the S-43 was Inter-Islands Airways (later Hawaiian Airlines). They bought four Baby Clippers including one with a twin tail, which they later sold to the Dutch airline, KLM. Pan Am also used them on their route to Cuba and throughout Latin America. Other airlines also used them including Reeve Aleutian Airways in Alaska. They were used by the USAAC and US Navy. A few S-43/JRS-1 remain in various plane museums, as is the case with the one owned by the Pima Air & Space Museum pictured here. All the larger S-42's was either lost or written-off in accidents.

Supermarine Stranraer

Famed aircraft designer, R.J. Mitchell, designed the Supermarine Stranraers as biplane flying boats for the Royal Air Force. They entered service in 1937 on coastal reconnaissance duties armed with guns and bombs until 1941. In its last year in RAF service, they were used for pilot training for another year before their final retirement in 1942.

The Canadian Vickers company also built forty of the type under licence for the Royal Canadian Air Force who used them on the east and west coasts of Canada for defence work until 1946. The RCAF fleet was then sold off to local airlines for use in the passenger and freight operations role.

The aircraft of interest here is the world's sole remaining, fully intact Supermarine Stranraer. Ex-RCAF, it was first operated by Canadian Pacific Airlines until 1947 before it changed hands to Queen Charlotte Airlines based in Vancouver, British Columbia, which at one time, was the third largest Canadian airline. Queen Charlotte Airlines flew this Stranraer until 1952 when it remained in private ownership until damaged by a ship.

The RAF Hendon Museum in north London bought the Stranraer in 1970, shipped it to London where it is now on display in their museum. This is a very nicely preserved flying boat from the early days of the pioneering airlines.

The TEAL Flying Boats

Several flying boats were used by New Zealand's TEAL airline (Tasman Empire Airways Ltd) now Air New Zealand. First to enter service from 1930 to 1947 were the Short Sandringham and Short Solent.

In 1946, TEAL bought four Tasman Class Short S.25 Sandringham IV flying boats. One was the Short Sunderland (JM715), the military version of the Empire class flying boats, which was first delivered to the RAF who used it for maritime patrol duties from 1938. TEAL bought it from the UK's Air Ministry and had it converted at the Shorts factory in Belfast to a passenger-carrying Sandringham Mk.III. It was delivered to Auckland on 29 October 1947 registered as ZK-AMH and placed on the Auckland to Sydney run, a distance of 1,300 miles (2,100 km). In May 1950 it was sold to Australia's Barrier Reef Airlines and then to Ansett Flying Boat Services named as *Beachcomber*. It was retired from service in 1981 and returned to England and placed in the Solent Sky Museum, in Southampton. TEAL's Sandringhams were replaced by four S.45 Solent Mk.IV flying boats and later a Solent Mk.III was added to the fleet.

This Supermarine Stranraer was flown by Canadian Pacific Airlines before being acquired by Queen Charlotte Airlines of British Columbia. It is now displayed by the RAF Museum Hendon, near London.

This Short S.25 Sandringham IV was operated by New Zealand's TEAL airline on its trans-Tasman services to Australia and later by Ansett Flying Boat Services as the 'Beachcomber'. Now a museum item in the Solent Sky Museum in Southampton, UK.

The Short Solent flying boat (ZK-AMO) used by TEAL on its trans-Tasman route to Sydney and its Coral Route island-hopping route to Tahiti. It is now a long-term resident in the MOTAT Museum's new hangar after many years of outside storage.

The single Solent Mk.III, registered as ZK-AMA, was the last flying boat to be operated by TEAL on the trans-Tasman service from Wellington's Evans Bay (near the airport) to Sydney. It was also used as a back-up plane on the Coral Route service. The service to Sydney ended when the new Wellington Airport opened in 1957 as a domestic terminal (but now a full International Airport) which brought about the end of all flying boat operations by TEAL from the capital, Wellington.

The last TEAL Short Solent Mk.IV (ZK-AMO) named *Aranui* was operated by TEAL from 1949-1960. It is now held on view by the Museum of Transport & Technology (MOTAT) in Auckland. All TEAL flying boat operations were replaced by Douglas DC-4 and DC-6 aircraft and in turn, they were replaced by Lockheed L-188 Electras as the company moved towards the jet age as Air New Zealand.

TEAL's Coral Island route flew from Auckland via Fiji, Samoa and the Cook Islands to Tahiti. A leisurely 30-hour trip hopping between South Pacific tropical islands to Tahiti; some pilots have all the luck! The jets today fly the route Auckland direct to Tahiti in about five hours or so. The service ended on 15 September 1960 bringing an end to all flying boat services on major international air routes.

The Royal New Zealand Air Force retired its last Sunderland in 1967 and replaced them with the Lockheed P-3 Orion, which they still operate as of 2023.

The Flying Tigers Line

The Flying Tigers Line was the USA's first dedicated cargo-carrier airline, established on 24 June 1945 by Robert William Prescott. Based at Los Angeles International Airport, the airline commenced cargo operations using a fleet of fourteen Budd Conestoga freighter aircraft bought as surplus property from the US Navy.

The first ten company pilots were de-mobbed fighter pilots from the USAF American Volunteer Group, known as the Flying Tigers, who all partly invested in the company and gave the company its name. The Flying Tigers Line specialized in flying cargo and later, passenger charter work across the USA and later still, to overseas destinations using a variety of aircraft types. They also made charter flights for the US Military flying supplies and military personnel to overseas bases including Japan, Southeast Asia during the Korean War and also to northern Canada and Alaska supplying the equipment to establish the Distant Early Warning Line sites. In fact, the airline operated world-wide flying to fifty-eight countries on scheduled cargo flights to become the world's largest air cargo carrier by 1980, exceeding Pan Am's cargo volume. On 1 October 1980, it bought out Seaboard Airlines who also flew cargo flights. However, by the end of 1988, the Flying Tigers were bought out by the Federal Express Company who merged the two companies and the Flying Tigers named was no longer used.

This Budd Conestoga was the first type used by the Flying Tigers Line between 1945 to 1948. This is all that remains of the twenty Conestoga that were built. This sole remaining exhibit was donated to the Pima Air & Space Museum, Tucson, Ar., in July 1978.

The Budd Conestoga RB-1 transport plane was ordered in large numbers (600) by the USAAF and US Navy but only twenty were built. Stainless steel was used in its construction due to an expected shortage of aluminium. It first flew on 31 October 1943, powered by two P&W R-1830 Twin Wasp radial engines of 1,200 hp each. At the front was an elevated cockpit, Boeing 747 style; cargo was loaded via doors on each side of the fuselage or through the rear cargo ramp with clamshell doors. It had a wing span of 100 feet (30 m), a maximum weight of 33,860 lb (15,359 kg) and could fly a distance of 700 miles (1,100 km) while cruising at 165 mph (266 km/h). A variety of aircraft types were used by the Flying Tigers Airline from the Conestoga right up to the Boeing 747.

A Flying Tigers' Boeing 707 made a world flight via the North and South Poles in 1965. (See the 'Rockwell Polar Flight' in section 12).

Douglas Piston-engine Transports

The Douglas DC series started with the sole prototype DC-1. It made its maiden flight on 1 July 1933 but was lost in an accident not long after. This was replaced by the improved DC-2, which made its first flight on 11 May 1934. Douglas built 198 DC-2's, which went to the USA airlines of TWA, Pan Am and the Dutch airline KLM. The DC-2 was replaced by the very popular DST, DC-3/C-47 Dakota transports. The Douglas DST (Douglas Sleeper Transport) carried passengers across the USA with 14 to 16 sleeping berths. After changing the sleeping berths for twenty-one seats, the aircraft was designated as the true DC-3. Seven DST's were built before the first DC-3 came off the production line for the American Airlines fleet.

The DC-3 model had greater dimensions than the DC-2 and although they look similar, it was not a simple case of making the DC-3 bigger, it required a completely new redesign. The first DC-3's were powered by two Pratt & Whitney R-1830 Twin Wasp radial engines developing 1,000-1,200 horsepower giving a cruise speed of 207 mph (333 km/h) while carrying up to thirty-two passengers or 6,000 lbs (2,700 kg) of freight.

The DC-3 made its maiden flight on 17 December 1935, thirty-two years after the Wright brother's famous first flight. Although an improvement on earlier aircraft designs, they still used the conventional, tail-dragger undercarriage. The DC-2 and DC-3 paved the way for the pioneer airlines to fly routes of longer distances and with greater capacity in the 1930s. They also gave great service throughout WWII as the C-47 and Dakota, as freight transporters and Paratroop carriers, etc. The DC-2 and DC-3 both played a

The Flying Tigers flew a diverse fleet of transport aircraft ending with the Boeing 747. This nose section represents the last remains of their fleet.

First flown by Pan Am and later by Mexicana, and Aviateca, this is a rare Douglas DC-2 that was restored to an airworthy condition in 2007 and preserved in the colours of the Transcontinental & Western Airlines/Lindbergh Line. Note the landing lights on the nose; relocated to the wings on the DC-3. This example is now displayed in the Museum of Flight, Seattle.

major part in establishing the modern airline industry we have today and they still remain in service as utility, cargo and passenger transports, skydiving and top-dressing aircraft, etc; in fact, the DC-3 has been put to many uses and can be found all over the world earning themselves the well-known title of the '*ubiquitous DC-3*'.

Over 16,000 of all versions of the DC-3 were built from 1935 until the last one came off the production line after the war ended and they were also licence-built in Russia and Japan. They were replaced by the DC-4 to DC-7 series, all four-engine aircraft with greater load carrying ability, greater range and speed. The DC-4 introduced in 1942 was the first Douglas transport to be equipped with a nose wheel for easier pilot handling. They were pressed into US military service with the new designation of Douglas C-54 Skymaster for the USAF and R5D for the US Navy. The C-54's were the most used type during the Berlin Air Lift in 1948-49. In 1944, a sole Douglas C-54C was redesignated as a VC-54C; it was the first aircraft to be converted especially for the USAF Presidential Fleet. The first president to use it was President F.D. Roosevelt (1882-1945) and later President Harry S. Truman (1884-1972). In October 1961, it was downgraded to other duties in the USAF and replaced by a Douglas VC-118 (a DC-6 version). It was nick-named the *Sacred Cow* for security reasons and is now exhibited in the NMUSAF at Dayton, Ohio.

A retired Douglas DC-6 Liftmaster was given a new lease-of-life when it was converted into a restaurant at Coventry Airport, England.

The Douglas DC-3 was used by many of the early airlines in America and across the world, which helped them to become established. This DC-3 was built in 1940 for American Airlines and in 1942, it was transferred to the TWA/Lindbergh Line. It is now in the colour scheme to represent the DC-3's flown by Alaska Airlines. It is seen here suspended in the Museum of Flight in Seattle, Washington, USA.

The Douglas DC-4 was also used by the USAAF, as shown here designated as a C-54 Skymaster. This DC-4/C-54 is located in the Pima Air & Space Museum in Tucson, Ar.

The DC-5 was unique in the Douglas line-up with only twelve aircraft built. It was a twin-engine plane with a tricycle undercarriage and a high-wing, the only high-wing plane in the DC series. Five were built as the civilian DC-5 version and the remainder were C-110 and R3D built for the US military in WWII. The prototype was bought by William Boeing for personal transport with the remaining four DC-5's going to the Dutch airline KLM who based two in the Dutch West Indies and the remaining three with their subsidiary airline KNILM in Batavia in the Dutch East Indies Indonesia (Jakarta).

From the DC-3 onwards, all the Douglas transports were a market success, with the exception of the DC-5. The DC-6 and DC-7 were the last of the Douglas piston-engine transports which all helped the early airlines to become established, leading the way to future jet transport fleets around the world. Continuing the DC series, the Douglas DC-8 was the first jet transport produced by Douglas followed by the DC-9 and DC-10. In 1967, Douglas Aircraft merged with the McDonnell Aircraft Corporation to become the McDonnell Douglas Corporation until 1997 when the company was merged with the Boeing Company. It is interesting to note, the Douglas DC-9 was renamed as the Boeing 717 after the company mergers, taking the unused 717 designation first allotted by Boeing for the air refuelling tankers built for the USAF, which the Air Force named as the Boeing KC-135.

Boeing 307 Stratoliner

The first Boeing 307 Stratoliner was built right from the start as a production model, no prototype was built and it made its first flight on 31 December 1938, however, it was lost in a fatal accident on 18 March 1939. The accident happened during a flight-test side-slip manoeuvre which caused the plane to enter a spin and the main wings and tail plane both failed from overstressing during the attempted recovery. The Stratoliners were built using the same main wings, tailplane, undercarriage and engines as used on the Boeing B-17C Flying Fortress bomber. The fuselage was relatively wide at 12 feet (3.6 m) giving the plane a short and fat appearance, allowing sleeper berths and reclining seats to be fitted for its thirty-three passengers, later modified to carry thirty-eight seated passengers or 28 in bunks. It had a crew of six, including a flight engineer, the first airliner land-plane to have one; some flying boats had flight engineers.

Ten Stratoliners were built including the first one that was lost in an accident; three went to Pan Am and the other five were flown by Transcontinental & Western Air (TWA) upon entering airline service in July 1940. The first one to be delivered went to TWA owner, Howard Hughes, as his own personal business plane in which he planned a world flight but was thwarted by the outbreak of WWII. The Boeing 307 was one of the first four-engine airliners to enter passenger service and it was also the world's first pressurized airliner. It could cruise at 14,700 feet (4,480 m) with a pressure differential of 2.5 psi giving a cabin altitude of 8,000 feet (2,440 m), which became the standard cabin altitude for most modern aircraft since then. Power was delivered by four, Pratt & Whitney GR-1820 radial engines of 1,100 horsepower each. They gave a cruise speed of 215 mph (344 km/h)

During WWII, Pan Am continued to fly its Stratoliners under the direction of the USAAF Air Transport Command to South and Central America as cargo aircraft on long-range flights. TWA's fleet were bought by the US government and were also operated as part of the USAAF and flown mostly by TWA pilots. In 1944, the Stratoliners were returned to TWA and Pan Am, where they returned to civilian passenger service for a few more years before being sold on to other secondary airlines.

This is the sole surviving Boeing 307 Stratoliner, ex Pan Am, in flying condition. The 307 was the first pressurised airliner to enter passenger service and is now exhibited in the Udvar-Hazy Center.

The Stratoliner in the attached photo was initially operated by Pan Am named the Clipper Flying Cloud and later sold to the Haitian Air Force as its presidential aircraft for President Francois Duvalier (1907-1971). The aircraft later returned to the USA and was restored by Boeing in 2001 and presented to the Smithsonian Museum where it is now on display in their Udvar-Hazy Center. It is the world's sole remaining, complete Stratoliner and still in flying condition. In fact, it was lucky to survive a take-off accident during its initial delivery flight to the museum. It was back to the workshop for repairs, before it was finally delivered to Washington.

Lockheed Constellation

The Lockheed Constellation, typically known as the Connie, was the last of the big piston-engine airliners. With its fuselage cross-section varying in dimension along its length, it had a very distinctive appearance. Its fuselage droops down at the front to enable a shorter nose gear leg and rises at the rear to place the tailplane in a higher position and gain an extra 3 mph of cruise speed. Three vertical fins provide better directional stability and control and also reduced the plane's height to fit into hangars.

The last of the big piston-engine airliners, the Lockheed Constellation. The few remaining Connies are now mostly based in aviation museums, such as this one in the Pima Air & Space Museum in Tucson, Ar. It started life as a military C-69 before its conversion to a passenger aircraft for TWA.

It was first intended to be an airliner designated as the Lockheed L-049 Constellation, but WWII intervened and after its maiden flight on 9 January 1943, they were used by the US military as transports, who gave it the designation of C-69. The C-69/L-049 Constellation was powered by four Wright R-3350 Cyclone radial engines developing 2,200 horsepower each, which gave it a good cruise speed of 313 mph (504 km/h) over a range of 3,995 miles (6,429 km). Several designations were used for the various models which followed during the production run right up to the L-1649 Starliner, the last of the passenger variant.

After the war, it was favoured by many airlines with TWA taking the first deliveries on 1 October 1945. TWA made their first trans-Atlantic passenger flight from New York to Paris on 6 February 1945, stopping for fuel at Gander and Shannon. Pan Am also used the Connie for its around-the-world scheduled service, which started on 17 June 1947 until 1982. Many of the major airlines operated Constellations until the arrival of the new jet transports, when Connies took second place and were relegated to secondary services and freight runs up to the 1990s.

The Constellation has a unique place in aviation history as the last of the pioneer piston-engine airliners.

De Havilland DH.114 Heron

The de Havilland DH.114 Heron was a post-war design developed from the twin-engine DH.104 Dove, which itself had replaced the pre-war Dragon Rapide, a 1930s biplane with a tail wheel. The Heron had a longer fuselage than the Dove, with a length of 48 feet 6 inches (14.78 m) to carry more cargo or seating for seventeen passengers. Four, de Havilland Gipsy Queen 30 engines of 250 horsepower each powered two-blade de Havilland constant-speed propellers, mounted on a new wing with a span of 71 feet 6 inches (21.79 m). The Herons cruised at 183 mph (295 km/h) with a range of 915 miles (1,473 km). Some were later converted to turbo-prop power giving a good improvement in flight performance and prolonging their useful life.

De Havilland built 149 Herons, the first of which made its maiden flight on 10 May 1950 flown by company test pilot, Geoffrey Pike. The Heron was first flight-trialled by BEA on its Scottish routes before the first production Heron Series 1 were sold to launch customer, National Airways Corporation (NAC), New Zealand's domestic airline before its merger to form Air New Zealand. The NAC fleet of Herons were replaced in 1957 by Fokker Friendships and Vickers Viscounts. Herons were also flown by the RAF for The Queen's Flight.

The de Havilland Heron Series 1 can be identified by its fixed, tricycle gear; the Series 2 has retractable gear. This Series 1 Heron shown here, is now owned by the Newark Air Museum, UK.

The Herons were equipped with a tricycle undercarriage – tail-wheels were a thing of the past for modern airliners. It was the world's smallest four-engine airliner! However, it was an ideal size for the emerging domestic airlines post-war.

Vickers Viscount

The days of the piston-powered airliners were coming to an end, to be replaced by turboprop and pure-jet transports. The Vickers Type 630 Viscount entered airline service in 1953 as the world's first turboprop airliner, which became the mainstay for many short-haul airlines starting-up after the war years.

The Viscount was developed from the piston-engined Vickers Viking, which itself was developed from the Wellington bomber. A Vickers VC.1 Viking was flight tested with a pair of Rolls Royce Nene turboprop engines in place of its original Bristol Hercules piston radial engines and it was first flown in this configuration on 6 April 1948 to claim the status of the world's first turbo-prop powered transport. The Viscount's design work starting in 1945 by its designer Rex Pierson as a 32-passenger airliner. Later versions carried up to seventy-five passengers plus two pilots and a hostess at a relatively high maximum speed (for the time) of 352 mph (566 km/h) when compared to the older piston-engine airliners. Its range was a respectable 1,380 miles (2,200 km) while cruising at around 20,000 feet with the comfort of pressurisation and the smoother running of its turbine engines.

The Viscount made its maiden flight flown by Joseph 'Mutt' Summers, chief test pilot for Vickers on 16 July 1948 from the factory at Brooklands, near London, England. Vickers produced 445 Viscounts in three basic versions, the 700, 800 and 810 series; the difference being evident mainly in the number of passenger seats and engine power. Power came from four, Rolls Royce RB.53 Dart turboprop engines initially developing 1,400 shaft-horsepower which was increased on later versions up to 1,630 shaft horsepower each, an engine that proved very popular in those early days of turbine power. [Note, power on turboprops is measured as shaft horsepower and for pure jet engines it is measured in pounds of thrust].

The success of the Viscounts was well-proven by the numerous orders from several airlines around the world. Other aircraft manufacturers have now turned to building turboprop and pure jet transport aircraft; the days of the pioneering piston-engine airliners are now well and truly over.

The Viscount was the world's first turboprop airliner debuting in 1953. This Viscount Type 724 pictured here, was the first turboprop airliner to fly in North America; it was operated by Trans Canadian Airlines from 1955. It is now parked in the grounds of the Pima Air & Space Museum, at Tucson, Ar

19 – Pioneers of Jet & Rocket Propulsion

Beyond the Piston Engines

The internal combustion engine was developed by the German engineer, Nicolaus August Otto (1832-1891), which became the modern diesel or petrol engine with which we are familiar with today. The first piston engines installed on aircraft were the in-line or V-type configuration engines usually built by pioneer pilots themselves. To produce greater power, the rotary engine was introduced working on the principle of the cylinders rotating around the stationary crankshaft. Several pioneer aviators built rotary engines; however it was the French brothers Laurent and Louis Sequin who had the first success with rotary engine production. Their Gnome rotary, introduced in 1907, was one of the most common types of engine in use, the other being the Le Rhone rotary and the engines most commonly used on the WWI fighter planes. It had several advantages in its design over the in-line type but by the early 1920s the rotary engine became redundant to be replaced by the better-known radial engines, which were used on heavy transport aircraft up until the introduction of the jet turbine engines in the 1950s.

The invention of the piston engine enabled pioneering flight to be achieved by the first pioneer pilots as we saw earlier in this work. And today, the piston engine is still quite suitable for the lower-powered light aircraft fleet flying world-wide. However, when speeds above 250-400 mph were required, the piston engine had reached its limit of power production. An alternative power source was required and this was eventually presented to the aviation world during the 1930s. Two men were individually working to develop a practical jet-powered engine, both unknown to each other at the time. The two pioneer engine designers were of course, Hans von Ohain (1911-1998) in Germany and Air Commodore Frank Whittle (1907-1996) in England; both found success with their work.

Sir Frank Whittle

Sir Frank Whittle (1907-1996) KBE, OM, CB, FRS and FRAeS, was an RAF pilot officer and an inventor of the jet engine. Frank Whittle had an early interest in aviation and he first applied to join the RAF at the age of fifteen years but was initially turned away due to his small physique, but determined, he reapplied and was eventually accepted the following year in 1923. He joined as an apprentice at the School of Technical Training at RAF Cranwell and he excelled at his studies in the engineering classes and earned his way to become a pilot, training on Avro 504's and moving on to flying Bristol Fighters and later still, he became a pilot-instructor at the Central Flying School.

His advanced studies required him to present a thesis, in which he introduced his theory on jet propulsion as an alternative method to piston-engine/propeller power, as the most efficient way to fly at high altitude and high speeds on long-distance flights, leading to him being issued a patent for his turbojet engine design in January 1930. His jet engine design was not readily accepted due to claims it was impractical and so, the Air Ministry had no initial interest in his jet engine design.

However, he continued to work on his design without any assistance from the RAF or Air Ministry and eventually he formed his own company Power Jets Ltd., on 27 January 1936 with two friends from the RAF and with financial help from backers as partners. His jet engine made its first bench-testing run on 12 April 1937 and eventually, the Air Ministry realised Whittle was onto something and in March 1938 issued funds to support the project.

The Whittle Type W.1 was of a centrifugal design with air directed from the compressor through to the turbine via the combustion chamber on a convoluted path. It was flight tested in a purpose-built aircraft designed and built by the Gloster Aircraft Company known as the Gloster E.28/39 (W4041/G) making its very historic first flight on 15 May 1941 from RAF Cranwell. This was the first jet turbine-powered aircraft to fly in England piloted by Gloster's chief test pilot and Britain's first pioneer jet pilot, Flight Lieutenant Gerry Sayer (1905-1942).

Whittle's second, improved jet engine was also flight tested in the prototype E.28/39 reaching a speed of 505 mph (810 km/h) at 30,000 feet (9,200 m). The E.28/39 was developed into the Gloster Meteor which became the RAF's first jet aircraft powered by the Rolls Royce Welland jet-turbine engine, an improved version of Frank Whittle's original design. The Welland was itself replaced by the Rolls Royce Derwent engine.

A replica of Frank Whittle's first jet engine displayed in the Jet Age Museum, England.

The first British jet aircraft to fly, the Gloster E.28/39 in which Whittle's jet engine was flight tested. It is displayed in the London Science Museum, England.

This Gloster Meteor is the prototype of Britain's first operational jet fighter; it first flew on 5 March 1943. It is on display in the Research Aircraft section of RAF Cosford Museum.

The Gloster E.28/39 aircraft, along with its original engine, has been on display in the London Science Museum since its retirement in 1946. The enclosed photographs show a replica of the Whittle W.1 engine in the Jet Age Museum in Gloucestershire.

Although Whittle's jet engine flew nearly two years after von Ohain's engine, Frank Whittle has received the credit for pioneering the jet turbine engine and therefore, he is recognised as the 'father of jet propulsion'.

Hans von Ohain

The German physicist, Hans Joachim Pabst von Ohain (1911-1998) is credited with designing the first operational jet engine. Von Ohain was born in Dessau in Germany and attended the University of Gottingen where he studied and gained his PhD in Aerodynamics and Physics with coaching from the famed Ludwig Prandtl.

Ohain conceived his jet engine idea and successfully developed it to produce the first operational jet engine to fly. His engine design was of a different layout to Whittle's engine; he introduced the axial-flow engine, which soon became the preferred engine design and now powers all modern jet aircraft today. The airflow through the axial-flow type of engine is more straight forward compared to a centrifugal type engine with its flow reversal.

Frank Whittle and von Ohain both developed their own engine designs around the same time, in the 1930s. Although von Ohain was unaware of Whittle's actual pioneering work, he was aware of Whittle's patent which he had received for his engine design in 1930.

The Whittle-designed centrifugal compressor engine, was a more basic design compared to the axial-flow type of engines, which were built with more durable materials prolonging engine life between overhauls to about 150 hours or more and with better fuel consumption and a greater power/weight ratio. However, after the war the British manufactures eventually moved to axial flow engines, no doubt from what they had learned from the Germans after the war ended.

Unlike Whittle who had to form his own company, Von Ohain had the backing of the Heinkel Flugzeugwerke. He had started on his own research work and with his associate, Hahn, were employed by Heinkel in April 1936 to continue their engine development work. It was the world's first jet-turbine engine to run during bench-testing leading him to receive the credit for the axial-flow design.

On 27 August 1939, a Heinkel HeS jet engine was test-flown for the first time installed in a Heinkel He 178 prototype test plane. It was the world's first jet powered aircraft to fly, flown by the world's first pioneer jet pilot, Erich Warsitz (1906-1983). He also flew the first rocket-powered aircraft, the Heinkel He 176, on 20 June 1939.

Although von Ohain developed the first jet engine and received the credit, other German designers, including Herbert Wagner working for Junkers Aircraft & Motor Works, were building more successful engines and von Ohain's engines never progressed much further. The success of both German jet engine pioneers, enabled the German Air Force to introduce operational Messerschmitt Me 262 jet fighter aircraft during July 1944. The Me 262 with its Junkers Jumo 004 engine, designed by Dr. Anselm Franz, proved more damaging (against British and American invading aircraft) than its British counterpart, the Gloster Meteor. The RAF Squadron 616, used their Meteors initially to intercept the German V-1 flying bombs over England. The Squadron later moved to bases in Holland and flew their Meteors mainly on ground attack and reconnaissance work.

Von Ohain and Frank Whittle became friends when they met after the war had ended. Von Ohain was employed by the USAF at Wright-Patterson AFB in Dayton, Ohio from 1947 where he became the Director of their Aeronautical Research Laboratory and Chief Scientist in their Aero Propulsion Lab in 1975. He continued to work on aircraft propulsion and other related projects. He also did other non-aeronautical research and received many awards for his work including the Charles Stark Draper Prize for his jet engine research, which he shared with Frank Whittle. He died in Florida in 1998.

The defeat of Germany in 1945, saw the combined American and British 'Operation Paperclip' retrieve valuable aeronautical technical information from the German research centres and many of their military aircraft were taken back to England and America as war trophies. The information helped both countries to further their aeronautical knowledge and to build more advanced aircraft, with the help of several German scientists who assisted the British and Americans in their research centres.

The Messerschmitt 262A was Germany's first operational jet fighter/bomber aircraft, which became operational in April 1944. This wartime trophy was taken to America for examination and is now displayed in the RAF Museum Cosford, UK.

American Jets

America's first jet was a secret war-time project when they designed and built the Bell XP-59A Airacomet for the USAAF 412th Fighter group, the USA's first fighter unit.

The American General Electric Company adopted the British Whittle/Power Jets W.1 jet engine to build their version of the engine as the General Electric J31. The J31 turbojets produced 1,250 lbf thrust each and two were used on the Bell Airacomet, which first flew on 1 October 1942. The Airacomet achieved a maximum speed of 404 mph (650 km/h) at 25,000 ft (7,620 m).

In collaboration with the British, the Americans sent one of their Airacomets to England for them to test in exchange for the first production Gloster Meteor, which proved to have far superior performance compared to the Airacomet. The Airacomet's poor performance can be attributed to its heavy airframe and the lack of performance of its early jet engines. Experience with engine design improved over the years and still continues to improve with more power produced for each new generation of jet engines.

Robert Morris Stanley (1912-1977) was the chief test pilot for Bell Aircraft (builders of the Bell XP-59A Airacomet) and he received the pleasure and distinction, of briefly becoming airborne during fast taxi tests at the Muroc Dry Lake testing facility, now Edwards AFB, in California. He was the first American pilot to fly a jet-powered aircraft. The first official flight was made the next day, 2 October 1942 by USAAC pilot, Colonel Laurence Craigie (1902-1994) to become the first American military pilot to officially fly a jet aircraft. After nearly sixty-hours of flight testing, the Airacomet proved the engine gave poor performance and was not the success hoped for. Although, it did provide the American designers with much needed data for developing their future jet aircraft.

From the sixty-three prototype and production aircraft built, all were grounded by 1950 and today, only six remain on display in American air museums. The one pictured here was the first prototype built and America's first jet aircraft to fly making it the ancestor of all American jet-powered aircraft. It is displayed in the National Air & Space Museum, Washington, D.C.

In America, the Boeing B-47 was in its early stage of design and building, originally with a straight wing; however, the German information proved a sweptback wing is more suited to high-speed flight and the B-47 design was changed accordingly. The swept wing paved the way for all Boeing jet transports to follow and all other high-speed jet aircraft. Swept back wings add to lateral stability and also delay the transonic drag rise at high Mach

This Bell XP-59A Airacomet is the ancestor of all USA jet aircraft. This one displayed here, was the first one to be built and made its first flight on 1 October 1942. It is shown here in the National Air & Space Museum in Washington, D.C.

The Boeing B-47 was the first jet bomber built for the USAF with sweptback wings designed from technical information recovered from the Geman research facilities at the end of the War. Note the unusual bicycle-type undercarriage with out-rigger wheels. This one is parked in the Pima Air & Space Museum grounds, in Arizona.

numbers allowing higher cruise speeds. The Boeing B-47 prototypes were powered by six General Electric J-35 jet turbine engines while later models used the GE J-47 engines. The Boeing B-47 became the first American jet bomber for the USAF Strategic Air Command, entering service in June 1951.

The use of rockets in warfare first appeared in China between the 10th and 13th centuries, before their use spread across Asia to Europe. But it was in America where rockets were seriously studied by pioneer rocket man, Robert Goddard.

Dr. R. Goddard

Doctor Robert Hutchings Goddard (1882-1945) was an American student studying at the Worcester Polytechnic Institute of Clark University when he realised the potential for rocket-powered flight. This was the start of his life-long interest and vocation in developing rocket science. In the course of his studies, he received the first of his US patents in 1914 for inventing the multi-stage rockets. He first used solid-fuel rockets and later introduced liquid fuel as the better option, which he used on the world's first liquid fueled rocket to be launched on 16 March 1926 at Auburn in Massachusetts. Again, at Auburn, he launched the first scientific payload by rocket in 1929. In 1937, he developed vanes and a gyro system to control the guidance and steering of his rockets.

His work was initially recognised as significant and was subsidized by the Daniel Guggenheim Foundation and the Smithsonian Institute. Although the US government were slow to realize the potential of rockets, it was to be many years later before his work was officially recognized. As such, his rocket invention allowed the USA to build inter-continental ballistic missiles (ICBM's), rocket-propelled research aircraft, missiles and to enter the space age. In recognition of his work, the NASA Goddard Space Flight Center in Greenbelt, Maryland, USA, was established on 1 May 1959 and named in his honour, thirty-five years after his first liquid fueled rocket was launched. Dr. Goddard had died in 1945, but his wife Esther was at the Space Flight Centre when it was opened and dedicated to him in 1959.

Dr. Robert Goddard is the pioneer and 'father of modern rocket propulsion'.

The German Pioneers of Rocket Planes

Rocket-propelled aircraft were first flown in Germany under the Fritz von Opel (1899-1971) and Max Valier's (1895-1930) Opel-RAK rocket programme during 1928. The first aircraft was a rocket-powered glider designed by a team led by German pioneer of aerodynamics, Dr. Alexander Lippisch (1894-1976). The Opel-RAK Ente (Duck) made its maiden flight on 11 June 1928 flown by test pilot Fritz Stamer (1897-1969) at Wasserkrupe, Germany. However, its lifespan was very brief, catching fire on its second flight after its rockets malfunctioned. Fritz Stamer was able to land the plane safely and abandon it, but the Ente was destroyed by fire. The Ente was followed by the Opel-RAK 1, which proved more successful, as was the Heinkel He 176 a few years later.

Hellmuth Walter

Hellmuth Walter (1900-1980) and Von Braun were both pioneers of rocket propulsion in Germany. In 1936, the first Heinkel experimental rocket plane, the Heinkel He 176 was flown by Heinkel test pilot, Erich Warsitz (1906-1983) on 20 June 1939. The Messerschmitt Me 163 Komet made its first flight on 1 September. The Yokosuka Ohka flying bomb was used by the Imperial Japanese Navy Air Service for suicide attacks on the American fleet in the Pacific. They were carried by a mothership and deployed using its rocket engine to dive-bomb its target ships.

An Me 163B Komet captured from Germany at the end of the war and taken to America for inspection and research into Germany's war-time rocket plane production. The Udvar-Hazy Center, now exhibits this aircraft.

After the war, British and American companies built research fighter/
interceptors with mixed-propulsion engines (jet and rocket) but none went
into production. However, the Americans used rocket-powered research
aircraft from the Bell X-1 through to the North American X-15 to further their
research towards the space age; these aircraft are covered next in section 20
– The Pioneers of Supersonic & Space Flight.

Wernher von Braun

Wernher von Braun (1912-1977) was born in Germany and he became
their leading pioneer rocket scientist during WWII where he worked on the
development of the V-2 ballistic missiles, which were launched from their
site at Peenemunde in Northern Germany at British targets starting on 7
September 1944. [Note, the V-1 Flying Bombs were powered by pulse jets,
not rockets.] Post war, Von Braun was transferred to the USA to assist in
their rocket programme which led on to the ICBM's mentioned above and
the USA's space programme.

Messerschmitt Me 163 Komet

The Messerschmitt Me 163 Komet was Germany's rocket-powered defensive
fighter built to counter the allied bombers attacking Germany. It was designed
by Dr. Alexander Lippisch (1894-1976) one of Germany's top aeronautical
engineers. The Me 163 made its first flight in September 1941 to become the
first and only rocket powered fighter plane to be built and mass produced,
with approximately 370 examples delivered to the German Luftwaffe. It
went into operational service with the Luftwaffe in 1944 and was not all
that successful, suffering fourteen losses due to various causes for only nine
bombers brought down. Having a rocket engine consuming a relatively large
amount of fuel, reduced its fuel endurance time to 7½ minutes allowing it to
climb up to attack the incoming bombers within its 50-mile combat radius
before gliding back to base. Its rocket engine was a Helmuth Walter HWK
509A-2 of 3,748 lbs thrust, which gave it a phenomenal rate of climb for its
day, at 16,000 feet per minute, after a fast take-off speed of 170 mph (275
km/h). It was a relatively small but heavy aircraft with a wingspan of 30 feet
6 inches (9.3 m) and a length of 18 feet 8 inches (5.7 m) with a maximum all
up weight of 9,500 lbs. (4,309 kg).

The photograph of the Me 163, a war-time trophy, with its rocket engine at
the lower right, was first exhibited at the Canada Aviation & Space Museum
in Ottawa before its transfer to the Udvar-Hazy Center.

Titan ICBM Rockets

During the Cold War era, both the Soviet Union and America had nuclear missiles ready to launch a counter attack against the opposing country, a deterrant that worked. America had fifty-four missile sites on standby alert 24 hours a day from 1963 to 1987. At the end of the Cold War, each country disbanded their missiles and rockets except for one, which is kept open with agreement from the Russians as the Titan Missile Museum in Green Valley, Arizona. The museum displays a dummy/practice ICBM Titan II rocket in its 104 feet (32 m) deep silo and the underground accomodation and operations room, which are now open to the public. Also on display in the grounds is a rocket engine built by Aerojet General, the type used for the USAF Titan II ICBM rockets. Their Stage One thrust is rated at 430,000 lbs and Stage Two is rated at a mere 100,000 lbs of thrust, produced by a special mix of liquid Hypergolic fuel and and an oxidyzer. Each missile site was top secret during its operational days, but now the Green Valley site is a National Historic Landmark.

A Titan II rocket motor on display at the last remaining Cold War ICBM missile site in the USA, located at Green Valley in the Sonoran Desert near Tucson, Arizona.

20 – Pioneers of Supersonic & Space Flight

The Search for Mach One

The first few years of the 20th century, saw many pioneer aviators attempting to increase the performance of their aircraft. By 1913, Maurice Prevost (1887-1952) was the first pilot to exceed 100 mph (160 km/h) and he was also the winner of the first Schneider Trophy air race.

The speed of aircraft continued to be increased and by the start of the Second World War, the piston-engine fighters were reaching speeds around 400 mph (650 km/h) and faster still in steep dives reaching around 550 mph (900 km/h). And this is where they encountered unexpected problems with the effects of compressibility making itself known in a nasty way. After entering a high-speed dive, the airflow over the wings entered into the transonic region where the wing's centre of pressure moved rearwards across the wing chord and caused the aircraft to pitch-down (known as Mach tuck) which quite often was unrecoverable. Lockheed's test pilot Ralph Virder, was the first pilot to die, possibly due to Mach tuck when conducting high-speed dives in the company's second prototype P-38 Lightning in November 1941. Some fighters were fitted with dive brakes, not for dive-bombing attacks but to alter the airflow over the wings in the transonic region and enable safe recoveries.

High-speed flight was initially studied by English and German aerodynamacists but generally ignored by the Americans. In 1935, at the National Physics Laboratory in London, Scientist W.F. Hilton explained to news reporters he was trying to find what caused a barrier to prevent aircraft from flying faster as they approached the speed of sound. The reporters wrongly interpreted his statement and gave it the name of 'sound barrier' and that incorrect name is still used today. There is no such thing as the sound barrier; the 'compressibility barrier' would be more appropriate because it is the increase in drag caused by compression of the airflow that prevented the early piston-engine aircraft from exceeding the speed of sound.

During WWII, the Germans were quite advanced in their supersonic research, which resulted in their production of the Messerschmitt Me 262 Schwalbe, the world's first operational jet fighter and the Me 163 Komet interceptor rocket plane capable of speeds up to 621 mph(1,000 km/h), very close to the speed of sound at 661 mph or Mach 0.94 at the standard temperature of 15° Celsius.

Both England and the USA used their research aircraft and their knowledge gained from Germany on supersonic flight to take two slightly different approaches to future supersonic aircraft. The USA built supersonic fighters and large bombers (the North American XB-70 Valkyrie and Rockwell International B-1B) and entered into the era of Space exploration. Conversely, the British built supersonic fighters and smaller fighter/bombers such as the ill-fated BAC TSR-2 and the successful Panavia Tornado and with the French, they produced the supersonic Concorde passenger jet transport.

Chuck Yeager

At the end of the WWII, benefiting from the technical information gained from Germany on high-speed flight, it was used to great advantage in America, which ultimately resulted in the production of the rocket-powered Bell X-1 research aircraft. On 14 October 1947, history was made when USAF test pilot General Charles (Chuck) Yeager (1923-2020) pioneered supersonic flight when he flew the Bell X-1 to exceed the speed of sound or Mach 1.06 to be precise, in level flight.

Chuck Yeager was a USAAF fighter pilot seeing action in Europe where he claimed 'ace' status with twelve enemy aircraft to his credit, which included the German's first jet fighter, a Messerschmitt 262. At the war's end, he enrolled in test pilot training at the Wright Field air base in Dayton, Ohio. He flew America's first jet fighter, the Bell P-59 Airacomet and their first jet-bomber, the Boeing B-47 followed by 180 other types of aircraft, which of course, included making the world's first supersonic flight, mentioned above.

The Bell X-1 research rocket plane was built by Bell Aircraft under contract to the USAAF and NACA for the purpose of research into the aerodynamic problems associated with compressibility when aircraft approach the speed of sound or Mach One.

The Bell X-1 was the first of an ongoing series of X-planes built solely for research purposes. It made its maiden flight on 19 January 1946 with seven

The historic Bell X-1 was the first aircraft to exceed Mach 1, in October 1947, flown by Chuck Yeager. It is seen here suspended from the ceiling in the Smithsonian National Air & Space Museum, Washington, D.C.

The Douglas D-558-2 Skyrocket was flown by Scott Crossfield, the first pilot to gain the record for exceeding Mach 2 in November 1953. It is now a museum exhibit in the Smithsonian National Air & Space Museum, Washington, D.C.

versions being built. The fuselage was shaped similar to .50 caliber bullet with straight wings of 28 feet (8,53 m) span. Swept back wings were still in their infancy in America at the time and knowledge of their aerodynamics was limited. The maximum all up weight of the Bell X-1 was 12,250 lbs. (5,557 kg). Power was provided by a single Reaction Motors XLR11-RM-3 rocket engine developing 6,000 pounds of thrust to push the plane through Mach One, the speed of sound.

All research flights were conducted at Muroc Air Base, now known as Edwards AFB in California, where the rocket planes were launched from their mothership, initially using a Boeing B-29 Superfortress and later a Boeing B-52N converted bomber was used later for launching other rocket planes.

Scott Crossfield

Supersonic speed was increased step by step until 20 November 1953, when Mach 2 was claimed by US Navy test pilot Albert Scott Crossfield (1921-2006) flying the rocket-powered Douglas D-558-2 Skyrocket to a speed of 1,291 mph (Mach 2.005). This was the only Mach 2 flight made by this aircraft. He made ninety-nine flights in rocket powered aircraft including the Bell X-1 and the North American X-15, to become the pilot with the most hours in rocket-powered aircraft.

Milburn Apt

The next target to achieve was Mach 3, which was gained on 27 September 1956 by US Air Force test pilot Captain Milburn Apt (1924-1956) while flying the Bell X-2. He reached a speed of Mach 3.196 (2,094 mph). Unfortunately, his plane went out of control soon after exceeding Mach 3, caused by inertia coupling (violent flight gyrations) and Captain Apt was knocked unconscious and was killed when his plane fell out of control and crashed.

Robert White & Pete Knight

Flying the special purpose-built North American Aviation X-15 research aircraft, USAF test pilot Captain Robert M. White (1924-2010) gained the next three Mach records claiming Mach 4, 5 and 6; the first record was gained on 7 March 1961 and Mach 6, on 9 November 1961. The highest speed recorded, which still stands today for non-space aircraft is Mach 6.70 (4,520 mph) gained by US Air Force pilot, Major William J. 'Pete' Knight (1929-2004) flying an X-15 rocket plane. Speeds above Mach 5 are classed as hypersonic speeds.

Joe Walker

Not only were high-speed flight records gained, but high-altitude flight was just as important with several test pilots gaining altitude records in the North American X-15. NASA test pilot Joe Walker (1921-1966) gained an altitude record of 271,000 feet (82,600 meters) on 17 January 1963. On 22 November 1963, he went on to claim the ultimate altitude record of 354,200 feet or 67.08 miles (108 km) above sea level, a record which still stands for a manned, non-space aircraft with conventional flight controls.

The edge of space, known as the Karman Line (after Theodore von Karman) is defined by the French, Federation Aeronautique Internationale as an altitude of 62 statute miles (100 km) or 330,000 feet above mean sea level. Any USAF pilot now exceeding this altitude qualifies as an astronaut and receives military astronaut wings. However, NASA's civilian pilots Joseph A. Walker, Bill Dana and Jack B. McKay were not recognized as astronauts until they received their NASA astronaut wings on 23 August 2005. Joseph Walker and Jack McKay had passed-on and their wings were accepted by family members. A great and well-deserved tribute to the pioneers of supersonic flight.

All of these high-speed and high-altitude flights provided flight data on the physiological aspects of high-speed/high-altitude flight and its effect on the aircraft's structure, flight controls and the effect of aerodynamic heating due to skin friction and shockwave formation, etc. All the research flights mentioned above and many more, culminated in NASA's space programme involving the flights into space performed by the Mercury, Gemini, Apollo and Space Shuttle programmes.

Peter Twiss

Across the Atlantic to England, Fleet Air Arm pilot, Lieutenant Commander Lionel Peter Twiss (1921-2011) OBE, DSC and Bar, was a Naval fighter pilot and civilian test pilot with the honour of being the British first pilot to exceed 1,000 mph (1,620 km/h).

Peter Twiss applied to join the Fleet Air Arm (FAA) before the start of WWII but his application was initially rejected. He was later accepted for training at the RNAS Yoevilton in the south of England, before seeing active war service in North Africa and Europe. He flew many of the early biplanes during his training and on wartime operations including the Fairey Battle, Hawker Harts, Gloster Gladiators and many others. He also served in the Merchant Ship Fighter Unit, flying Hawker Hurricanes that were catapulted

This X-15 was equipped with jettisonable fuel tanks attached to the side of the fuselage, below the wings. Their purpose was to increase the fuel capacity for a longer engine burn-time to boost the aircraft to its ultimate hypersonic record speed of Mach 6.70. It is seen here in the USAF Museum at Dayton, Ohio, with the North American Aviation XB-70A Valkyrie supersonic bomber to the rear of the X-15.

The first jet-powered aircraft to exceed 1,000 mph was this research aircraft, the Fairey Delta 2 flown by Peter Twiss. It is displayed in the Fleet Air Arm Museum at Yoevilton, England, in its nice, dark blue colour scheme. In the background is the prototype Concorde 002, the first British-built Concorde to fly on 9 April 1969 with BAC test pilot Brian Trubshaw at the controls.

off the ship to protect the convoy from enemy action. The mission ended by ditching in the sea to be picked up by a passing ship. During the North African landings, he was based on the aircraft carrier *HMS Furious* flying Seafires (the Naval version of the Spitfire). He was promoted to Lt Commander at the end of the war.

In 1945, Peter Twiss turned to test flying after attending the third course of the Empire Test Pilots School held at RAF Cranfield, followed by a posting to the Naval Squadron at the Aeroplane & Armament Experimental Establishment at Boscombe Down.

Peter Twiss found employment with Fairey Aviation as their test pilot from 1946-1959, flying many of their different types of aircraft. However, it was to be the delta-winged, Fairey Delta 2 research aircraft, that brought him fame. The Delta 2 was built to gather flight-test data for the Concorde, then under development.

The 10 March 1956 was to become a memorable date for Peter Twiss. After two-years of extensive flight testing, Peter Twiss flew the Delta 2 to a world speed record for jet-propelled aircraft, when he reached 1,131.76 mph (1,811 km/h or Mach 1.7). After several attempts, it was on the 10 March 1956 that he made aviation history for being the first British pilot to exceed the 1,000-mph mark. He had exceeded the previous jet aircraft speed record by nearly 300 mph (480 km/h), but the Americans regained the record some eighteen-months later. It was the last flight-speed record to be gained by a British pilot. The reader may recall that Scott Crossfield exceeded had previously exceeded the 1,000 mph mark before reaching 1,200 mph in his rocket plane in November 1953.

Peter Twiss had a very interesting and varied career from his days of flying the old and slow biplanes to his record-breaking flight in the Delta 2.

William M. Magruder

Ask a layman, "what was the first airliner to fly supersonic" and they will most likely answer, "it was the Concorde". However, they would be wrong. It was in fact, a Douglas DC-8, one of the world's first jet propelled airliners. On 21 August 1961 during a test flight, the DC-8 exceeded the speed of sound reaching Mach 1.012 (660.6 mph) during a dive starting at 50,000 feet and reaching Mach One at 41,088 feet. Aircraft designer and test pilot, William M. Magruder (1925-2021) was at the controls on this history-making flight. He was awarded the Ivan C. Kinchelo Trophy for his outstanding flight test performance.

His flying career started with his time as a WWII pilot flying with the Army Air Corps. Post-war, he attended the University of California where he earned his aeronautical engineering degree. In 1949, he returned to military flying in the USAF until 1956 where he flew as a test pilot on the Boeing B-52 Stratofortress, an eight-engine bomber that is still in operation today, seventy years after its maiden flight in in 1952. He was also on the design team for the Lockheed L1011 Tristar, one of the first airliners in the Jumbo-jet class. After spending time as the leader of the USA's Federal SST supersonic passenger transport project in 1971, he became the vice-president of Piedmont Airlines in 1973. For his services in the aviation industry, he received the Legion of Merit.

Brian Trubshaw & Andre Turcat

From the Fairey Delta 2/BAC 221, the Concorde was developed jointly between France and England with each country building their own aircraft. The test pilots for the British Concorde, which was the second one to fly, were the Englishmen Captain Brian Trubshaw (1924-2001) BAC's chief test pilot, with co-pilot John Cochrane (1930-2006). The Director for Aerospatiale flight-testing was French test pilot Captain Andre Edouard Turcat (1921-2016) and his co-pilot Jacques Guignard flying the French-built Sud Aviation (later Aerospatiale) Concorde. The four pilot were the pioneers of supersonic transport aircraft flight.

Andre Turcat had joined the Free French Air Force as a transport pilot and later flew as their test pilot from 1951. He is noted for his flights in the Nord 1500 Griffon II, a scram-jet research aircraft and its predecessor the Nord Griffon I. [A scram-jet is a cross between a ram jet and a jet engine, designed for supersonic flight]. On 2 March 1969, Turcat made the pioneering flight of the Anglo/French supersonic airliner, Concorde 001. The Russian Tupolev Tu-144 supersonic airliner (coincidently of very similar appearance) had made its first flight a month earlier on 1 February 1969. Although the Tu-144 supersonic transport was the first to fly, the Anglo-French Concorde was more successful remaining in service for twenty-seven years from 1976 to 2003.

Concorde 202 pictured here, was the last of the six Concorde prototypes to be built and flown. This Concorde flew the most hours of all six Concorde test aircraft, a total of 1,284 hours before its last flight on 24 December 1981. This Concorde conformed to the final design of the fourteen production Concordes, which were flown by British Airways and Air France.

Concorde 202 (G-BBDG) was the British development Concorde and was the last of the six prototypes to fly and flew the most hours of test flying. It is now displayed in the Brooklands Museum near London, UK.

Concorde passenger flights with British Airways and Air France both commenced on the same day, 21 January 1976, with BA flying from London to Bahrain and Air France flying from Paris to Rio de Janeiro in Brazil. Concorde made its final commercial flight on 24 October 2003 with its return flight from New York to London.

The Pioneers of Space

The aim of the research flights mentioned above, was to increase aircraft speed into the supersonic and hypersonic regions and venture to ever higher altitude, not just to make records, but to gain technical information for furthering aircraft design and also in preparation for future space travel.

The Russian artificial satellite *Sputnik 1*, was sent into earth orbit on 4 October 1957 to become the pioneer of the world's first spacecrafts and space travel. It remained in orbit for nearly three months before re-entering the Earth's atmosphere and burning up. From Sputnik 1, the next major space venture of importance was the Earth orbit of Russia's first Cosmonaut.

Yuri Gagarin

Yuri Gagarin (1934-1968) was a Soviet Air Force pilot and made world history for being the first man to fly in space as Russia's first astronaut, or cosmonaut as they are known in Russia. He was one of five pilots selected from a long list of Air Force pilot applicants to become the first pioneer of space flight.

Flying in the Vostok 1 space capsule, he made one orbit of the Earth on 12 April 1961, which lasted for 108 minutes. On his return from space, he ejected from his capsule as planned at 23,000 feet (7,000 m) to make a safe landing. It was the only space flight he was to make, although he was on the stand-by crew for the Soviet's Soyuz 1 space flight, but he was not selected; the mission had a fatal ending.

Gagarin received many honours for his space flight including 'Hero of the Soviet Union'. He became a national celebrity and visited about thirty countries; however, he was banned from the USA by President John F. Kennedy. The world's first space flight was recognized as a FAI record.

Returning to flight duties, he was killed in a training accident with his instructor while flying a MiG-15 in March 1968. The cause of the accident was never officially found.

Alan B. Shepard

The first American pioneer astronaut was US Navy Commander Alan B. Shepard (1923-1998) who flew on a sub-orbital space flight on 5 May 1961 in the space capsule *Freedom 7*. Launched from Cape Canaveral by a Mercury-Redstone (MR-3) rocket, the short, 15-minute duration flight reached an altitude of 116 Miles (185 km). He was commander on the *Apollo 14* moon mission in 1971 and became the fifth astronaut to walk on the moon and also the oldest to do so. US astronaut, John Glen made the first American full-orbital flight on 20 February 1962.

The Moon Mission

The Apollo 11 mission to the Moon is a well-known story and has been well-documented; what follows is just a short recap on this most famous Moon mission.

The Apollo 11 three-stage Saturn V rocket departed Kennedy Space Centre in Florida on 16 July 1969. After lift-off, it made one and a half orbits of Earth before aiming for the moon, approximately 238,900 miles (384,400 km) away, which they reached after three-days of travel and entered Moon orbit. After one day in orbit, Neil Armstrong made the famous descent down the steps from their Lunar Lander *Eagle* to become the first human to stand on the Moon, followed shortly after by Buzz Aldrin. Michael Collins remained in Moon orbit for 21-hours in the Command Module *Columbia*. The three astronauts returned safely to Earth splashing down in the sea off Hawaii on 24 July 1969, to a hero's welcome; they were the ultimate pioneers of Moon missions and space flight. Over the next 3½ years, ten other American astronauts set foot on the Moon, with Gene Cernan as the Moon mission commander on the last flight to the Moon in December 1972. Will the US return to the Moon in 2024? That remains to be seen.

Neil Armstrong (1930-2012) will forever be remembered as the first man set foot on the Moon. He became a US Navy pilot in 1950 seeing combat service in the Korean War flying Grumman F9F Panthers off the aircraft carrier *USS Essex*. Leaving the Navy, he became a test-pilot for NACA/NASA based at the High-Speed Flight Test Centre at Edwards AFB in California. He was also an aeronautical engineer and later a university professor as well as the aforementioned fighter pilot, test pilot and astronaut.

Edwin E. (Buzz) Aldrin Jr., (1930-20?) was an astronaut, engineer and a USAF fighter pilot in the Korean War making 66 combat missions claiming two MiG's shot down. He had joined NASA in 1963 and made his first space flight as a crew member with Jim Lovell on the Gemini 12 mission on 11 November 1966; he also made three space-walks. In 1969, he descended onto the Moon's surface with Neil Armstrong as the second astronaut in the Lunar Lander module *Eagle*. He was the only astronaut to hold a doctorate degree (in Astronautics). In 1971, he was appointed Commander of the USAF Test Pilots School.

The third Apollo 11 crew member was Michael Collins (1930-2021) an American national born in Rome, Italy. He was a 1952 graduate from the Military Academy and flew as a USAF fighter pilot flying the North American F-86 Sabre, the USA's first supersonic capable jet fighter. In 1960, he attended the USAF Experimental Flight Test Pilot School at Edwards AFB and the Aerospace Research Pilot School. He became a NASA astronaut in 1963 and made his first space flight on the Gemini 10 programme in 1966. In 1969, he flew as the third astronaut on the Apollo 11 Moon mission with Neil Armstrong and Buzz Aldrin, as the Commander of the command module *Columbia*, making thirty orbits around the Moon.

After leaving the USAF in 1970, he remained on the reserve pilot list until 1982, holding the rank of Major General. He entered US Government politics until 1978 when he became the Director of the National Air & Space Museum in Washington, D.C., before starting his own consulting business.

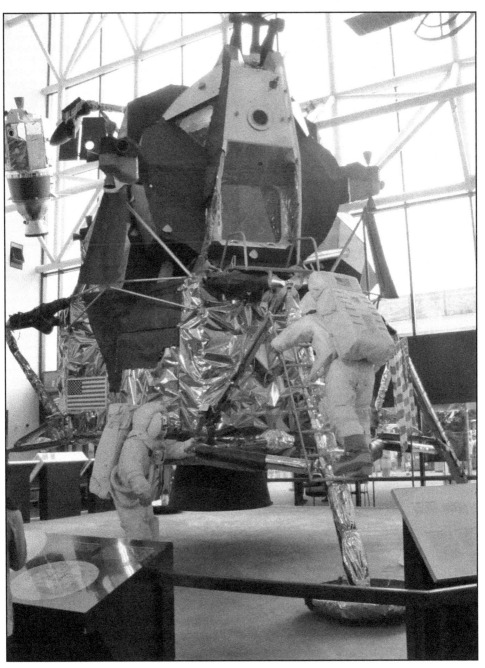

A Lunar Lander Module modified to look like the LM-2 used by Neil Armstrong for the first moon landing. This diorama shows Armstrong standing beside the Lunar Lander as Buzz Aldrin descends the steps. This museum exhibit is in the Smithsonian Air & Space Museum in Washington, D.C.

Burt Rutan & Scaled Composites

Burt Rutan (1943-20?) was an American civilian pilot and aerospace engineer. He worked for the USAF from 1965 to 1972 as a civilian flight test project engineer at Edwards AFB.

In June 1974, he established his first company, the Rutan Aircraft Factory and in 1982, Scaled Composites, both based at Mojave, California. His company Scaled Composites was famous for its many unique and unusual-looking designs of light aircraft, well-known to all home-built aircraft enthusiasts. Burt Rutan also designed his record-breaking world, non-stop, unrefueled aircraft, the Voyager in 1986 (featured in section 12 – The Circumnavigators) and the Virgin Atlantic Global Flyer in 2006.

Burt Rutan pioneered the first private venture to enter space when his SpaceShipOne won the Ansari X-Prize of $US10 million for making two flights into space within a two-week period in 2004. For his space flight success, he was awarded the 2004 Collier Trophy and of course, other awards came his way over the years. The first SpaceShipOne was the prototype for a small fleet of sub-orbital craft intended to carry tourists into space, at $US25,000 per ticket. The craft can carry a single pilot plus two passengers.

SpaceShipOne had low-aspect ratio wings with a short span of 16 feet (5 m) and wide chord. Twin tail booms attached to each wing tip folded upwards during re-entry for stability and they increased the drag to reduce speed. The SpaceShipOne was air launched from its mothership at approximately 50,000 feet (15,000 m) and then used its own rocket power to climb to the fringe of space reaching a height of 62.5 miles (100 km) above sea-level. Engine burn time was about 80 seconds allowing about three minutes in space before gliding back to Earth.

The craft made several test flights, with company test pilot Michael Melville venturing into space on the fifteenth flight. He became the world's first commercial astronaut and the pioneer of private venture space flight.

Burt Rutan also designed the mothership which was named *White Knight* for the North America X-15 pilots, Captain Robert M. White and Major William J. 'Pete' Knight.

The world's first private-venture spacecraft was pioneered by Burt Rutan and his team at Scaled Composites in Mojave, California. It is shown here in its re-entry configuration with its tail-booms raised for increased drag. His SpaceShipOne is now displayed near to the Bell X-1 and Lindbergh's Ryan NY-P in the National Air & Space Museum in Washington, D.C.

21 – Human-powered Flight

The Almost Impossible

We saw at the beginning of this work where Greek mythology tells the story of Daedalus and his son Icarus, who attempted to fly using home-made wings, which they flapped with their arms. Although the story is a myth, man has dreamed of flying like a bird ever since. One of the first designs put forward was drawn by Leonardo da Vinci, circa 1485. During the 13th century, Roger Bacon, a far-sighted English Friar believed ornithopters would one day become a reality allowing man to fly as free as the birds; he is considered as the 'father of ornithopters'. In later years, the inventors moved away from the idea of man-powered flight believing it was impossible to perform, as indeed it was at the time. Man-powered flight was one of the first methods of flight to be mooted, however, it was the last method to be achieved.

Moving forward to more recent times, serious attempts have been made to fly human-powered aircraft. Three types that come to mind are the SUMPAC in 1961, the MacCready Condor in 1977 and the Snowbird Ornithopter in 1991.

SUMPAC

In England, the SUMPAC (Southampton University Man Powered Aircraft) was a project for the university's post-graduate students. Their brief was to design, build and fly a human-powered aircraft capable of flying a figure of eight course over a distance of one mile. If successful, they would receive the Kremer Prize of £50,000 from the Royal Aeronautical Society.

The SUMPAC aircraft has a very high-aspect ratio wing of 21 to 3 built with lightweight materials of plywood, balsa and aluminium; the wings and fuselage are covered with a plastic, transparent skin to keep the weight as low as possible. The aircraft's empty weight is 128 lb (58.2 kg); the weight of the pilot brings the craft up to its gross weight and obviously, a pilot of light weight was preferred. The wingspan stretches out to 80 feet 1 inch (24.4 m) and is fixed in the high-wing position. Power is supplied by the pilot turning the propeller via bicycle-type pedals and chain-drive.

The test pilot chosen to make the flight was Derek Piggott, a glider pilot instructor. He made the first flight from Lasham Airfield on 9 November 1961 where he flew a distance of 210 feet (64 m) at just six feet above the ground. The SUMPAC made forty-flights with the greatest distance recorded at 1,950 feet (594 m) and a height of 15 feet (4.6 m). Turning flight, as the Wright brothers and others discovered in the early days, was not easy to accomplish; although the SUMPAC did manage turns up to 80-degrees, it was unable to complete a figure of eight course and therefore, failed to claim the Kremer Prize.

The SUMPAC was damaged in an accident in 1963 and retired from service. It is now on display in the Solent Sky Museum in Southampton, England.

The human-powered SUMPAC aircraft built by students from the Southampton University. It is displayed suspended from the ceiling of the Solent Sky Museum in Southampton, UK.

MacCready Gossamer Albatross

The Gossamer Condor was the first human-powered aircraft to fly the prescribed figure-of-eight course of one-mile (1.6 km) long and to clear a ten feet high barrier at the start and finish of the course. The record flight was made at Minter Field in Shafter, California, flown by Brian Allen, to win the Kremer Prize on 23 August 1977. The Kremer Prize was instigated in 1959 by Englishman, Henry Kremer, an industrialist.

The Condor was designed by the American, Dr. Paul MacCready and his team as his first human-powered design and was built by his company, the AeroVironment. MacCready is noted for being a world soaring champion, aeronautical engineer and designer. MacCready's second human-powered aircraft, the Gossamer Albatross featured here, was the first to cross the English Channel to win the second Kremer Prize, in remembrance of Louis Bleriot's English Channel crossing back in 1909.

As with other human-powered aircraft, the Albatross was built with light weight carbon fibre materials and covered with myler, a thin lightweight,

The Gossamer Albatross I claimed the second Kremer Prize for crossing the English Chanel in 1979. It is now displayed in the Udvar Hazy Centre.

The first successful human-powered ornithopter, the UTIAS Snowbird,
built by Toronto University students is now a museum exhibit in the
Canada Aviation & Space Museum in Ottawa, Canada.

transparent plastic. A high aspect ratio wing with a span of 96 feet (29.25 m) was used with the pilot's cabin mounted underneath the wing. A large canard in front maintained longitudinal stability. Pedal power applied by the pilot turned the prop. The Albatross empty weight was 71 lb (32 kg) much lighter than the SUMPAC mentioned above which had an empty weight of 128 lb (58.2 kg). The use of composites greatly reduced the weight.

The pilot for the Channel flight was again Brian Allen who departed from Folkstone in England on the 12 June 1979 and reached the beach at Cape Gris-Nez in France after a flight of two hours and 49 minutes of non-stop pedalling, to claim the second Kremer Prize. MacCready was awarded the Collier Trophy for his successful Channel flight plus the prize of £100,000.

Two Albatross aircraft were built, the first one used on the Channel flight is now owned by the Udvar-Hazy Center. The second craft was a back-up plane which is now displayed in the Museum of Flight in Seattle, Washington.

UTIAS Snowbird Ornithopter

The first successful human-powered ornithopter flight was made on 2 August 2010 at the Great Lakes Gliding Club in Tottenham, Ontario. An ornithopter has man-powered flapping wings, unlike the SUMPAC and Albatross where the pilot used-pedal power to turn the propeller. But we are moving into the 21st century here, way beyond the early pioneering days of flight, which has been our main interest throughout this work. The name ornithopter is taken from the Greek words *Ornis* meaning bird and *pterion* meaning wings.

Final words...

From the mythology of Daedalus and Icarus flying with their ornithopter wings to the Snowbird Ornithopter built by the students at the UTIAS, man has conquered the problems of human flight progressing from hot air balloons to airships and gliders and finally powered flight in a large variety of different aircraft types and also, not forgetting the achievements of space flight.

It is a tribute to all those pioneer aviators who persevered to make flight a reality and without their determined efforts, we would not have the aviation industry that we know today. And we must not forget those pioneers who lost their lives while trying to further the advance of aeronautics. The pioneer aviators from the past have all contributed to the history and advancement of the world's aviation.

Appendices

1: Pioneers of Aerodynamic Discoveries

Within this work, we have looked at numerous pioneer aviators and the planes they flew from the beginning of flight up to the end of the 20th century. Since the Wright brothers first flight in 1903, a great deal of progress has been made in improving aircraft performance and safety. But, how did these improvements come about? The success of the airplane can be attributed to a number of pioneer aviators who through trial and error, endeavoured to make workable airplanes, followed by the dedicated scientists and aerodynamicists, mainly in Europe and North America who discovered the mysteries of aerodynamics to make safe and efficient aircraft.

The following is a brief selection on the pioneers who developed the various parts of aircraft that we take for granted today. If the reader desires to delve further into aerodynamics, *The Encyclopedia of Aerodynamics* by this author is recommended.

Frenchman, Jean Charles Borda (1733-1799) discovered interference drag.

In 1784, the term aerostat was given to mean a lighter-than-air aircraft, e.g., airships.

Sir George Cayley (1773-1857) was named the 'father of the aeroplane' in 1846, due to his serious study of the beginnings of aerodynamic theory. He designed the first 'modern' airplane with a main wing in front and a tailplane at the rear. He introduced the term of centre of pressure and stated the wing should be designed with a cambered upper surface. In 1799, he studied lift, drag, streamlining and the power-to-weight ratio and stated that lift, control and power be treated separately as the forces of lift versus weight and thrust versus drag. He also contributed to aircraft stability.

The term 'aviation' was coined by John Wise (1808-1879) in 1850. He was the first person to discover the existence of the jet stream on one of his balloon flights.

William J.M. Rankine (1820-1880) in 1865, founded the propeller axial momentum theory for ship's propellers; the theory is also applied to aircraft propellers.

In 1871, the Frenchman Alphonse Pénaud (1850-1880) improved the theory of aerodynamics and wing contours. He introduced the requirement for longitudinal stability where the tailplane is set at a lower angle of attack than the main wing (known as longitudinal dihedral). He also gave us the term 'angle of incidence', the angle between the wing's chord line and the plane's longitudinal axis.

Francis Herbert Wenham (1824-1908) discovered the forward part of a wing at around 25% MAC (a quarter of the way from the wing's leading edge) produced more lift than the rear portion. Francis Wenham with John Moses Browning (1855-1926) invented the wind tunnel in 1871, which provided new aerodynamic data for aircraft design. John Browning also invented the Browning machine gun.

William Froude (1810-1879) introduced the propeller's blade element theory in 1878.

English born, Australian aviator, Lawrence Hargrave (1850-1915) invented the box kite in 1894. He used four of his box kites attached to a seat to lift himself to a height of sixteen feet.

The term 'aviator' was coined by Frenchman, Guilloume Gabriel de La Londelle (1812-1886).

The UK physicist, Lord John W.S. Rayleigh (1842-1919) introduced the drag equation.

Louis Bleriot's plane, the Bleriot VIII of 1908-09, was the first plane to use the control system now common on most airplanes today, using a control-stick or yoke, for elevator/aileron control and a pivoted foot-bar for rudder control.

In 1907, Dr. Frederick Lanchester (1868-1946) studied advanced aerodynamic theories, such as wing tip vortices, lifting line and vortex lift theories.

In 1911, Deperdussin built the world's first wood monocoque fuselage on production aircraft.

The engineer and thermodynamacist, Hugo Junkers (1859-1935) pioneered the use of all-metal airframes, which he first used on his Junkers J.1 designed by Professor Hans Reisner. It first flew on 23 May 1912. Dornier built the first metal monocoque planes.

The world's first four-engine aircraft was the Russian-built Sikorsky S.21 Russian Knight, previously known as the Great Baltic. It was designed by Igor Sikorsky as a biplane airliner and built by the Russo-Baltic Wagon Works. It first flew on 10 May 1913.

Horatio Phillips (1845-1924) was a main contributor to the science of aerodynamics, proving the theories of aerodynamic lift put forward by Sir George Cayley and Francis Herbert Wenham (1824-1908).

Wing warping was the first method used by the pioneer aviators to keep their aircraft wings level. It was soon replaced by ailerons with their invention credited to various pioneers including Henri Farman (1874-1958) which he used on his Farman III biplane in 1909. Englishman Mathew Pier Bolton (1820-1894) in 1868 also received the credit, as did Robert Esnault-Pelterie who patented the use of a joystick for both roll and pitch movements in 1907.

The American, Dr. William W. Christmas (1865-1960) claims the elevon invention. A combined elevator and aileron as found on delta wing aircraft.

In 1925, Jacob Ackeret (1895-1981) introduced the term Mach number, in honour of Ernst Mach. Ackeret was the first person to study supersonic airflow past a two-dimensional infinite wing (a wing stretching from wall to wall in a wind tunnel).

NACA scientist, Dr. Robert Rowe Gilruth (1913-2000) invented the all-flying tailplane to reduce Mach tuck on jet fighter aircraft. It is now used on jet airliners and light aircraft such as the Piper Cherokee. He also introduced the term aerodynamic centre.

Drooped wing tips were invented by Dr. S.F. Hoerner to reduce wing tip vortices.

One of the world's greatest aerodynamicists was Professor Ludwig Prandtl (1875-1953). He discovered that induced drag is proportional to the wing's aspect ratio; he also made many other important aerodynamic discoveries.

High performance airfoils and their boundary layers and laminar flow were studied by E. Jacobs.

Professor N. Joukowski (1847-1921) studied the lift on airfoil sections and flow circulation over the wing. He built the first wind tunnel in Russia. He is considered to be the 'father of Russian aviation'.

The term aeroplane (airplane in America) was coined by Frederick Edme Marriott (c1905-1984). He also discovered that speed is squared in the lift and drag equations.

Dr. Hugh L. Dryden (1895-1965) researched laminar and turbulent flows, boundary layer and wind tunnel design.

William F. Durand (1859-1958) performed considerable study on propeller aerodynamics.

Harlan D. Fowler (1895-1982) invented Fowler flaps now common on jet transport aircraft.

Professor Ludwig Prandtl (1875-1953) and Herman Glauert (1892-1934) combined their research into biplane aerodynamics and introduced the Interference Factor on biplane wings. Prandtl also made further study on the centre of pressure and its movement on aircraft wings. Prandtl also discovered induced drag and many other aerodynamic features.

Sydney B. Gates (1893-1973) at the Royal Aircraft Establishment at Farnborough, UK, researched the problems of aircraft entering into a spin and discovered the required pilot-input actions to recover.

Orville Wright (1871-1948) and James M. Jacobs invented split flaps in 1920, which were first used on the Northrop Gamma.

Jack Northrop (1895-1981) was the first to use spoilers on his night-fighter, the Northrop Black Widow design. All jet transport now use spoilers/airbrakes.

Theodore Von Karman (1881-1963) studied advanced aerodynamics discovering several important aspects which we take for granted today.

2: Aeronautical Terms

Aerodynamics: A branch of aerology. The term was introduced in the *Popular Encyclopedia* in 1837.

Aerology: The study of flight theory. Now known as aerodynamics.

Aerostatics: The branch of aerodynamics covering the science of gases at rest, in particular as applied to lighter-than-air aircraft (hot air balloon and airships).

Angle of attack: The angle between the wing's chord line and the relative air flow.

Aviation: From the Latin words, *avis* (bird) and action was introduced by Frenchman Gabriel la Landelle in 1863.

Aviatrix: A female aviator (pilot) from the pioneering era.

Buoyancy: Its application in aerostatics refers to the displaced mass of air equal to the balloon or airship's own weight. The word is from New Latin and was introduced in 1784.

Centre of pressure: The air pressure varies over an aircraft's wing and is assumed to act at one point on the wing's surface and to move fore and aft with changes in angle of attack.

Constant-speed props: Modern props have governors to maintain a constant RPM by automatically adjusting the angle of attack to suit the speed of the aircraft.

Departure stall: A stall caused on take-off after an engine failure, with the aircraft in a nose-high attitude.

Dihedral: The angle between the transverse horizontal plane and the wing's up-tilt towards the tips.

Dirigible: A French word applied to airships meaning 'steerable'.

Hp: Horsepower.

Infinite wing: An infinite wing stretches across a wind tunnel from wall-to-wall.

Lateral stability: The stability of the aircraft in the rolling plane.

Ornithopter: A flying machine powered by manually operated flapping wings.

Orthogonal wing: A biplane's wings, one directly above the other, not staggered.

Single-surface wing: Early airfoils had only an upper, single surface to produce lift. Cambered airfoils came later having both upper and lower surfaces, both contributing towards the lift.

Standard temperature: The average temperature around the world is considered to be 15° C. The standard temperature is used for comparing aircraft performance data and meteorological issues, etc.

Tandem wings: A pair of wings of similar size, mounted on the fuselage one behind the other.

Variable pitch props: VP props have two settings, fine and course, for take-off and cruise, respectively. Their RPM varies as it does on a fixed-pitch prop. Constant speed props came later, which automatically maintain a constant engine RPM, within a given range.

Wing warping: An early form of lateral roll control before ailerons were introduced.

3: Bibliography

Christopher Chant, *Pioneers of Aviation,* Grange Books

David Nevin, *Epic of Flight, the Pathfinders,* Caxton Publishing Group

Fia O. Caoimph, *The Aviation Book*, Chronicle Books, San Francisco, USA 2006

Francis Hitching, *The World Atlas of Mysteries,* Pan Books

Jim Winchester, *A Chronology of Aviation,* Grange Books Ltd

John W.R Taylor & Kenneth Munson, *History of Aviation,* Octopus Books 1973

R.G. Grant, *Flight, The Complete History,* Dorling Kinderslet Ltd

Riccardo Niccoli, *History of Flight,* White Star Publisher

Ron Dick & Dan Patterson, *The Early Years,* Boston Mills press

Rowland White, *The Big Book of Flight*, Bantam Press

4: About the Author

Frank Hitchens was born in Birmingham, England and he joined the British Merchant Navy at the age of seventeen years, as a ship's steward and travelled the world. He settled in New Zealand in 1965 and while working on the coastal ships, he joined the Wellington Aero Club and gained his Private Pilot Licence and later, he gained his Commercial Pilot Licence. Flying charter flights and joy rides for the aero club he enjoyed the challenges of air navigation on cross-country flights around scenic New Zealand, flying mostly single-engine light aircraft, which also included flights in a flex-wing microlight and gyrocopter. Flying the Boeing 737-800 flight simulator in later years brought him new and more challenging flight experiences.

Marriage to his wife Deirdre reduced his active flying but his love for aviation and flying never ceased. His interest in photography naturally included photographing aircraft of all types and his technical interest in aeronautical subjects turned to writing. Travelling in later life, took him to many countries where he visited plane museums to see and photograph the aircraft in their collection. He has written a few magazine articles published in Australia and New Zealand and also six other books, *Range & Endurance, Formulas for the E6-B Air Navigation Computer, Encyclopedia of Aerodynamics, Propeller Aerodynamics, Aircraft Museums of the United Kingdom, Special Purpose Aircraft and Pioneer Aviators & the Planes They Flew,* written for aircraft enthusiasts and pilots of all levels.

Also from Frank Hitchens

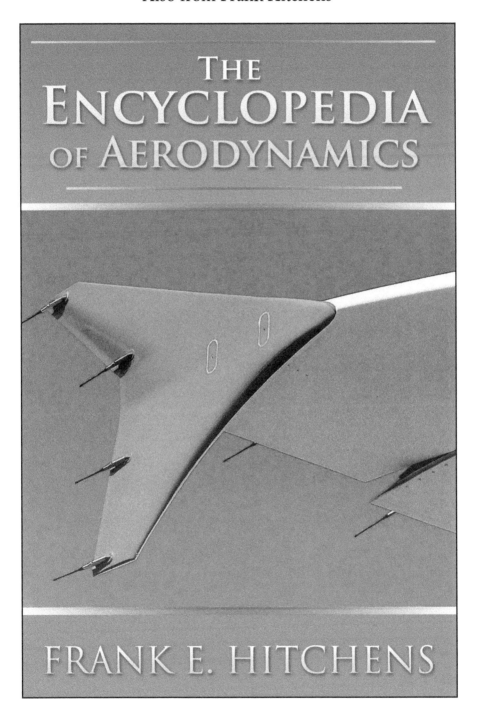

THE
ENCYCLOPEDIA
OF AERODYNAMICS

FRANK E. HITCHENS

You may also enjoy...

AIRCRAFT MUSEUMS
OF THE
UNITED KINGDOM

FRANK E. HITCHENS

Milton Keynes UK
Ingram Content Group UK Ltd.
UKHW022222180823
427045UK00001B/6